PS
3562
.E42
Z96

Ursula K. Le Guin,
voyager to inner
lands and to outer
space

DATE			

URSULA K. LE GUIN

Finally, I do not pretend to have set down, in Baconian terms, a true, or even a consistent model of the universe. I can only say that here is a bit of my personal universe, the universe traversed in a long and uncompleted journey. If my record, like those of the sixteenth-century voyagers, is confused by strange beasts or monstrous thoughts or sights of abortive men, these are no more than my eyes saw or my mind conceived. On the world island we are all castaways, so that what is seen by one may often be dark or obscure to another.

Loren Eiseley, *The Immense Journey*

Kennikat Press
National University Publications
Literary Criticism Series

General Editor
John E. Becker

URSULA K. LE GUIN

Voyager to Inner Lands and to Outer Space

Edited by
Joe De Bolt

With an Introduction by
Barry N. Malzberg

National University Publications
KENNIKAT PRESS // 1979
Port Washington, N.Y. // London

Manufactured in the United States of America

Published by
Kennikat Press Corp.
Port Washington, N.Y. / London

Library of Congress Cataloging in Publication Data
Main entry under title:

Ursula K. Le Guin, voyager to inner lands and to outer
space.

(Literary criticism series) (National university
publications)
Bibliography: p.
Includes index.
1. Le Guin, Ursula K., 1929– –Criticism and
interpretation–Addresses, essays, lectures.
2. Science fiction, American–History and criticism–
Addresses, essays, lectures. I. De Bolt, Joe.
PS3562.E42Z96   813'.5'4   78-20916
ISBN 0-8046-9229-7

TO LIZZIE
She has voyaged and endures.

CONTENTS

INTRODUCTION
  CIRCUMSTANCE AS POLICY: The Decade   5
    of Ursula K. Le Guin / Barry N. Malzberg
PART ONE: THE VOYAGER
  A LE GUIN BIOGRAPHY / Joe De Bolt   13
PART TWO: VOYAGE TO INNER LANDS AND TO OUTER SPACE
  A SURVEY OF LE GUIN CRITICISM / James W. Bittner   31
  SOLITARY BEING: The Hero as   50
    Anthropologist / Karen Sinclair
  SCIENCE AND RHETORIC IN THE FICTION OF   66
    URSULA LE GUIN / Peter T. Koper
PART THREE: THE EARTHSEA VOYAGE
  FOUR LETTERS ABOUT LE GUIN / Rollin A. Lasseter   89
  "But Dragons Have Keen Ears:" On Hearing "Earthsea"   115
    with Recollections of Beowulf / John R. Pfeiffer
  THE EARTHSEA TRILOGY: Ethical Fantasy   128
    for Children / Francis J. Molson
PART FOUR: VOYAGE TO ANARRES
  TAOIST CONFIGURATIONS: 153
    The Dispossessed / Elizabeth Cummins Cogell
  POSSESSED SOCIOLOGY AND LE GUIN'S   180
    DISPOSSESSED: From Exile to Anarchism /
    Larry L. Tifft and Dennis C. Sullivan
  NOTES   198
  A SELECTED LE GUIN BIBLIOGRAPHY   211
  CONTRIBUTORS   215
  INDEX   218

ACKNOWLEDGMENTS

Several persons aided me by reading and commenting on material in this book; I give my thanks to Jim Bittner, Nancy Leis, John Parke, John Pfeiffer, Ronald Primeau, and Norm Rasulis. Also, I want to thank the reference librarians and the interlibrary loan department of Central Michigan University. Without them, this project, and all my writing and research tasks, would have been incalculably more difficult. Above all, however, it is to my wife, Denise, that I owe the most gratitude.

URSULA K. LE GUIN

Frequently cited and quoted works by Ursula K. Le Guin have been abbreviated throughout the text, except for their initial appearance in each selection. The abbreviations for these works are listed below. In addition, if Le Guin's works are quoted in an essay, an initial note informs the reader of the specific editions used.

DBR	"The Day before the Revolution"
DIS	*The Dispossessed*
LHD	*The Left Hand of Darkness*
LOH	*The Lathe of Heaven*
ORT	*Orsinian Tales*
OWW	"The Ones Who Walk Away from Omelas"
TFS	*The Farthest Shore*
TOA	*The Tombs of Atuan*
VTE	"Vaster Than Empires and More Slow"
WOE	*A Wizard of Earthsea*
WTQ	*The Wind's Twelve Quarters*
WWF	"The Word for World Is Forest"

BARRY N. MALZBERG

CIRCUMSTANCE AS POLICY
The Decade of Ursula K. Le Guin

Le Guin's first stories appeared in the science fiction magazines as early as 1962, and three early novels appeared in Ace paperback format in 1966/7, but it was in 1969 with *The Left Hand of Darkness,* which won all the best novel of the year awards within science fiction, that this writer became prominent. Since that novel and all through the 1970s she has moved on to become perhaps the most successful and critically admired writer ever to produce a substantial body of work within the genre limits of science fiction. In terms of critical recognition, only Vonnegut and Bradbury come close, but Vonnegut's novels were published as literary, not genre, works, and the short stories that made Bradbury famous in the 1940s and 1950s appeared in mass circulation magazines. And neither has won a National Book Award as did Le Guin for juvenile literature, although Vonnegut's *Slaughterhouse Five,* as Le Guin's *Orsinian Tales,* did appear short listed in the fiction category of the NBA.

This book on Le Guin is, hence, already overdue and much to the point. In order for us to understand the science fiction of this decade, its most honored writer must be investigated.

Another way of putting this, perhaps, is to say that an important writer is important by that fact alone ... that even if Le Guin's work did not bear serious investigation on its own merits (and it does) it would do so because of the estimation it has reached within science fiction.

This essay, neither critical exegesis nor appreciation (although I admire the writer's accomplishments), is an attempt, deliberately superficial, to assess the reasons for Le Guin's importance and success within contemporary science fiction. It is not an attempt to explicate or criticize the work in detail; that will be well taken care of by others in this volume. It is an essay by a contemporary (my own work began to receive some attention at about the time *LHD* was published) more interested in what this writer's prominence implies about modern science fiction itself.

Le Guin's focus, from the outset, has been detailed and anthropological. From the beginning of her career she identified herself, then a woman in her mid-thirties, as the daughter of two anthropologists. Moreover, *LHD* in its careful documentation of a society whose mores superseded the individual choice of its members, was perhaps the most distinguished example since Hal Clement's *A Mission of Gravity*, in which the background became the main character of a science fiction novel. In her 1971 *Lathe of Heaven* Le Guin backed off momentarily from these concerns into a kind of psychological, solipsistic subtext (and that novel will be discussed later), but in 1974 *The Dispossessed*, considered a work even more successful than *LHD*, shifted into a novelistic modus operandi where not only was cultural background novel-foreground, but the nominal protagonist was merely a vessel through which the real conflict of the novel, that between cultures, could be enacted. It may be argued that *DIS* is a metaphor; a kind of climactic East/West novel of the future or even a two-culture Vietnam novel, but I think that argument would be specious; *DIS* like the aforementioned Clement novel or an even older antecedent, the Venus Equilateral technological series of G. O. Smith, is about merely what it is about . . . two invented, imaginary subcultures. It is a novel which could not have been done in any way other than as science fiction; it needs those devices in order to work and this, surely, is the central definition of a "good" science fiction novel.

It is the concentration upon detail of culture which interests me so much and is probably the best means to understanding the significance of the work. We are, I believe, in a post-ideological time in science fiction and in the world: the great thrashings of the sixties have been overcome, and many of the nakedly dialectical or polemical approaches of the new writers of the last decade have almost entirely lost their audience. Certainly, if J. G. Ballard, Robert Silverberg, Thomas Disch, Michael Moorcock (some of the time), John Brunner (some of the time), Samuel R. Delany (most of the time), Norman Spinrad, and this writer were committing a literature of exhaustion in the late sixties to early seventies, sculpturing templates for a time of perceived collapse, then what has happened is that the repudiation of the last decade in most of the institutions of that culture has been reflected in the field itself. (Which is of course only a minor institution of the culture.) The literature of process, then, has given way yet again to the literature of product, of which Le Guin is a major exponent. The basic statement of the anthropologist is that the individual is essentially helpless, forced to enact in varying degrees the folkways and mores of his culture; the message of Le Guin is that culture predominates. No Ballardian wasteland here, no Dischian landscape of dread, no *Bug Jack Barron* in which the systems' interstices can be found and destroyed. In Le Guin the connection between individual and culture is seamless; and the character bears less responsibility for his acts than he does in the fiction of these other writers. One does not want to push this point too far. Le Guin is a fine writer of decent range and sophistication; like all fine writers she would resent being categorized or used as a demonstration of anyone's theorem. Her work, like that of any important writer, must perversely resist labeling. Still, there are clues, consistencies, certain indications that Le Guin is reaching a large audience and is becoming science fiction's most successful writer both within and without the field because her work is centered around a point which a seventies American audience may need to consider: the individual responds only to the flux of culture; the individual no longer has ultimate responsibility for his/her acts. "The Word for World Is Forest," Le Guin's long novella originally published in 1972 (and appearing by itself in book form four years later) opens with one of the classic plots of science fiction: Earthmen are colonizing another planet, dealing with the natives, and the suspicion is that the natives are highly civilized, highly intelligent, and that colonization of them amounts to genocide. This fact is brutally repressed by the administrative hierarchy, of course, but it eventually will surface. What makes *WWF* particularly interesting is its direct (and I would claim, absolutely conscious) construction as a paradigm of Vietnam—the American occupation of Indochina taken to a science fictional context. Here, in short, is a clearly political work, but what renders it more interesting than most of this sort is not only its careful and patient crafting, its extensive limning of the alien subculture (Le Guin is nothing if not thorough), but the fact that its principals can take no action whatsoever to alter the system. The tragedy of cultural confrontation is the tragedy of history, Le Guin is saying, and the culture with weaker technology will always lose.

Beyond that bleak conclusion is little more; before it are only the thrashings of the principal as he first resists and then accepts this knowledge. *WWF* is many things, and not the least of them is a distinguished and well-imagined work of fiction, but its ultimate point is even more horrid than that granted by Ballard's wasteland: no human impress can be left upon the social abstract. Nothing will change. *Terminal Beach* gives indication that ultimately the spirit does exist separately from the devices of culture, bearing witness; Le Guin sees "spirit" as merely another sociological folkway, inseparable from the cultural context in which it would arise.

LOH, by general agreement the least successful novel of Le Guin's mature period, fails, perhaps, because the vision is in the forefront and not to be subsumed by the detail. The dreamer, as in folklore, dreams real; he creates the world piece by piece. He seeks therapy and transfers his solipsism, ironically enough, to the psychiatrist. This novel, which seems in synopsis little more than a whimsy taken to extraordinary length, is at first puzzling and then frightening: the world and all its creatures seem merely to be a device, an incidental extension of the interrelation of the two characters (there are only two), but what is happening outside this single transaction cannot matter and eventually does not. The word for world in *LOH* is not forest. It is clutter.

Le Guin is a difficult and complex writer, it must be said again. She can not be categorized in order to make a point. She has written short stories, two of which have won awards in science fiction. "The Ones Who Walk Away from Omelas," the Hugo winner, is a Borges pastiche which is very much fixated upon the single transaction as it describes an idealized society pivoting only on necessary brutalities to one child (echoes of Schwartz-Bart's thirty-six Just whose sufferings and witness make possible God's tolerance of existence). Some citizens can not accept such an unjust society and must leave it—although Le Guin does not say to where. "Vaster Than Empires and More Slow" (not an award winner; "The Day before the Revolution" won a Nebula in 1975), a story written at about the same time as *LHD,* deliberately represses detail and shrouds truths for the sake of denouement. And the Earthsea trilogy, the last novel of which won a National Book Award for children's literature, is fantasy. (The previous novels had won children's book awards.) They are characteristically Le Guin and the style is consistent, but any understanding of these books must be accomplished outside the context of modern science fiction; they are linked to the far older tradition of fantasy and have access to antecedents which *DIS* does not.

It is, of course, the NBA—both the prize in 1973 and the short ballot in 1977—which has led to major critical attention outside the genre limits of science fiction and which has raised Le Guin's stock enormously within her own field. It is no small accomplishment. Le Guin is probably the first writer to emerge solely within the confines of the genres to win significant literary recognition in my time. Children's literature is not adult fiction, of course, and it is clearly impossible for a novel by a science fiction writer published as science fiction to win in the latter category (Harper kept the category label from *Orsinian Tales,* and much of the contents had appeared in literary magazines); still it is a remarkable achievement and of itself would justify this book.

I do not think that acclaim for Le Guin is transferable to other science fiction writers. In the fifty-year history of this genre as a discrete literary form, unusual regard for a few writers has done nothing for the mass. As a matter of fact, until Le Guin's ascendancy in the mid-seventies there had been no change in almost twenty years in the names of the five science fiction writers who reach an audience outside the genre. Isaac Asimov, Ray Bradbury, Robert Heinlein, Arthur Clarke, and Kurt Vonnegut each reached that point for reasons which had nothing to do with the success of their works within science fiction and everything to do with what they had achieved *outside* it, and such is likely to be the case with Le Guin, whose career now seems to be taking her out of science fiction entirely. (I may be wrong; good writers have a way of making prognosticators fools, but I would be almost sure that her next novel will not be science fiction or at least will not be published at all as science fiction; that eventually Le Guin will be writing complex fantasies comparable with *Watership Down* or *Shardik* or the Tolkien trilogy . . . important work all, but work having nothing to do with science fiction.)

It is thus, at what might be the logical conclusion of her career within the perimeters of the genre, that this book has been assembled and is being published at the right time. I have, in sum, and as may be clearly inferred, certain reservations about Le Guin and the eventual estimation of her work. She may be seen, some time from now, as less a perpetrator of visions than their mirror. Still, this does not take away from the essence: she is, as of the date of this essay, the most important contemporary writer of science fiction, and this field cannot be understood if she is not. No writer could ask for or receive better tribute.

PART 1

THE VOYAGER

. . . I have not stopped dreaming.

Dreams Must Explain Themselves

JOE DE BOLT

A LE GUIN BIOGRAPHY

Ursula Kroeber Le Guin treasures her privacy, believing that her public self can be found in her books while her private self is the interest only of herself and her family.[1] Moreover, she doesn't want her works to be autobiographical. She prefers to distance herself from her books, and writing science fiction provides that opportunity. She writes about aliens, she says; she likes the alien point of view.[2] Many Le Guin readers seek to narrow their distance from this writer of beautiful, powerful, and meaningful tales, to diminish the alienness of this person who is the daughter of illustrious parents, achiever of recognition in both science fiction and mainstream literature, and who strikes those who have met her as being so extraordinary. Where, then, can the curious turn?

Fortunately, bits and pieces and even a few sizable chunks of information have been placed in the public record by Ursula Le Guin and her family, enough to be assembled, without rude invasion of Le Guin's life or dubious psychologizing about her works, as a portrait. This will be a family portrait, for Ursula is not only a daughter, but a sister, a wife, and a mother, as well; family is important to her. And it will be ambiguous, with elements of a storybook childhood, a contemporary woman, and a gifted artist. Finally, the portrait will be incomplete, more a sketch than a detailed, finished study. Despite this, the outline seems clear enough; this is not an alien, but a person, very human.

In photographs one often notes the famous pipe and pixie, the full lower lip, and, when they're turned upward, the large bright eyes. Reporters have seen her as slender, slightly tall, with uncluttered lines and soft, dark hair beginning to gray. There's an easy laugh, warmth, and whimsy; grace, but tempered by an inner tension. Gestures are deliberate,

clothes are practical.[3] The inner person has been described by Harlan
Ellison as "witty, strong, emphatic and empathic, wise, knowledgeable,
easygoing, and electric, seraphic, gracious, sanguine and sane."[4] Le Guin
sees herself as an introvert who communicates through her works, which
spring from her subconscious. She says she has a poor memory, that she
is a "congenital non-Christian," and that she has faith in human nature's
capacity for goodness.[5]

She doesn't want to be swamped by people; "I like it kind of dull,
basically. I live a very regular life."[6] And maturity came slowly; "Coming
of age is a process that took me many years; I finished it, so far as I ever
will, at about age 31; and so I feel rather deeply about it."[7]

The road to that coming of age began on October 21, 1929, St. Ursula's
Day, when Le Guin was born in Berkeley, California, the only daughter
and youngest child of Theodora and Alfred Kroeber.[8] To say that these
parents were remarkable would be a severe understatement. Alfred
Kroeber was well on his way to becoming one of the world's leading
anthropologists. Born in June, 1876, he took a B.A. and M.A. in literature
at Columbia University, but was converted to anthropology by Franz
Boas, considered by many to be the founder of modern American anthropology. He soon moved west, formed a permanent attachment there,
took a position at Berkeley, and built an outstanding department of
anthropology. Besides the more professionally related areas of history
and biology, Alfred Kroeber maintained a lifelong interest in art and
literature, and Ursula, quite appropriately, dedicated her collection of
poems, *Wild Angels,* to him. He was multilingual, with some facility in
classical, modern European, and several American Indian languages.

Theodora Kracaw was born in Denver, in March, 1897, and moved with
her family at age four to the mining town of Telluride in southwestern
Colorado, where she grew up. She graduated cum laude from Berkeley
in 1919 and received an M.A. in psychology in 1920. Meanwhile she had
married and borne two sons, Clifton and Theodore, but her husband
died in 1923 and she returned to Berkeley to consider graduate work.
It was then that Theodora met Alfred, himself a widower of several years,
and they were soon married. Before Ursula she bore another son, Karl.
By the time of their daughter's birth, Alfred was in his early fifties and
Theodora in her early thirties. It was to this "redhead from Telluride"
that Ursula Le Guin dedicated *The Tombs of Atuan,* the second book
of her Earthsea trilogy. By then Theodora Kroeber too was a successful
author, having published *The Inland Whale* (1959), a collection of Indian
myths, and *Ishi in Two Worlds* (1961), the biography of Ishi, the last
"wild" Indian in North America and the close friend of Alfred Kroeber
following his "capture" in 1911 to his death in 1916. Theodora Kroeber

later wrote several beautiful children's books, published by Parnassus Press, as well as additional works in anthropology, a biography of her husband, *Alfred Kroeber: A Personal Configuration* (1970), and poems and other essays. Remarkably, she began writing seriously only in 1955, when she was nearly 60, and she is still at it.[9]

The two Kroeber parents, their four children, and other household members, including Marciano, the houseboy and children's major playmate, settled into their newly purchased family home on Arch Street in Berkeley. It is a "sturdy, ample" house, built in 1906 by Bernard Maybeck, and constructed inside and out of untreated redwood without finished or painted trim. The high western windows look across San Francisco Bay and through the Golden Gate.

But the Arch Street house was for the winters and the school year. Come summer and vacation, the Kroebers were off to their country place, forty acres in the hills of the Napa Valley's west side, which they had purchased in 1930. It had a redwood house, a barn, and dry-rock walls. The land, once vineyard, had gone back to brush or served as pasture; it faced St. John's Mountain. They named it Kishamish. As Theodora Kroeber recalls, it was "a world for exploration, for reading, for one's own work, for swimming and playing games, for sitting by the outdoor fire until late in the night talking, telling stories, singing; for sleeping under the stars."[10]

Through these settings moved a continual flux of stimulating people, such as Robert Oppenheimer and Clyde Kluckhohn, graduate students and American Indians, and so many refugees from Europe, Le Guin recalls, that the house seemed always full of people speaking German.[11] Of these, the anthropologists seemed to have had special impact on Le Guin:

The people that I met as a kid—that generation trained by Boas, and the next generation—they were exciting people. They had this intense interest in individuals and individual cultures, and then also this kind of broad range of trying to put large ideas together. They were not culture-bound types, I must say; they were pretty free souls, those anthropologists. They loved the variety of mankind, they just ate it up![12]

But above all, there were those remarkable parents. They were "neat people," Le Guin recalls, and spared her many "hangups." Despite being the youngest of the four children and the only girl, she experienced no differences in expectations for herself and her brothers; her parents were "totally nonsexist."[13] Their influence has been incorporated into her temperament,

like a willingness to get outside of your own culture, and also a sensitivity to how culture affects personality, which is what my father was concerned with. My father felt very strongly that you can never actually get outside your own culture. All you can do is try. I think that feeling sometimes comes out in my writing. My father studied real cultures and I make them up—in a way, it's the same thing.[14]

In the home of scholars there are books, and the children of scholars usually take to them as a matter of course. Le Guin reports reading everything she could get hands on. Besides absorbing anthropology by "osmosis," she had Lady Frazer's *Leaves from the Golden Bough,* which she read "like Peter Rabbit";[15] she read the Norse myths, which meant "incomparably" more to her than did the Greek or any others, and they became part of her "childhood lore," shapers of her imagination;[16] her brothers and she read science fiction in the early 1940s, *Thrilling Wonder Stories* and *Astounding.* Her favorite author was "Lewis Padgett," but she got off science fiction in the late 1940s—"It seemed to be all about hardware and soldiers"—and moved on to Tolstoy.[17]

From this reading Le Guin made a discovery that strongly affected her entire life. On the living room book shelves she found Dunsany's *A Dreamer's Tales;* it was her father's book, one of his favorites. He had often told Indian legends to the family, and she had nurtured herself on the myths of the past in her other reading, but here was a thing new to her—people were *still* creating myths. It came to her "as a revelation"; she had found the "Inner Lands," her "native country."[18] She dwells there yet.

From the perspective of many of us looking at these fragments through the filters of time, Le Guin's family and early life take on the aura of a child's storybook tale. They hurdled the Great Depression handily; they survived World War 2 intact. There were deaths at the family's periphery, other problems undoubtedly existed, but surely this close family, with its cosmopolitan and stimulating experiences, its rich physical environment, and its economic and psychological security, must produce outstanding offspring.

This appears to be the case. Of the three sons, Clifton, Karl, and Theodore, one is a psychologist, one a historian, and one an English professor. But it is the daughter, Ursula, with her writing, who has made the greatest public impact to date.

Le Guin's original ambitions were to be a biologist and a poet, and, although her inability to handle math caused her to drop biology,[19] her writing career was launched early. Her first completed short story, written at age nine, was a fantasy in which a man is persecuted by evil elves. By ten or eleven years of age, she had written her first science fiction, involving time travel and the origins of Earth life, which she submitted to *Astounding.* It was rejected, and Le Guin would not submit a work again until she was 21. She can still remember the day that rejection slip arrived. But throughout her youth she continued to produce "prolific and derivative adolescent scribblings."[20]

In 1947 Le Guin entered Radcliffe College; a member of Phi Beta Kappa, she received a B.A. in 1951, then went on to graduate work at Columbia, where her father was teaching following his retirement from Berkeley in 1946 and his one-year visiting professorship at Harvard. Le Guin earned an M.A. in 1952. She specialized in French and Italian Renaissance literature; science courses were "carefully" avoided because of her math deficiency. She began work on a Ph.D. at Columbia in 1952, and soon won a Fulbright grant to study the poet Jean Lemaire de Belges, in France. While crossing the Atlantic on the *Queen Mary* in 1953, she met Charles A. Le Guin, then an assistant professor at Mercer College, who was also on a Fulbright to France. They were married in Paris on December 22, of that same year.

"And that," Le Guin said, "was the end of the doctorate!"[21] Well, perhaps that and the concern that, even with a Ph.D., as a woman she might be limited to teaching freshman French; "So I got out."[22] Returning to the United States, the Le Guins did not settle long in one place, as Charles moved from teaching at Mercer, to Emory, to the University of Idaho in Moscow. He earned a Ph.D. in history from Emory in 1956, and in 1957, while the Le Guins were living in Idaho, their eldest daughter, Elisabeth, was born.

During this time Ursula continued writing. For years she had worked at poems, short stories, and even novels, the first of which was finished when she was 21. Some of the poems and one short story, "An die Musik," were published in little magazines, but five novels and several other stories could not find print despite efforts beginning in 1951. Most of these works, the ones Le Guin considered her best, were set in an invented but "nonfantastic" central European country; thus, they were neither fantasy nor science fiction, nor were they realistic. In short, they had no market.[23]

As the turn of the decade approached, a second daughter, Caroline, was born to the Le Guins, and they moved again, this time to their present home in Oregon, where Charles began teaching at Portland State University in 1959. But in the next year two events were to occur which would mark major turnings in the lives of both the Kroebers and the Le Guins. One would be an ending, the other a beginning. And that was to be the time when, Ursula Kroeber Le Guin feels, she finally came of age.

In Paris on an October's night in 1960, Alfred Kroeber, in his mid-eighties, suddenly died. Theodora was with him.[24] In writing of his final years, she tells of a giant intellect at the peak of its creative powers: "... Kroeber's mind and imagination spread, like the delta of a great stream, over the whole plain of culture history, probing its vastness and variety, testing, playing with possibilities; gathering new data or rearranging, freshly interpreting old data; viewing the phenomena of history in ways as yet not philosophically accepted, sometimes not named."[25] The loss of this vital man must have profoundly affected his family, including Ursula, who wrote this poem the next summer:

ALFRED

This old notebook I write in was my father's;
he never wrote in it. A gray man,
all my lifetime, with a short gray beard;
a slight man, not tall.
The other day I saw five elephants,
big elephants, with palm-trunk legs
and continents of sides, and one,
the biggest one, had bent tusks bound
about with brass. They were waiting,
patient, to be let outside
into the sunlight and the autumn air,
moving about their stall so quietly,
using the grace of great size and the gentleness,
swaying a little, silent, strong as ships.
That was a great pleasure, to see that.
And he would have liked to see the big one making water,
too, like a steaming river,
enough to float ten bigots in.
O there is nothing like sheer quantity,
mountains, elephants, minds.[26]

Le Guin had not read science fiction for about fifteen years; then a friend in Portland loaned her some works from his collection, including a copy of *The Magazine of Fantasy and Science Fiction* which contained a story by Cordwainer Smith.[27] Le Guin had rediscovered science fiction, and with it, she candidly tells us, a way into print:

You must either fit a category, or "have a name," to publish a book in America. As the only way I was ever going to achieve Namehood was *by* writing, I was reduced to fitting a category. Therefore my first efforts to write science fiction were motivated by a pretty distinct wish to get published: nothing higher or lower. The stories reflect this extrinsic motivation. They are kind of amiable, but not very good, not serious, essentially slick. They were published by Cele Goldsmith Lalli, the kindly and courageous editor of *Amazing* and *Fantastic* in the early sixties.[28]

Ursula Le Guin had crossed a watershed in her life.

A fantasy story, "April in Paris," appeared in the September, 1962, *Fantastic,* one of science fiction's lesser magazines. This was Le Guin's first sale—she was 32—and the first genre piece she had written since the story rejected by *Astounding* in 1942.[29] The next year her first published "genuine authentic real virgin-wool" science fiction story, "The Masters," appeared in the February *Fantastic.*[30]

With her revived interest in science fiction, Le Guin attended the Oakland Worldcon in 1964. Science fiction fandom's existence had come as a surprise, for she had not participated in it during her youthful days of science fiction reading, and, although later she occasionally wrote letters to fanzines, gave some interviews, and was guest of honor at a Vancouver science fiction convention, Le Guin generally preferred to remain on the margins of the science fiction fan community. She did not attend another Worldcon until 1975, when she was guest of honor at "Aussiecon" in Melbourne, Australia.[31]

Nineteen sixty-four also saw the appearance of "The Word of Unbinding" and "The Rule of Names," both in *Fantastic;* these were significant stories, for their creation marked the imaginative genesis of Earthsea, the archipelago world of Le Guin's superb trilogy.[32]

But before producing these major works of fantasy, Le Guin wrote three entertaining but undistinguished science fiction novels, *Planet of Exile, Rocannon's World,* both published in 1966, and *City of Illusions,* which saw print in 1967. These were published in paperback by Ace Books, a traditional market in the genre for novels by new writers. They were tied loosely into the Hainish universe, the same "future history" which provides the settings for most of Le Guin's science fiction.

Meanwhile the Le Guins' youngest child, Theodore, had been born in 1964. Since the late 1950s Le Guin had had young children to care for in addition to her writing and other activities. However, her motherhood was apparently coincidental to her entrance into a new field—books for young persons—a type of writing she had never tried before.

In 1967 Herman Schein, the proprietor of Parnassus Press, asked Le Guin to write a book for older children; she was to have complete freedom of subject and approach. Le Guin found the request "exhilarating," for she had never been commissioned to write something for a publisher. Her thinking returned to her archipelagic world, and the result was *A Wizard of Earthsea* (1968).[33] The quality of this work marked Le Guin as someone special among contemporary fantasy writers and gained for her her first national recognition by winning a *Boston Globe-Horn Book* Award for Excellence. It was also named an American Library Association "Notable Book." She dedicated *WOE* to her three brothers.

Recognition in the smaller world of science fiction soon followed. In 1969 Ace published *The Left Hand of Darkness* as one of its Science Fiction Special series, and the following year it won both the Nebula, selected by science fiction writers, and the Hugo, the field's highest fan award. Set in the Hainish universe, it described an intriguing race of androgynous humans. Le Guin's dedication here was to her husband, Charles, "sine quo non." As with the Earthsea books, *LHD* was foreshadowed by an earlier story, "Winter's King," which appeared in Damon Knight's *Orbit 5,* one of the original anthologies which were increasingly becoming Le Guin's new, and higher paying, market for shorter fiction. Interestingly, in "Winter's King," the people were not androgynous; that surfaced from Le Guin's subconscious only with the novel.[34]

Androgyny's antithesis, *Playboy,* published Le Guin's "Nine Lives" the same year that *LHD* appeared and, ironically, presented Le Guin with her most serious sexist experience as a writer. The magazine, after purchasing the story, requested that it be published under the name "U. K. Le Guin," thereby disguising the author's sex. Le Guin agreed, but this reduction of "Ursula" to "a simple, unthreatening, slightly enigmatic shape—a U," still rankles with her.[35]

Le Guin's development as a professional writer advanced further when, wondering how one goes about getting a book published in hardcover, she approached the agent Virginia Kidd. Kidd rapidly arranged for a hardcover edition for *LHD* to be published by Walker, and she has been representing Le Guin ever since.[36]

Two unusual novels appeared in 1971, *The Lathe of Heaven,* the least typical of all Le Guin science fiction novels, and *The Tombs of Atuan,* the second Earthsea book and her only novel with a female as the lead character. Philip K. Dick, with his novels of multiple realities, has often been mentioned by Le Guin as her favorite science fiction writer, and *LOH* seems highly influenced by his work. Never much interested in "wiring diagram" science fiction—Le Guin admitted in 1970 to having never read John W. Campbell, Jr.'s, *Analog*[37]—her taste also ran counter to general contemporary opinion in the genre with her admiration of Britain's D. G. Compton and, later, Poland's Stanislaw Lem. But Le Guin's stature in the field continued to grow, for, although it didn't win, *LOH* was nominated for the Nebula and the Hugo; moreover, the story "Vaster

Than Empires and More Slow," published that same year, also received a Hugo nomination.

Le Guin took an interest in the development of new writers in the genre, too. In 1971 she taught a writer's workshop on science fiction and fantasy for children and adults held at Pacific University and, starting that same year, was a writer-in-residence at several Clarion West workshops on writing science fiction.

The Earthsea books continued to be popular; *TOA* won a Newbery honor medal and was nominated for the National Book Award for Children's Literature. The following year the third and final Earthsea novel, *The Farthest Shore* (1972), won the National Book Award in the children's literature category, a great honor but one perhaps somewhat dismaying to its author, who had only so recently turned to writing for young people after having tried so long to sell her serious adult fiction.

Coming of age was the topic of the first Earthsea novel, sex of the second; but *TFS* concerned death. Is this a suitable subject for young readers? Yes, says Le Guin, "since in a way one can say that the hour when a child realizes, not that death exists—children are intensely aware of death—but that he/she, personally, is mortal, will die, is the hour when childhood ends, and the new life begins. Coming of age again, but in a larger context."[38] *TFS* is dedicated to her three children.

Le Guin's science fiction now became somewhat polemical; "The Word for World Is Forest" (1972), a novella written during Charles's 1968–69 sabbatical in England, was stimulated by her opposition to the Vietnam War. Although Le Guin has said of herself, "I'm not an activist and I'm not a joiner," she frequently translated her political beliefs into actions, including allowing her name to appear in print on a petition by science fiction writers opposing the Vietnam War, engaging in nonviolent protest marches against atomic testing and the war in Vietnam, and working for Eugene McCarthy and George McGovern in their primaries.[39]

Certainly her concern for human rights and freedom are quite strong, as her story "The Ones Who Walk Away from Omelas" (1973) demonstrates; if the contentedness of the many is purchased at a cost of a single individual's torment, the price is too high.[40] Le Guin has also spoken out against the extreme centralization of our modern society and the limitations it imposes on freedom: "Today, of course, we have government encouraging business growth, encouraging the large corporation that either makes money or war as against the individual consumer or soldier. The individual is treated only as a member of an enormous mass. I think this is essentially anti-democratic and disastrous, leading to a future of repressive control."[41]

In 1977 Le Guin protested an action by the Science Fiction Writers of America, an organization of which she had been a member for several years. In the German paper *Frankfurter Allgemeine Zeitung,* Stanislaw Lem had rendered a harsh assessment of science fiction in America; his essay was reprinted in the SFWA's private journal, and a furor resulted. As either a direct or an indirect consequence of the controversy, the SFWA withdrew an honorary membership it had bestowed upon Lem some time before. In retaliation Le Guin publicly withdrew her story "The Diary of the Rose" (1976), already nominated for the Nebula, which the SFWA awards, from further consideration. For her, the SFWA had "condoned the deliberate dishonoring of a fellow writer," and, especially since her story was about "freedom of opinion, and stuff like that," she felt impelled to act.[42] But she didn't walk away from membership in SFWA. Instead, she chose to stay and fight from within.[43]

Both "The Word for World Is Forest" and "The Ones Who Walk Away from Omelas" won Hugos. However, Le Guin was at work on another major and remarkable novel, *The Dispossessed* (1974), which, as had *LHD,* won both the Hugo and Nebula, making her not only the first woman to receive the Hugo and the Nebula for the year's best novel, but the only writer to receive *both* awards twice for best novel. Interestingly, *DIS* was picked only for runner-up for the John W. Campbell Memorial Award, a prize chosen by science fiction critics, losing to Dick's *Flow My Tears the Policeman Said.* More importantly, the work itself is unique, being an extraordinarily realistic, "ambiguous" utopia reflecting a rich blend of the thoughts of the anarchists, such as Kropotkin, and the ancient Chinese philosophy of Taoism (see the Cogell and the Tifft and Sullivan essays in this volume). *DIS* was Le Guin's attempt, like Kropotkin's, to "inject a gentle antidote" into her generation to counteract the individualistic, social Darwinist "crap," such as in Robert Ardrey's works and in the film *2001,* that still abounds.[44]

The philosophy of the anarchists in *DIS* was developed by Odo, a nearly legendary woman revolutionary. After finishing the novel Le Guin found that Odo too needed her story told.[45] The result was "The Day before the Revolution" (1974), an exquisitely beautiful piece of polemical art. It won Le Guin a Nebula, but, probably due to its genre label, has yet to receive the wider recognition it deserves.

This situation applies not only to much of Le Guin's work but to that of many other fine science fiction writers, as well. To counter this problem, a movement began in the sixties among some scholars to give serious attention to science fiction. It soon culminated in the founding of two scholarly journals in the United States, *Extrapolation* and *Science-*

Fiction Studies, and the creation of the Science Fiction Research Association.

Le Guin has received a great deal of recognition from these scholars—including invited appearances at SFRA meetings and a special Le Guin number of *Science-Fiction Studies* in 1975—but increasing attention is being paid her by critics outside science fiction (see the Bittner essay in this volume). This parallels Le Guin's recent professional development, which has advanced on several fronts: first, her polemical science fiction continued, with such stories as "The New Atlantis" (1975); second, a collection of her fantasy and science fiction short stories, *The Wind's Twelve Quarters* (1975), was published; third, she wrote a short novel for juvenile readers, *Very Far Away from Anywhere Else* (1976); fourth, and most important, there appeared *Orsinian Tales* (1976), a collection of stories set in that invented central European country that Le Guin had been exploring since the early fifties. Whether because she had finally established a name, or because the publishing field had changed, these long ignored stories, some undoubtedly written years earlier, finally saw print. In perhaps the greatest irony of her career, *Orsinian Tales* received a 1977 National Book Award nomination, not in children's books, but, simply, in fiction. Le Guin was 47 years of age.

As reporters have described it, the Le Guin house, a tall Victorian structure built around the turn of the century, is warm and orderly; there are light wood floors, oriental rugs, and comfortable chairs. The fireplace will be going in cold weather and candles are scattered about. It is spacious, yet it has a lean, spare quality with just enough dust to be homey. A cat is likely to be curled in a corner. The neighborhood is pleasant, a residential area along Thurman Street in northwest Portland, Oregon.[46] The mountains can be seen from the back porch.

The house reflects the home. Like the Kroebers, the Le Guins seem close, solid, secure. Charles and Ursula have been married for twenty-five years. She has said: "Long term pair bonding—sexuality plus affection that lasts—seems to me one of the most important things human beings can do." She adds that it isn't for everyone, however.[47]

Charles A. Le Guin, a history professor, is a native of Macon, Georgia, and has the appearance of a southern intellectual, with a heavy mustache, gentle eyes, longish brown hair, and southern tones.[48] He sews patchwork coverlets and shares the household chores. The Le Guins also share an enthusiasm for music, and they attend local opera and symphony productions.[49] Charles has always encouraged Ursula in her writing, even reading the first typed drafts of her works. In Ursula's words:

He could always make time to give me an hour or two when I couldn't find it any other way. It wasn't like he would say, "Well, I feel good today so I'll stay with the kids." I'd say, "I've got to finish this story; and he'd say, "Okay, I'll take them." That kind of thing is very important and I don't think you can make it work with marriage contracts. Your heart has got to be in it. One person cannot do two full-time jobs, and we had three of them: my writing, his teaching and writing, and mothering. But two people can do three full-time jobs. They really can. That's why I'm so strong on partnership. It can be a great thing.[50]

In eloquent testimony of the Le Guins' relationship, *DIS* carries the simple dedication, "for the partner."

In 1975 a reporter cameoed the three Le Guin children: Elisabeth, a student studying cello at San Francisco Conservatory of Music; Caroline, called "Carlie," wild about horses; Theo, small and faintly elfish like his mother.[51] Only rarely have items about the Le Guin children appeared in print, but the evidence indicates a close family with charming children and concerned, sophisticated parents. Ursula Le Guin has spoken about her relationship with her children, and it gives additional insight into her political beliefs:

I believe that nobody should have any authority over anybody else except what can personally be developed and maintained. There are situations in which somebody has to be in control, but it has to be somebody who deserves to be there—and when the occasion is over, the authority is gone. . . . You can't always button yourself into a uniform, because there will come a day when you want to take it off and you can't undo the buttons.[52]

Le Guin has been taken to task by some persons in the women's movement for her infrequent use of women as leading characters and an inadequate feminine point of view in her works. Le Guin labels herself a feminist, although her beliefs in this area appear to have evolved throughout the seventies. At first, in 1970, she was reluctant to go on record on the subject; she did point out that she was taking no part in the movement herself. To her sexism seemed "an injustice which is less evident than many others" and the feminist movement itself was too general; the anti-male bias of some feminists, much of the ranting, and the movement's middle class bias turned her off. She had never experienced any discrimination as a woman writer except for the *Playboy* episode with "Nine Lives," which she seemed to shrug off.[53] In 1971 Le Guin said that she was for the movement in so far as it is a move toward economic equality and human brotherliness or charity, and part of this century's effort toward civilization. Every step away from civilization, such as National Socialism, included a strong element of male domination and this was no coincidence, she pointed out.[54] In 1974 she explained her use of a male lead in *LHD* as the result of her fear that men would "loathe" the book and "be unsettled and unnerved by it." But a male lead character, "and a rather stupid and slightly bigoted" male character at that, would make it easier for male readers to "work in with and sort of be changed." While she did not consider herself to be a "radical" feminist, she couldn't see "how you can be an intelligent woman and not be a feminist."[55] That same year she said: "I'm a feminist; I think the woman's movement is going very much in a good direction, for everyone. . . . Listen, I know there's a lot of shouting, but, well, you have to make noise to get listened to."[56] In her "Aussiecon" speech in 1975 Le Guin pointed out that perhaps only one in thirty science fiction writers are women—a figure given her by her agent, Virginia Kidd—and she would like to see more women writing: "The practice of an art is, in its absolute discipline, the experience of absolute freedom. And that, above all, is why I'd like to see more of my sisters trying out their wings above the mountains. Because freedom is not always an easy thing for women to find."[57] By 1977, when Le Guin was asked about the trend in feminist science fiction, she replied that it was "great": "Now more women are reading it, and that's good because a lot of women can't do anything much more than dream and propose alternatives, and science fiction is a great way of doing it." But what about the anti-male tone in some of this work? "It's inevitable that some people are mad. My basic judgment has to be aesthetic and I don't think anger inspires the highest type of literature. But it's got to be done. Some of these things have to be said for the sake of sheer justice."[58]

With the responsibility of a family, when does Le Guin find the time to write? "If you have little kids—babies—you don't." You wait awhile. From 1957 to 1967, when there were babies in the house, Le Guin wrote at night after they were in bed. Once the children reached school age, the mornings were free for writing, and she got to work by 8:45, saving the chores for other times. In summer, when school was out, she would return to night writing. In short, she had to work on a schedule. Today, with children still in school, Le Guin gets in about six hours of writing a day.[59]

Finding it difficult to think at a typewriter, Le Guin writes first in longhand, as her father did. Short stories tend to come to her as a whole, and she just writes them down. With novels, she generally knows where she will end, but most of the story is "uncovered" as she writes.[60] Sometimes she makes notes on plot and character, but these are seldom relied on; she doesn't write out descriptions beforehand. It's all part of herself; she knows her characters as well as she knows herself, and she "discovers," not invents, her worlds.[61]

Le Guin prefers novels to short stories, both to write or to read, unless the stories are by Borges or Chekhov.[62] She writes relatively fast, with a short story taking perhaps a week, but revision can take a month to six weeks; "Nine Lives" took most of a year. Novels take about a year for initial drafting (this was the case with *LHD*), but research and revisions add additional time.[63] Thus, unlike John Brunner, Barry Malzberg, or Robert Silverberg, Le Guin has never been a volume producer. But, then, neither has she had to support herself and her family by writing: thus, she has escaped the output/income bind that plagues so many other fine writers in the genre.

Works on how to write have always been avoided by Le Guin; the *Shorter Oxford Dictionary* and Follett's and Fowler's manuals of usage are her entire tool kit.[64] These are shelved above her desk in her high ceilinged work room at home–her writing retreat. She is fond of paraphrasing Virginia Woolf: "I have a room of my own."

For the last several years, people have been suggesting that Le Guin will leave science fiction and pursue her career in mainstream fiction. Le Guin has continually rejected this notion, but recent statements indicate some indecisiveness concerning her future. Did she have the desire to enter mainstream fiction, she was asked in 1970. "Not really. To a large extent science fiction is where it's at anyway, so I'm perfectly happy with it."[65] Again, in 1973 she said, "The limits, and the great spaces of fantasy and science fiction are precisely what my imagination needs. Outer Space, and the Inner Lands, are still, and always will be, my country."[66] Yet in 1975, having been "written out" after *DIS,* she seemed less certain: "I'm just beginning to write again, but it's going in all sorts of different directions so I don't really want to talk about it because I don't know quite what's going on."[67]

Likewise, her love of fantasy offers another route somewhat away from science fiction (see the Malzberg preface to this book). Fantasy is the language her imagination speaks, she has said;[68] "When in difficulties [in writing] I fall back into my native tongue, which is that of non-intellectualized fantasy, daydreams, symbol, myth."[69]

But realistic mainstream fiction offers no attraction to Le Guin:

... the reality of our lives and times has become quite unmanageable in terms of conventional literary realism. Most realistic, naturalistic novels nowadays are so limited as to be positively quaint; they are the true escapist literature. It is only the genuinely great artist—a Solzhenitsyn— who can encompass all the terrible fantasies of which our lives are made and make us see that they are not only real, but meaningful. The rest of us can only come at reality by hints, by flashes, through symbols and through dreams.[70]

There is yet another alternative: the mainstream may come to Le Guin. She believes that the dichotomy between science fiction and the mainstream no longer exists: "There is a spectrum, now, not a chasm. The SF label is a remnant of the ghetto wall, and I'll be very glad to see it go. Oh for the day when I can go into any library and find *The Man in the High Castle*, not shelved next to *Barf the Barbarian* by Elmer T. Hack, but by author's name, Philip K. Dick, right next to Charles Dickens—where it belongs."[71]

Whatever Le Guin's future plans, she has been a strong and positive voice in defense and explication of science fiction: "If science fiction has a major gift to offer literature, I think it is just this: the capacity to face an open universe. Physically open, psychically open. No doors shut."[72] And again: "At its best—when its practitioners take it seriously—it is a new integrative effort, a way of enabling the contemporary, scientific, individualistic consciousness to achieve the collective creative power of myth, to cope with thunder and suffering by aesthetic, integrative means."[73] And yet again:

SF is not a great art form yet, and I rather think it never will be. It has certain inherent limitations which may keep it always on the fringe of the greatest potentialities of the novel. But there is something about it that I like tremendously and will defend in it against all comers, and this is its effort to include in art, in fiction, a whole new—truly new—field of vast complexity: that is, of course, the field of science, including modern technology. Science and technology, as they affect human beings, of course. Here is a case where "life's job" as I call it is crying to be done; where the harmony of art, the ordering process, is very badly needed, where the complexity of our experience has become a terrible confusion. A whole great area of knowledge and experience, very intense and important experience, is omitted from literature, because most writers still shy away from science, as if it was going to bite them.[74]

The subtitle of *DIS* is "An Ambiguous Utopia"; for Le Guin, the subtitle of her career might be "An Ambiguous Success." As she reflects on her accomplishments, the conflict between her goals and means sharply appears:

I have found, somewhat to my displeasure, that I am an extremely moral writer. I am always grinding axes and making points. I wish I wasn't so moralistic, because my interest is aesthetic. What I want to do is make something beautiful like a good pot or a good piece of music, and the ideas and moralism keep getting in the way. There's a definite battle going on.[75]

Whatever the outcome of that battle, Ursula K. Le Guin is certain to have Odo at her side, a gentle command in her ear, to remind her of who she is: "One who, choosing, accepts the responsibility of choice." And that, too, is maturity.

PART 2

VOYAGE TO INNER LANDS
and to
OUTER SPACE

I'll make my report as if I told a story, for I was taught as a child on my homeworld that Truth is a matter of the imagination.

The Left Hand of Darkness

JAMES W. BITTNER

A SURVEY OF LE GUIN CRITICISM

Critical evaluations of Ursula K. Le Guin's individual works and formulations about the shape of her development must be provisional. She is, after all, still writing, still "pushing out towards the limits—my own and those of the medium," as she once said.[1] Each new work she creates will affect the meanings of those that preceded it; each new publication will alter, subtly perhaps, perhaps dramatically, the configurations of her creative achievement.

The publication of *Orsinian Tales* (1976), a collection of stories "written, & rewritten, over a span of 20 years," is a case in point.[2] These tales, set in an imaginary Central European country, are neither science fiction nor fantasy nor realism. As the dust jacket on *The Farthest Shore* (1972) tells us, "Most of her books are about imaginary countries inhabited by imaginary people with real problems"; we might call them prose versions of Marianne Moore's "imaginary gardens with real toads in them."[3] Le Guin's "imaginary countries" (the title of the last story in *ORT*) include not only the science fiction worlds Rokanan, Werel, Terra, Athshe, and Anarres-Urras, but also Orsinia, Earthsea, the castle in the poem "Coming of Age" in *Wild Angels* (1975), Owen Griffiths's Thorn in *Very Far Away from Anywhere Else* (1976), and the other shore in *The Water Is Wide* (1976). It is now more apparent than ever that Le Guin cannot be narrowly categorized as a science fiction writer. Criticism that concentrates on her science fiction can produce only a partial view of her creative range and artistic powers.

Even if a comprehensive overview of Le Guin's writing—fiction, poetry, and nonfiction—is not yet possible, there can be little doubt about the quality of her individual achievements. Her place as a major figure in

twentieth-century science fiction is already secure. The Earthsea trilogy—
A Wizard of Earthsea (1968), *The Tombs of Atuan* (1971), and *The
Farthest Shore* (1972)—has joined the works of J. R. R. Tolkien and
C. S. Lewis as one of the best fantasies of recent times. As the general
reading public and the academics continue to discover her fiction, she will
be accepted as a significant voice in contemporary literature regardless
of generic boundaries. Translations of her work into Finnish, Polish,
Swedish, German, Norwegian, Danish, Dutch, French, Spanish, Italian,
and Japanese are creating a world-wide audience of admirers. Indeed,
as of this writing, more than half of the significant comment on Le
Guin has come from critics living outside the United States.

Le Guin's fiction did not attract wide notice until after her fourth
and fifth novels appeared. Her first novel, *Rocannon's World* (1966),
was published in an Ace Double paperback and was reviewed in a few
science fiction magazines as the flip side of Avram Davidson's *The
Kar-Chee Reign*. Her next two novels, *Planet of Exile* (1966) and *City
of Illusions* (1967), were generally ignored and soon went out of print.
Only after the success of *WOE* and *The Left Hand of Darkness* (1969)
were they reprinted and reviewed. With those two novels Le Guin's reputation began its rapid rise; her subsequent books were not only reviewed
in science fiction magazines but were also noticed in national magazines.
Since 1971 all her books have been continuously in print, most of them
going into several printings both in hardcover and paperback. Her first
three novels, out of print in 1968–69, have been reissued in hard-
covers, and may finally attract the attention they deserve.[4]

Acclaim for Le Guin's fiction came first from writers and readers of
children's literature, from science fiction fans (who award the Hugo,
the Science Fiction Achievement Award), and from her colleagues in the
Science Fiction Writers of America (who award the Nebula). Each volume
of the Earthsea trilogy has been honored: *WOE* received the *Boston Globe-
Horn Book* Award for Excellence in juvenile fiction in 1969; *TOA* was
named a Newbery Honor Book in 1972; and *TFS* won the National
Book Award for children's literature in 1973. Le Guin is one of six
science fiction writers to win both the Nebula and the Hugo for the best
novel of the year; she is the *only* one to do it twice, for *LHD* and *The
Dispossessed* (1974). She has also won Hugos for "The Word for World
Is Forest" (1972) and "The Ones Who Walk Away from Omelas" (1973),
and a Nebula for "The Day before the Revolution" (1974). In 1977
ORT was a National Book Award nominee.

Except for some early assessments in fanzines, the first serious criticism
of Le Guin's fiction was Eleanor Cameron's talk at a 1969 meeting of the
New England Round Table of Children's Librarians, "High Fantasy: *A*

Wizard of Earthsea."⁵ After a brief discussion and definition of "high fantasy," Cameron surveys Le Guin's writing career through *LHD.* She praises Le Guin's aesthetic uses of anthropology in *WOE,* recognizes the completeness with which Le Guin creates a world of mages and magic, and draws on Sir James Frazer and Carl Jung to illuminate the themes of "names and shadows" in *WOE.* Noting that "Le Guin must herself be a wizard at naming," Cameron shows how Le Guin, unlike Walter de la Mare and Tolkien, combines known names with strange ones. She concludes with some remarks on the uses and value of high fantasy, and writes that Le Guin "takes us beyond magic to an understanding of truths which illuminate our difficulties in the world of reality." American critics of Le Guin, who value her science fiction more than her fantasy, have yet to match Cameron's graceful, sensitive analysis of *WOE* and her sympathetic understanding of Le Guin's fantasy. In fact, when the *New York Times* finally recognized the trilogy, it printed a review by a British poet.⁶

For critical insights into Le Guin's fantasy, one must go to England, where the American preference for science fiction over fantasy is inverted. The *Times Literary Supplement,* which had covered *LHD* and *The Lathe of Heaven* (1971) in a couple of paragraphs and written off *DIS* as "a novel of conversations, often in sixth-form polemics,"⁷ published full reviews by Naomi Lewis of each volume of the trilogy as it appeared.⁸ Lewis, who also reviewed the trilogy for the *Observer,*⁹ welcomes *WOE* as "a new quest-story, an original allegory" with none of the "theological quiddities of C. S. Lewis." Like Cameron, she praises the "wholeness" of Le Guin's artistry. She finds *TOA*'s "unerring detail," its "total realization of place, time, customs, laws of beahviour, of magic," and its "complex terrain" to be as "closely realized as the Brontës' imagined worlds," and commanding the same belief. (That N. Lewis's appreciation of "imagined worlds" closely resembles Le Guin's own became apparent when *Very Far Away from Anywhere Else* appeared in 1976. Angria and Gondal, the Brontës' imaginary countries, have a prominent place in Owen Griffiths's story.) In *TFS,* says N. Lewis, Le Guin shows herself to be a "writer of phenomenal power" who poses and meets "audacious problems with a seductive style." *The Economist* supported Lewis; sandwiched between photographs of Tolkien and Le Guin is its judgment that the Earthsea trilogy is "a true saga of serious purpose, worth taking seriously."¹⁰

In "*A Wizard of Earthsea* and the Charge of Escapism,"¹¹ Wendy Jago, a British writer and editor of children's books, uses Tolkien's "On Fairy-Stories" in *Tree and Leaf,* Jerome Bruner's essay "Identity and the Modern Novel," and an analysis of *WOE* to support her argument for the moral relevance of juvenile fantasy. Quoting Bruner, Jago contends that we turn to literature in general not for "'mythic models for action [but] for models or images or paradigms of awareness and its paradoxes: it is not objective reality and what to do when up against it, but subjective reality and how to discern it.'" We enjoy children's books in particular, says Jago herself, because their "'pared-down-ness' may allow us back into a world which is [as] sharp and significant . . . as are the moments of intensity in adult life." Jago illustrates this with a glance at how *WOE* relates to "developmental stages and crises," and shows how *WOE* "is concerned with morality, and with the enactment of morality in choice." This last statement is directly applicable to almost everything—fiction and nonfiction—Le Guin has written. More than that, Jago's argument for the relevance of children's literature is very nearly congruent with the ideas Le Guin herself expresses in "The Child and the Shadow," a lecture presented at the Library of Congress in 1974.[12]

The same journal that published Jago's essay also includes Geoff Fox's "Notes on 'Teaching' *A Wizard of Earthsea.*"[13] Having collected many teachers' approaches to *WOE*, Fox shows how, "through talk, choral work, drama, paint, game making and the writing of prose and verse," teachers can help a young reader gain "greater understanding, keener enjoyment of *[WOE]* itself: perhaps greater understanding, even keener enjoyment, of his own experience."

The first extended discussion of Le Guin in the British science fiction journal *Foundation* was not a treatment of her science fiction; it was instead an appreciation of her fantasy: Peter Nicholls's review-essay of *TFS*, "showing children the value of death."[14] Like most other writers on the trilogy, Nicholls argues that it transcends the boundaries of children's literature. His comparisons of Le Guin with Tolkien and Lewis are intended to demonstrate that Le Guin has deeper resources of language than Tolkien, uses fewer black/white moral dualisms than Tolkien, and has a metaphysic more satisfyingly *this*-worldly than Lewis. Nicholls regards the Earthsea trilogy as Le Guin's "finest achievement to date"; he praises her stylistic accuracy, her "honesty and depth of feelings," and her "transparently subtle intellect."

Critical interpretations of Le Guin's science fiction—what she calls her "Outer Space" to distinguish it from the "Inner Lands" of her fantasy[15] — opened with essays on *LHD*. From the beginning, debate about the artistic quality of *LHD* has centered on whether the plot, variously construed by different critics, is integrated with the most striking thing in the novel, Gethenian androgyny and ambisexuality, and whether Le Guin succeeded in creating really androgynous aliens or just thinly disguised males. The world-famous Polish science fiction writer Stanislaw Lem, while grateful that a work of science fiction had finally come along to which he could apply the criteria of great literature, found several shortcomings in *LHD*.[16] The sexual ontology of the Gethenians, he argues, has very little to do with the plot of the novel, which concerns the entry of Gethen into the Ekumen, a loose confederation of eighty-three inhabitable worlds. He charges, moreover, that Le Guin avoided grappling with the "cruel harshness of the individual's destiny in [the Gethenian biological and social] system." Like many feminist critics in the United States, Lem sees only men in *LHD*: "Karhider garments, manners of speech, mores, and behaviour, are all masculine." One of those feminist critics is Joanna Russ.[17] She is sorry to see that "family structure is not fully explained" and that "child-rearing is left completely in the dark." Those omissions, together with Le Guin's use of a male hero and her use of the word "he" to refer to Estraven and the Gethenians, give Russ the impression that in *LHD* we have "a world of men."

In a rejoinder to Lem the Australian novelist and critic George Turner observes that Lem confuses plot and theme in *LHD*: "The theme is communication, the plot is the means of achieving it, [and] the fable, not to be confused with the plot, is the purely external matter of entry" into the Ekumen.[18] And, adds Turner, Le Guin may have had defensible aesthetic reasons for not treating every aspect and implication of Gethenian sexuality. Le Guin herself answered Lem.[19] She refers him to passages in the novel which negate some of his criticisms, and defends her (Genly Ai's, really) use of the English masculine pronoun. She reminds Lem and her feminist sisters in the United States that the novel's narrative consciousness is a "'normal,' and male, Terran observer," and further, that she "will not deform English [by using an invented neuter pronoun] even to make an ethical point. . . . The intransigence of the medium is, after all, the joy of it."

Replying to Le Guin's answer to Lem, Brian Aldiss writes that Le Guin "wrote a science fiction novel, not an ordinary novel, and in a science fiction novel one does expect such a dramatic donnée to have some pivotal function."[20] There are two issues in this debate: we should realize that Le Guin speaks through Genly Ai no more than Swift does through Gulliver, and we should also be conscious of how generic assumptions control our aesthetic judgments. We can either judge *LHD* as a flawed science fiction novel, or we can recognize that Le Guin has indeed extended the limits of the medium by confounding generic assumptions.

At about the same time that Lem's and Russ's essays appeared, David Ketterer delivered "*The Left Hand of Darkness*: Ursula K. Le Guin's Archetypal 'Winter-Journey'" at the 1971 Toronto Secondary Universe Conference.[21] Like Lem, though for different reasons, Ketterer believes the "inconsequential plot element is a serious weakness in the novel."[22]

Because Ketterer approaches the novel through archetypal myth criticism, and because he reads *LHD* as a nearly pure example of his theory that science fiction effects epistemological apocalypses, he concludes that the plot, which he claims can be summarized without reference to the sexuality of the Gethenians, is controlled by Le Guin's conscious use of mythic-apocalyptic patterns. Le Guin answered Ketterer (and Lem again) in a symposium on Ketterer's *New Worlds for Old*, admitting some defects in the construction of the novel, but pointing to the difficulties she set herself, the paramount one being the effort to bring the "archetypal figure of the Androgyne" to consciousness, and embody its power in aesthetic form.[23] Le Guin has pursued these matters in other places, outlining her intentions and methods, particularly her use of the "thought-experiment."[24]

Ketterer's fellow Canadian Douglas Barbour, whose dissertation includes a 100-page chapter on Le Guin's first six novels,[25] has published three articles on various aspects of her fiction. In *"The Lathe of Heaven: Taoist Dream,"* he demonstrates the degree to which Taoist ideas permeate *LOH* by citing the many quotations from and allusions to Lao Tzu and Chuang Tzu.[26] In another essay Barbour discusses four aspects of Le Guin's novels as they appear in *WOE:* the quest, Taoism, the creation of a total culture, and light/dark imagery as an index to the theme of wholeness and balance.[27] A much fuller treatment of this theme in *Rocannon's World, Planet of Exile, City of Illusions, LHD, WWF,* and *DIS* may be found in Barbour's "Wholeness and Balance in the Hainish Novels of Ursula K. Le Guin," and in "Wholeness and Balance: An Addendum."[28] This two-part essay, the first to study a large portion of Le Guin's fiction, identifies not only the themes and images that appear throughout her novels, but also notices how these are embodied in different ways in the individual texts. Barbour implicitly counters Ketterer when he says that "the whole [of *LHD*] is a masterful example of form creating content."

Though a native of Yugoslavia, Darko Suvin is another Canadian who was an early critic of Le Guin. Regarded by many as the best science fiction critic writing today, Suvin judges *LHD* "the most memorable novel of the year" in his survey "The SF Novel in 1969," contributed to *Nebula Award Stories 5.*[29] Placing Le Guin in a group of writers he calls "the 'New Left' in SF," Suvin reads *LHD* as a "truly civilized parable on human love and trust independent of (though deeply concerned with) maleness or feminity." On another occasion Suvin spoke at greater length on the value of science fiction in general and *LHD* in particular.[30] Although he thinks that the absence of political economics in *LHD* is a "very bad gap," he praises Le Guin's "extremely realistic psychological, sociological, even political insight" into the way two people overcome barriers to communication and create mutual understanding: it is through cooperative labor. In *LHD* this is embodied metaphorically in Ai's and Estraven's pulling a sledge across the Gobrin Ice.

After lively discussions of Le Guin's fiction had been going on for some time in circles rarely touched by American academics, academic recognition of Le Guin in the United States got underway with Robert Scholes's "The Good Witch of the West."[31] With all the prestige of his earlier achievements—Scholes is the author of *The Nature of Narrative* (with Robert Kellogg), *The Fabulators,* and *Structuralism in Literature*—he asserts that Le Guin is "the best writer of speculative fabulation working in the country today, and she deserves a place among our major contemporary writers of fiction." Intending to initiate a "full and serious critical scrutiny" of her work, Scholes demonstrates Le Guin's virtues in an extended comparison of *WOE* and Lewis's Narnia stories. The bulk of his essay, however, is devoted to *LHD.* Unlike Lem and Ketterer, Scholes believes that the novel "interweaves all its levels and combines all its voices and values in an ordered, balanced, whole . . . everything is summed up in the relationship between the two main characters, and the narrative is shaped to present this relationship with the maximum intensity." Since Le Guin herself says that the germ of the story was a "vision of two people hauling a sledge, seen from a distance in a great waste of ice,"[32] Scholes may have his finger on the heart of the novel. In another essay Scholes enthusiastically presents Le Guin as a writer who has done as much as anyone, in or out of science fiction, "to create a modern conscience."[33]

The first extended analysis of *DIS* was Turner's "Paradigm and Pattern: Form and Meaning in *The Dispossessed,*" an essay which won Australian fandom's William Atheling Award.[34] Turner explains that his systematic and detailed exploration of the connections between the two narrative strands in *DIS* was prompted by his memory of the structure of George Eliot's *Daniel Deronda.* Like Eliot's novel, which uses a single hero "as a connecting link" to display "two cultures, Jewry and upper-middle-class English," *DIS* uses Shevek to connect Urras and Anarres. Along with the rest of Le Guin's writing, says Turner, *DIS* is concerned with the theme of communication. It is a novel "about the conflict between man the individual and man the group-member," and the whole point of the two plots is to express "the failure of cultural systematisation." Rather than being the masterpiece that Suvin's dust jacket blurb claims it to be, *DIS* is just an "originally conceived and executed novel operating on levels unfamiliar to conventional s f . . . it is a solid and, in the main, successful attempt to break the mold." One could say, then, that like *LHD, DIS* overturns generic assumptions and extends the limits of the medium. Except for Turner's admitted ignorance of political theory, which probably accounts for his repeated use of the word "state" to refer to the govern-ment on Anarres; except for his irritation with Le Guin's "overstressed women's-libbery"; and except for his conclusion that *DIS* "is totally anti-utopian, dystopian," Turner's detailed and careful attention to Le Guin's *form* may be taken as a model for further study of her novels.

Two reviews, by Le Guin's fellow science fiction writers Joanna Russ and James Tiptree, Jr., are notable. Russ detects a "rift between authentic and inauthentic" throughout *DIS*.[35] Contending that utopias and dys-topias are more poetic than prescriptive, and that Le Guin's talent is lyrical rather than dramatic, Russ argues that Le Guin's forays into "Big Subjects," particularly the insurrection scene on Urras, mar the book. For Russ there is entirely too much telling and not enough showing in the novel. Like Lem, she believes that Le Guin has earned the right to be judged by the highest standards and, like Lem, she sees her falling short. Le Guin is, says Russ, still trying to find her voice. Tiptree's belated review of *LOH* is intended to draw attention to a book she feels was passed over.[36] *LOH* reminds her of the "principle of Japanese art which teaches that one must never close a design so completely as to lock infinity out." This novel, Tiptree senses, will be seen as a real turning point in Le Guin's career.

Like Tiptree, the British science fiction author and critic Ian Watson believes *LOH* has a crucial position in Le Guin's development as a science fiction writer. In "Le Guin's *The Lathe of Heaven* and the Role of Dick,"[37] Watson charts Le Guin's increasing preoccupation with paranormal com-munication in the first five Hainish novels *(Rocannon's World, Planet of Exile, City of Illusions, LHD,* and *WWF),* and argues that she used "the Dickian mode" in *LOH* to discharge the paranormal theme's accumulating energy, which was carrying Le Guin toward "a quasi-mystical escape route from real problems." As Le Guin reversed chronology in her exploration of the Hainish worlds, she needed to discharge "schismogenic thematic tensions" so that the way would be clear to write *DIS.* Watson's essay, one of the first to erect a theory to explain the configurations of Le Guin's career, is suggestive, and needs to be tested in the light of her other fiction. Perhaps the most useful item in Watson's essay is his fairly accurate internal chronology of the Hainish cycle.

In a long two-part study—the first part entitled "Malaise dans la science-fiction," and the second "Ursula Le Guin ou la sortie du piège"—Gerard Klein, a French economist, science fiction author, and editor, reaches conclusions reminiscent of Matthew Arnold's in *Culture and Anarchy* or Karl Mannheim's in *Ideology and Utopia.*[38] In the same way that Arnold and Mannheim saw powerful ideologies driving their cultures toward disaster, and called for disinterested thinkers able "to see life steadily

and see it whole" (Arnold) or "free-floating intelligentsia" (Mannheim),
Klein anatomizes the ideological sources of pessimism in Anglo-American
science fiction in the 1960s, and then argues that Le Guin offers a way out
of this pessimistic trap because she is uncontaminated by the ideologies
that created it.[39]
    Klein begins with the hypothesis, taken from Lucien Goldmann's
sociology of literature, that "the real subject of a literary work (or group
of works) is the situation of the social group the author belongs to." Most
science fiction writers, says Klein, belong to "a scientifically and tech-
nologically oriented middle class." In the 1960s the economic and social
structures of the whole world changed in a way that threatens the identity,
the power, and the values of this social group and the science fiction
authors who belong to it. Klein's second thesis is that "literary works (all
works of art) are attempts to resolve through the use of the imagination
and in the aesthetic mode, a problem which is not soluble in reality."
He then examines the aesthetic solutions to the imminent dissolution of
the middle class in the science fiction of Roger Zelazny, Norman Spinrad,
Philip K. Dick, Frank Herbert, and John Brunner, and concludes the first
part of the essay by discussing one metaphor in which the death-anxiety
of the "social group of SF tragically perceives its destiny": a return
to nature, "a way of life modelled on the social insects," extreme reifica-
tion.
    Le Guin does not belong to the social group which advocates a uni-
formity-producing technology, and thus she is not affected by the
pessimism that group feels when its values are threatened. Instead, she
grew up in anthropological and historical milieus and therefore affirms
cultural diversity and relativity. Unlike the members of the "social group
SF," Le Guin does not fall into the trap of confusing the destiny of her
social group with the future of all mankind; thus, she is not vulnerable to
the despair that afflicts the social group SF when it sees all humanity
perishing as it perishes. Klein locates the sources of Le Guin's hope in the
dynamics of personal and cultural interaction and communication which
we see in her novels. When one culture is confronted with another, ethics
develop. For Le Guin, man is an ethical animal, and remains ethical only
so long as he is capable of understanding some part of the experiences
and social structures of another culture. Le Guin's rich and tolerant ethic
guards itself against pretensions of universality by remembering its
origins in error and injustice. The Hainish, Klein notes, become sages
through acknowledging and remembering their crimes. Le Guin's fictional
world, like the worlds of other science fiction writers, is structured on a
scientific model: ethnology. Klein uses Lévi-Strauss's *Race et histoire* to
make explicit what is implicit in Le Guin's fiction: cultural diversity

is a natural phenomenon, civilization is a process not a linear progress, and all cultures help bring other cultures to fruition. Klein concludes by speculating that Le Guin's ability to create a world not dominated by one controlling or unifying system may be rooted in her being as a woman; this frees her from "L'affirmation obsessionnelle de la puissance du phallus."[40]

A high point in Le Guin's critical reputation is the November, 1975, issue of *Science-Fiction Studies*, wholly devoted to her fiction, except the Earthsea trilogy.[41] It opens with Suvin's introductory comparison of Le Guin and Philip K. Dick (who had been the subject of an earlier special issue of *Science-Fiction Studies*), and his statement of regret that no one could be found to "integrate the *Earthsea* trilogy with Le Guin's SF." Following Suvin's introduction are a select bibliography by Jeff Levin and Le Guin's "American SF and the Other," a polemical attack on science fiction's unwillingness to deal with sexual, social, cultural, and racial aliens.[42] The rest of the issue is composed of nine dense and closely argued scholarly essays exploring various aspects of her fiction, but concentrating on formal, generic, and thematic (political) matters. Most of the essays try to formulate a scheme for Le Guin's development: the words "period," "stage," "break," "evolution," and "progression" are common throughout. In many cases, the authors formulate a reading of Le Guin's most recent work, *DIS*, then read the earlier works as "proving grounds" which enabled her to write the next novel. This approach must be provisional; those essays which use it the least (Nudelman and Theall), or those which use it with caution and flexibility (Bierman and Suvin) will probably endure longer than those which tend toward the reductive and overly schematic (Huntington and Porter).

The Russian writer, critic, and theoretical physicist Rafail Nudelman opens the criticism with "An Approach to the Structure of Le Guin's SF." Using a flexible semiotic/ structuralist method, Nudelman analyzes Le Guin's textual structures, explores and defines the temporal and spatial relationships as well as the part/whole relationships in her novels, and detects a "strong musically organised form." Le Guin's essential structural principle, he discovers, is "*iconicity:* in it, the 'lower' level of the narrative form is a similarity, an image, the isomorphic sign of a more general or 'higher' formal level." After determining in his analysis of Le Guin's textual structure that "scattered elements strive toward oneness" in Le Guin's fictional worlds, Nudelman shows how the plot structure—the journey tale—is isomorphic with the textual structure, for it unifies the I and the Thou. Echoing Tiptree's reference to the openness of Japanese art, Nudelman notes that Le Guin's journey tales are neither tautological nor closed, but are a "symbolic sign for a mythopoetic Way, in

Lévi-Strauss's sense of myth as a search for mediation between opposing orders of being–which is always 'androgynous.'" Myth as plot in Le Guin is a source of historical optimism, but it is counterpointed by "a constant elegiac undercurrent."

In "World Reduction in Le Guin: The Emergence of Utopian Narrative," Fredric Jameson looks for "some structural homology" between four elements in *LHD* (Gethenian sexuality, politics and war, ecology, and myth and religion), and finds it in "the principle of systematic exclusion, . . . an operation of radical abstraction and simplification which [he calls] *world-reduction*," adding it to extrapolation and analogy as a third principle for structuring a science fiction narrative. In *LHD*, says Jameson, the cold isolates and reduces to extreme simplicity our sense of being, the religious practices reduce and simplify the mind, the ambisexuality removes all problematical aspects of sex, and the absence of war on Gethen rests on an "attempt to imagine something like a West which would never have known capitalism." Jameson's reading of the cold as something that isolates might be complemented with a reading that recognizes that the cold unites too, for that is what happens on the Gobrin Ice. Moreover, his interpretation of Karhide's history as Le Guin's attempt to reimagine the history of the West might be supplemented with the fact that Karhide's history derives in part from the actual history of the East.[43] Jameson concludes that Le Guin and her heroes offer a "liberal 'solution'" to the "vicious circle which is the option between feudalism and capitalism," and that the strategy of "*not* asking questions" is a way the utopian imagination protects itself from "historical contradiction." Because the "vicious circle" Jameson sees in *LHD* may not be there, his conclusions are moot.

Ian Watson's theory of the paranormal gets further development in his "The Forest as Metaphor for Mind." Watson argues that "The Word for World Is Forest" and "Vaster Than Empires and More Slow" are "necessary stages in [Le Guin's] development from ur-SF to the mystico-political theory of time and society in *The Dispossessed.*" Unlike *WWF*, in which the paranormal theme cannot find a full outlet because Le Guin's political and ideological purposes block it, *VTE* allows a full expression through the "forest-mind." Then, says Watson, Le Guin could proceed from detached mysticism in *VTE* to mysticism integrated with the social, political, and emotional in *DIS*. Watson's essay contains some valuable comparisons of Le Guin's "forest-minds" with those of other science fiction writers; comparative studies like this are uncommon in Le Guin criticism and could be a fertile area to cultivate.

For John Huntington the mainspring of Le Guin's development is not a theme like the paranormal; it is her treatment of the tension between public and private duty. In "Public and Private Imperatives in Le Guin's Novels," he writes that "in all her work, Le Guin probes in various ways for the point at which the public and private imperatives intersect, for the act that will allow them to be unified, if only momentarily." In *LHD*, says Huntington, Le Guin held the public and private in tension (he accepts Ketterer's reading of the split between plot and theme), then in WWF she shows the public dominating the private, an imbalance which she inverts in *LOH*, and finally in *DIS* she solves the problem by offering a new definition: she makes the "private totally a function of the public." Although Huntington begins by looking at "the typical Le Guin hero," he does not mention Ged and Earthsea at all.

The stages of existentialism, Taoism, and anarchism form the scaffolding on which David Porter builds his theory about "The Politics of Le guin's Opus." Le Guin's political development through these stages "represents a significant section of a whole generation of white radical American intellectuals, from the early 1960s to the present." Arguing that Le Guin has a "consistent though evolving political perspective," and that she is a "political writer-activist," Porter says that Le Guin offers a "critique and a positive alternative" in anarchism and parapsychology. Porter too easily infers from the text of Le Guin's National Book Award speech that she "defends the SF *form* as . . . political communication."

After Barbour's "Addendum" to his earlier *Science-Fiction Studies* article, Judah Bierman explores "Ambiguity in Utopia." Bierman's essay on *DIS* is the only one in this special issue which gives the Earthsea trilogy more than a passing mention, but even then he treats it in a digression as "the proving ground" in the "development that brought Le Guin to Shevek, Urras, and Anarres." Nevertheless, Bierman's knowledge of the trilogy and the rest of Le Guin's fiction aid him in making fundamentally sound statements of Le Guin's central concerns. In *DIS* Le Guin "establishes continuing choice as the human condition, burden, and joy"; the tale in *DIS* is "the structure of choice-making"; and "men are moral agents in Le Guin's universe." Bierman takes quite seriously the subtitle of *DIS*, "an ambiguous utopia," and thus reads the novel's two plot lines as embodiments of the traditional structure of the utopia, a "dialogue of criticism and a discourse of showing." This is reflected in the alternating chapters as "two journeys, combining romance and satire, quest and rejection." One might quibble with Bierman's frequent use of the word "allegory," preferring "fable" or "parable" if such a word is needed. The latter words are, as Suvin notes later in the issue, polysemous, and might better convey Bierman's accurate observation that Le Guin's universe is ambiguous, uncertain, and open-ended.

Donald Theall's "The Art of Social-Science Fiction: The Ambiguous Utopian Dialectics of Ursula K. Le Guin" covers some of the same ground that Bierman does. But Theall goes further in discussing, almost alone among the nine contributors to this issue, Le Guin's narrative voices, seeing Genly Ai in *LHD* and Shevek in *DIS* at the end of a line that begins with More's Hythloday in *Utopia* and Swift's Gulliver. Reading *LHD* and *DIS* in the tradition of More and Swift, Theall discovers in Le Guin a "double historical vision" which precludes "definite outcome" and therefore engages history, a conclusion at odds with Jameson's. Noting that balance is central to her fiction, Theall points out that Le Guin stresses "history as perpetually upsetting the balance and creating new tensions." He concludes with a word on uncertainty in Le Guin: "Uncertainty is an important aspect of the balance, for wholeness is only gained in a process of change and the process of change is only raised to consciousness through her ambiguous utopian dialectic."

Suvin's "Parables of De-Alienation: Le Guin's Widdershins Dance" is a highly allusive and difficult, yet rewarding, essay centered on an interpretation of "The New Atlantis" (1975). In the first of three parts Suvin reads the twin planets in *DIS* in terms of two forms of alienation, external (imperialist oppression) and internal (absorbed from the "all-pervading psychical eco-system of modern capitalism"), and he sees Shevek's simulsequentialist thought as "correlative to the ideologico-political breakthrough of Le Guin's identifying the privileged forms of alienation as propertarian possession." Suvin offers to "pursue and perhaps clinch this argument" in the second part of the essay as he applies to "The New Atlantis" the theory "that the centre of Le Guin's creation is the double star [i.e., widdershins dance] of identifying the neo-capitalist, individualist alienation and juxtaposing to it a sketch of a new, collectivist and harmonious creation." He concludes with some speculations on the courses Le Guin's anarchism might take, and thinks it might be in the direction of a "new libertarian socialism."

Robert Plank's "Ursula K. Le Guin and the Decline of Romantic Love" was crowded out of the special Le Guin issue of *Science-Fiction Studies,* but appeared in the next number.[44] Plank's psychoanalytical interpretations pass over evidence in Le Guin's text which might offer more sensible readings than the ones he produces. Shevek's vomiting at Vea's party, for example, might be connected with his vomiting on Anarres after the "prison-playing" episode, rather than to Pascal's stomach troubles or to the vomiting in Mailer's *An American Dream.*

Le Guin responded to the special *Science-Fiction Studies* issue by remarking that her critics overlooked her craft as they purused her ideas, by correcting some misconceptions she detected about Taoism, by speculating on why the Earthsea trilogy was ignored (too few ideas, too little politics), by rejecting the label "liberal" and disavowing a belief in ESP, and by listing some of her influences.[45] Anthony Wolk also responded: he objects to the political and philosophical limits and boundaries imposed on Le Guin's fiction, and he objects to reading the novels as way-stations to something else rather than appreciating them for what they are in themselves.[46]

Late in 1975 two review-essays of *DIS* with divergent approaches appeared on different sides of the Atlantic. In England Ian Watson offers high praise for the way Le Guin fits technique and theme together.[47] He analyzes the concept of permanent revolution in *DIS* and finds that the "pattern of dialectic interaction" pervades every aspect of the novel: social theory, scientific theory, structure, characterization, and theme. In an effort to show that the connections between the imaginary science in *DIS* and real science are strong, an effort probably intended to root *DIS* firmly in the ground of science fiction, Watson concludes his review with a discussion of "Action at a Distance Electrodynamics" and the concepts of succession, interval, and series in mathematics. *DIS* is significant, says Watson, "both as a social statement, and as a breakthrough to a new level of *science* fiction" (Watson's italics). This kind of criticism is precisely what Robert C. Elliott objects to in his review.[48] Elliott thinks that *DIS* has not received the attention it deserves because it was marketed and reviewed as a science fiction novel rather than as a utopian novel. Elliott, the author of *The Shape of Utopia*, a generic study of the utopia from More to Skinner and Huxley, regards *DIS* as a creative extension of that tradition. He dismisses the scientific content of the novel and anticipates "literary, political, [and] generic" discussions of *DIS* when it is removed from the science fiction ghetto.

Two essays comparing Le Guin to other authors are Angus Taylor's "The Politics of Space, Time and Entropy"[49] and Donna Gerstenberger's "Conceptions Literary and Otherwise: Women Writers and the Modern Imagination."[50] Taylor's comparison of Le Guin and Philip K. Dick addresses the content of their fictions: although they begin from different premises, they "both contend that a reified social structure is a mystification, and both affirm that a proper stance must be one of individual initiative coupled with community solidarity." Gerstenberger, on the other hand, is concerned more with the novelist's artistry than with her message. She sees Genly Ai's situation in *LHD* as a paradigm for the difficulties modern writers, especially women writers, must grapple with in order to communicate their visions of reality. The major block to communication between Ai and the Gethenians is "biological in origin, psychological in significance"; Ai must give meaning to unprecedented experiences for which his language is simply inadequate. Women writers have the same difficulties, says Gerstenberger, and the remainder of her essay is an analysis of how the Canadian novelist Margaret Atwood tries to overcome them in *Surfacing.* Gerstenberger's comparison of *LHD* with a mainstream novel shows how fruitful criticism of science fiction can be when it arches over the walls of the science fiction ghetto. Not only does it illuminate more clearly the artistry of *LHD,* but it also shifts the debate on the feminist content of *LHD* from superficial issues (whether Estraven is or is not "male") to deeper issues of feminist aesthetics.

Thomas J. Remington's "A Touch of Difference, A Touch of Love: Theme in Three Stories by Ursula K. Le Guin," uses "Nine Lives" (1969), *WWF,* and *VTE* to illustrate themes common to Le Guin's novels: "The loneliness of the self, the impossibility of understanding the self except through its relationship with the other, and the human need to establish that relationship through reaching out to the other in love."[51] Except for Remington's sound and sensible essay, and except for a few reviews,[52] Le Guin's short stories have not received the attention her novels have. Along with the Earthsea trilogy, Le Guin's two collections of short stories *(WTQ* and *ORT),* and the uncollected ones as well, still await the scrutiny of American critics.

By 1975-76 Le Guin's critical reputation in academia was strong and growing. There was a seminar on her fiction at the 1975 Modern Language Association Convention and three papers on her work at the 1976 Science Fiction Research Association Meeting. One of the three is Martin Bickman's "Le Guin's *The Left Hand of Darkness:* Form and Content."[53] After acknowledging that science fiction writers have difficulty unifying form and content in the way authors of "any fine work of literature" do, Bickman examines *LHD* to suggest ways it can be done. He begins by concentrating on Genly Ai as the structuring consciousness of the narrative; not only does Ai tell his own story, but his selection and arrangement of the myths, legends, and excerpts from Estraven's diary reflect the understanding he has gained from his experiences related in the novel. *LHD* is the dynamic interweaving of pairs of tensions—unity and diversity, and fact and myth being the main ones— into "complementary relationships without collapsing the important distinctions between them." Every aspect of the narrative, from the personal relationship between Ai and Estraven to the larger social and political relationships, participate in this movement. Bickman's convincing account of the structure of *LHD* makes it clear, eight years after the novel appeared, that the initial readings of the novel as badly flawed may themselves have been badly flawed.

One might think that Le Guin's anarchism would be the focus of an essay on her novels by George Woodcock, biographer of Godwin, Proudhon, and Kropotkin, and author of *Anarchism,* a standard history of the movement. But Woodcock is also the author of books on Huxley, Orwell, and Read. In "Equilibrations of Freedom: Notes on the Novels of Ursula K. Le Guin," Woodcock's literary and aesthetic interests crowd out his political and philosophical interests.[54] In artistic terms, says Woodcock, the Earthsea trilogy is Le Guin's finest achievement; *DIS* is "tendentious—far more a tract for our times—than any of Le Guin's earlier books." Le Guin's prose style draws Woodcock's attention: it is "a style of crystalline clarity and functional flexibility that has always reminded me of the limpid prose in which the great naturalist travellers of the nineteenth century revealed their discoveries to an astonished public . . . it has the lucid verisimilitude by which Swift in *Gulliver's Travels* made the unactual real." Woodcock does not regard Le Guin as a science fiction writer, but calls her "a highly accomplished fantasist and allegorist whose concerns are far more ethical and spiritual than with scientific development." After discussing all nine of Le Guin's novels through 1974, he concludes with an appreciation of her anarchism in the "imperfect but splendid" *DIS.* Le Guin, says Woodcock, "has studied anarchism and its history so closely that it is hard to exclude the possibility of at least a period of active involvement"—high praise coming from one of the greatest authorities on anarchism in our time.

George Slusser's *The Farthest Shores of Ursula K. Le Guin* is the first relatively complete survey of her novels.[55] As a general introduction for the nonscholarly reader, and as an attempt to integrate the Earthsea trilogy with Le Guin's science fiction, it is a useful complement to the essays in *Science-Fiction Studies.* Instead of focusing on formal and political matters, Slusser deals with thematic and moral elements in Le Guin's fiction. A leitmotif in the pamphlet is his attention to "the nature of human evil." Unlike those who receive an optimistic and liberating message from Le Guin, Slusser is quite sensitive to a pessimistic undercurrent. He plays down a political development in Le Guin's career, and speaks instead of a "growth" and "harmonious expansion" of the "organism" that is her writing. This approach yields Slusser's most valuable insights: an awareness of the relationships among Le Guin's first nine novels, especially those between the fantasy and the science fiction. Although Slusser dismisses *LOH,* the most explicitly Taoist of Le Guin's novels, as her worst, he nevertheless contends that Taoism is the "strongest single force" on her writing.

Slusser's introduction announces his theses. In Le Guin's nine novels from 1966 through 1974, there is a thematic shift from a celebration of balance to the problematics of balance, and there are formal shifts from stylized worlds to complex societies, from heroes to multifaceted characters, and from impersonal, straightforward narration to experimentation with point of view. These ideas, except the last one, are developed in detail in the four sections of the pamphlet: "The Early Hainish Novels," *"The Left Hand of Darkness,"* "The Earthsea Trilogy," and *"The Dispossessed."*

Slusser argues that there has been a gradual interiorization of evil from Le Guin's first novel to her most recent fiction. In *Rocannon's World* and *Planet of Exile* we see faceless enemies, but in *LHD* "the enemy within has proven itself far more dangerous than the enemy without. No one in the book is without folly or misunderstanding. And there is more than a whiff of some stronger, more stubborn perversion in man" (p. 31). Slusser does not call this perversion original sin, but that concept is close at hand when he characterizes *DIS* as Le Guin's "strenuous, almost Puritanical probing of man's social conscience," her investigation of "the problem of evil in a fundamentally monistic universe" (p. 47). His interpretations of *DIS* and "The New Atlantis" depart radically from most others. Slusser asks, rhetorically, "What hope is there for the creative man [Shevek], the visionary, faced with this unregenerate human nature [on Anarres]?" (p. 55). Very few, if any, of Le Guin's readers would claim for her a belief in "unregenerate human nature." And Slusser ends his conclusion, an analysis of "The Day before the Revolution" (1974) and "The New Atlantis," with another rhetorical question: "Has ambiguity given way to pessimism? In these two stories, the individual life ends in death, the collective existence in annihilation" (p. 58). That is a long way from Suvin's reading of "The New Atlantis" as "a sketch of a new, collectivist and harmonious creation."

Slusser's remark that Gethen's "sexless [sic] society seems a libber's dream come true" (p. 19) will not endear him to feminists, nor will his constant use of the word "man" to refer to all humanity. His study is, however, the first published work to provide a comprehensive view of Le Guin's first nine novels and is valuable for its readings of *Rocannon's World, Planet of Exile,* and *City of Illusions,* novels usually brushed aside as mere apprentice work, and for its close attention to the Earthsea trilogy as an integral part of Le Guin's oeuvre.

T. A. Shippey's "The Magic Art and the Evolution of Words: Ursula Le Guin's Earthsea Trilogy" is a weighty and somber investigation of the philosophical and religious implications of the trilogy.[56] Frequently referring to the *OED,* Shippey begins by showing how Le Guin erases the "sharpness and hardness of modern concepts" about magic, religion, and science, and notes that her "continuous and consistent use of words *not* familiar to the modern reader reminds him to suspend his judgment." Throughout the rest of his essay Shippey reads Le Guin's fantasy in terms of issues which engaged late Victorian thinkers, a frame of reference which may strike some as rather remote. Shippey interprets the magic in *WOE* as a radical critique of, and an alternative to, theories proposed by early modern anthropologists (Spencer, Tylor, Frazer, and Malinowski). In *TOA,* however, Le Guin does seem to agree with Frazer's model of the genesis of religion and T. H. Huxley's ethics. Underlying *TFS* Shippey finds the failure of belief and the lapse of faith that haunted nineteenth-century artists like Dostoevsky and A. E. Housman. Le Guin may be a mythmaker, concludes Shippey, but she is "at least as much of an iconoclast, a myth-breaker; . . . Mrs. Le Guin takes 'In the beginning was the Word' more seriously and more literally than do many modern theologians; but her respect for ancient texts includes no great regard for the mythic structures that have been built on them."

The metaphor of discovery guides Susan Wood's journey through Le Guin's novels in "Discovering Worlds: The Fiction of Ursula K. Le Guin."[57] The keynote of Wood's essay comes from Le Guin's "Dreams Must Explain Themselves": "the true laws—ethical and aesthetic, as surely as scientific—are not imposed from above by any authority, but exist in things and are to be found—discovered." In Le Guin's fiction, says Wood, this discovery of true laws is both process and result: it is the artist's journey into the creative unconscious to discover worlds and imaginary countries; it is the artist's effort to discover the right words, images, and sentences to communicate (to map) those discoveries; and it is the map itself, the novel, whose "central figure—scientist, wizard, designer, or traveller—embod[ies] aspects of the artist seeking truth and expressing its patterns." Wood's whole essay germinates from its first sentence, "Ursula K. Le Guin makes maps," probably the finest single sentence in all that has been written on Le Guin.

Wood seems to have used the same method. Rather than imposing a rigid interpretive scheme on Le Guin's fiction, she makes this discovery: underlying all Le Guin's work is a celebration and a joyful acceptance of the patterned richness and variety of life. Because Wood understands discovery and celebration to be the central activities in Le Guin's fiction, she regards Le Guin's "tendency to impose moral and ethical patterns on her work" as a violation of her fundamental principles which weakens, aesthetically, works like *WWF* and *DIS*. Along with Joanna Russ, Wood believes that *DIS* "relies too heavily on the idea expressed and analysed rather than embodied and shown." But the Earthsea trilogy, in which ideas rise organically from Le Guin's "specific knowledge of individual things," is "the major work of this mature writer."

In the last eight years criticism of Le Guin's fiction has seen a general movement from examinations of the specific content of individual works toward an appreciation of the ways Le Guin's stories and the storytelling process are intimately related. This movement may best be illustrated by the revision of early opinions about the flaws in *LHD*. Once critics began to pay attention to Genly Ai as the structuring consciousness of the narrative, rifts between form and content in the novel disappeared. At the same time, as the walls enclosing the science fiction ghetto were crumbling both from within and without, Le Guin's fiction began to be read alongside mainstream literature. Approaches like Turner's, which compares *DIS* and *Daniel Deronda,* and Gerstenberger's, which compares *LHD* and *Surfacing,* can illuminate Le Guin's fiction in a way criticism within the traditions of science fiction cannot. The converse, of course, is also true: we appreciate Atwood's novel more fully when we read Le Guin's novel with it. The cultural wall that has, until recently, separated science fiction worlds from other imaginary countries is built from the same stones that make up the walls between characters and cultures in Le Guin's fiction: fear, distrust, chauvinism, elitism, insecurity, and alienation. Readers who venture back and forth across these barriers, ignoring the generic boundaries between imaginary countries in science fiction, in fantasy, and in other literary modes, may discover that these countries are all part of the same world. Those readers are in a position to enjoy what Genly Ai offers to King Argaven as he invites Gethen to join the Ekumen: "the augmentation of the complexity and intensity of the field of intelligent life. . . . Curiosity. Adventure. Delight."[58]

KAREN SINCLAIR

SOLITARY BEING
The Hero as Anthropologist

It is not uncommon, as a literary technique, to employ a critical individual who narrates as the action unfolds. Ursula Le Guin takes this device one step further, making of her protagonists participant-observers; in short, she transforms them into anthropologists. Her heroes all seem to have characteristics that separate them from the worlds in which they find themselves: they are either off-worlders whose job may be explicitly that of an ethnographer, such as Rocannon (*Rocannon's World*) or Genly Ai *(The Left Hand of Darkness),* or they are the skeptics and freethinkers in their native society, as in the cases of Selver and Lyubov *(The Word for World Is Forest)* and Shevek *(The Dispossessed).*[1] Because they are outsiders with the outsider's critical viewpoint, they are cast in the mold of anthropologists, with the perspective and unique dilemmas of the discipline. Repeatedly in her fiction we confront individuals who are of society and yet not quite a part of it. The outsider, the alien, the marginal man, adopts a vantage point with rather serious existential and philosophical implications. For Le Guin this marginality becomes a metaphor whose potency is fulfilled in a critical assessment of society.[2]

Anthropologists, in their insistence upon fieldwork as a prerequisite rite of passage, maintain that the failure to be comfortable with a new environment enhances the perspective of the foreigner. In 1908 Georg Simmel[3] described such a person as "the stranger"—one whose unfamiliarity lent him objectivity. Similarly, Alfred Schutz[4] held that the objectivity of the foreigner ". . . lies in his own bitter experience of the limits of thinking as usual. . . ." Precisely because he is free of the commitments and prejudices of the group, the anthropologist or stranger may be successful in his role as researcher. Implicitly and explicitly, such a notion is evident in the explorations of Rocannon, Genly Ai, and Lyubov. Yet the success of Le Guin's protagonists is not that they are good researchers, or keen observers; it lies, instead, in their marginality and alienation. At no time, despite their intimate association with society, do they lose their detached point of view. Shevek appraises both "propertarian" Urras and anarchistic Anarres quite critically, while Lyubov not only sympathizes with and understands the Edenic Athshean natives, but bitterly rejects the colonial exploitation by those of his own culture, like Davidson. But if their success is in their ability to perceive more than one point of view, their failures are to be found in their inability to explain and to translate adequately: Davidson is far from illuminated by Lyubov's impassioned discourses in defense of Athshean culture and intellect, while Shevek meets with resistance and hostility in his refusal to leave untouched and unquestioned the social assumptions his fellows take for granted. Thus, the viewpoint of the anthropologist often turns him into an outsider in his own culture. As Pouwer has noted: "In the most advanced stage of this process of participant observation, a social anthropologist almost becomes a stranger to himself, even in his own society."[5]

Claude Lévi-Strauss writes most eloquently on precisely this point:

> The ethnographer, while in no wise abdicating his own humanity, strives to know and estimate his fellow-men from a lofty and distant point of vantage: only thus can he abstract them from the contingencies particular to this or that civilization. The conditions of his life and work cut him off from his own group for long periods together: and he himself acquires a kind of chronic uprootedness from the sheer brutality of the environmental changes to which he is exposed. Never can he feel himself "at home" anywhere: he will always be, psychologically speaking, an amputated man.[6]

It is from this "point of vantage" that Le Guin creates her characters and her stories. The "chronic uprootedness," the disconnectedness, endows the protagonists with a vision that transcends that of the others around them, who see the world through culture-bound categories and characterizations. Yet theirs is not a happy plight. Their vision isolates them, while their attempts to promote understanding seem only to remove them further from their compatriots. Ultimately, despite her concern with utopias, Le Guin's view is not optimistic. It can be argued that her heroes' lack of success is due in fact to the failures of society—a failure to examine, to reappraise, and to change.

Le Guin squarely confronts the isolation and loneliness of her protagonists. Themes such as xenophobia, a suspicion and mistrust of all that is different, are developed in all her work, but reach a clear culmination in 1972 in *WWF*. Here there is an explicit presentation of the heroes (Lyubov and Selver) as anthropologists in their roles as outsiders and translators. Consistently her portrayal is pessimistic. Such individuals suffer heartily. Abandoned, misread, and psychologically disoriented, they often sacrifice themselves or are sacrificed for their understanding. Yet often they represent the only hope.

Le Guin has, essentially, two modes for presenting her protagonists as outsiders: either they are true aliens (for example, Rocannon, Lyubov, Genly Ai, and Falk-Ramarren *[City of Illusions]*) or they are natives of a society, yet their perception of social life nevertheless sets them apart (for example, Shevek, Selver, Estraven *[LHD]*, Jakob Agat *[Planet of Exile]*, and George Orr *[The Lathe of Heaven]*). In either case, their problems, and more importantly their solutions, are of a similar nature. Their apartness precludes their complete membership in, or commitment to, any particular society. Yet their critical viewpoint gives them an insight into the nature of social relations that eludes their fellows.

In *Rocannon's World*, Le Guin's first published novel (1966), we are presented with two important and consistent themes: the hero as observer and the tension, the mutual distrust, that so often prevails in intergroup relations. Here Rocannon is actually called an ethnographer, an investigator of *hilfs*, "high intelligence life forms." His approach and his dilemmas are distinctly anthropological in nature. It is apt that Rocannon is given a place, over his objections and disclaimers, in the local mythology. His name is "The Wanderer." He is no mere wanderer in geographical terms; he moves as well, and perhaps more fundamentally, in cultural space and time. His position is that of seeker, or questioner—an outsider, who, like all outsiders, sees two sides to all questions. Displaying the relativism, if not always the objectivity, that marks the discipline, he queries the motivations of the League, under whose auspices his work is taking place. In pondering his affiliation with this organization, in the midst of strangers, his aloneness is only more evident:

And there, Rocannon said to himself as he watched the midmen unsaddle the windsteeds and loose them for their night's hunting, right there perhaps was the League's own weak spot. Only technology mattered. The two missions to this world in the last century had started pushing one of the species toward a pre-atomic technology before they had even explored the other continents or contacted all intelligent races. He had called a halt to that, and had finally managed to bring his own Ethnographic Survey here to learn something about the planet; *but he did not fool himself*. Even his work here would finally have served only as an informational basis for encouraging technological advance in the most likely species or culture. This was how the League of All Worlds prepared to meet its ultimate enemy. A hundred worlds had been trained and armed, a thousand more were being schooled in the uses of steel and wheel and tractor and reactor. But Rocannon the hilfer, whose *job was learning, not teaching*, and who had lived on quite a few backward worlds, doubted the wisdom of staking everything on weapons and the uses of machines. Dominated by the aggressive, tool-making humanoid species of Centaurus, Earth, and the Cetians, the League had slighted certain skills and powers and potentialities of intelligent life, and judged by too narrow a standard. (*Rocannon's World*, p. 36—italics added)

Rocannon is not blind to the detrimental consequences or motivations of his researches. Yet his curiosity goads him on. Not only are the Fiia and the midmen (Liuar) objects of his scrutiny, but he condemns as well the limited vision of his own sponsors. In his musings we see the true anthropological problem: he is a learner, not a teacher, and his acquired wisdom, whatever its bounds or limits, will be amassed, not applied. For his own edification, Rocannon concentrates instead on the delights of truly exploring the infinite variety of possibilities. "Would it not be well to learn a little of the different shapes minds come in, and their powers?" (*Rocannon's World*, p. 37).

The elfish Fiia hold as great a fascination for him as do the feudal Liuar. Yet the two groups have at best contempt for one another.[7] His inability to convince one group of the worth of the other underlines the impotence and powerlessness of the outsider whose perspective can bridge otherwise culture-bound characterizations. Ultimately his recognition of affinities serves only to increase his isolation. But he can not ignore those affinities any more than he can give unquestioning allegiance to the League. As the book reaches its dramatic conclusion, Rocannon saves both the planet which will now bear his name and the League itself.

In *City of Illusions*, Le Guin's third novel (1967), we are once again confronted with an alien, Falk, whose task is both to comprehend his surroundings and to overcome them. An amnesic interplanetary castaway, he is befriended by the forest-dwelling humans of a future Earth dominated by the evil, mind-altering Shing. Although a true outsider, he is not a fearsome creature; rather, he is an individual whose insights force comprehension upon others. Unlike Rocannon, however, Falk has a self-awareness, a contemplativeness, and a scrutiny of personal motivations that we will see again in Shevek and Genly Ai. In search of his identity, Falk sets out into the wilderness to learn the truth from the deceitful Shing. Intensely aware of his solitariness, he realizes he is alone in the forest, alone on a planet where nothing is familiar to him and where he is familiar to no living being. He in part surmounts his aloneness by finding within the alien culture a paean appropriate to his personal predicament:

> Everyone is useful
> only I am alone
> am inept
> outlandish.
> I alone differ from others
> but I seek
> the milk of the Mother
> the Way. . . .
> (*City of Illusions*, p. 41)

In his journey to the City of the Shing, his singularity is always emphasized. But intuitively he establishes relationships by seeking out commonalities, not by maintaining differences. Puzzled and perhaps even terrified of the Shing initially, his strategy is to understand and, by understanding, to oppose them. In this task the difficulties of finding a dubious and elusive reality are paramount. He has to decide how his past experience colors his perceptions of his present condition. In the process of overcoming the illusion, and in his ultimate recognition of the duplicity of the Shing, Falk (Ramarren) becomes a true participant observer. To survive, he must battle to separate two voices in his head. Falk, the identity achieved on this planet, resides simultaneously with his initial identity of Ramarren. His salvation lies in not forgetting either aspect of himself, while, at the same time, not permitting either personality to dominate or obliterate the other. The difficulties of the alien who has accepted, albeit forcibly, two ways of life are evident in the following passage:

There was of course no actual overlap of his two sets of memories. Falk had come to conscious being in the vast number of neurons that in a highly intelligent brain remain unused—the fallow fields of Ramarren's mind. The basic motor and sensory paths has [sic] never been blocked off and so in a sense had been shared all along, though difficulties arose there caused by the doubling of the sets of motor habits and modes of perception. *An object looked different to him depending on whether he looked at it as Falk or as Ramarren,* and though in the long run this reduplication might prove an augmentation of his intelligence and perceptive power, at the moment it was confusing to the point of vertigo. There was considerable emotional intershading, so that his feelings on some points quite literally conflicted. (*City of Illusions*, p. 140—italics added)

The difficulties described here are not really very different from those of the fieldworker who attempts to make sense of other people's situations while keeping his own cultural perceptions firmly under control. Inevitably a confusion and duality emerge that, in the words of Pouwer quoted earlier, force the anthropologist to become a "stranger to himself." But, as most anthropologists come to realize, underlying the apparent disparity there is unity. Le Guin recognizes this in Falk-Ramarren, for she writes in *City of Illusions:* "Yet even in this bewilderment there was the germ of interaction, of the coherence toward which he strove. For the fact remained, he was, bodily and chronologically, one man: his problem was not really that of creating a unity, only of comprehending it" (p. 140). In short, he has learned, as does George Orr in *LOH,* in a most painful way that there are many sides to reality.

In *City of Illusions* and *Rocannon's World,* the theme of the outsider, who is both blessed and cursed in his attempts to understand the subtleties of social life, is presented. In addition, by offering the outsider as a contrast Le Guin challenges the parochialism and xenophobia so often characteristic of the insider's point of view. However, the inability to fit in, the unwillingness to accept the world as it is rather than as it might be, can be equally true for insiders. In *LHD* (1969) Le Guin explores aliena-tion from both angles. Genly Ai is the alien ambassador to the planet Winter. Estraven, a native of Winter, has surmounted the ethnocentrism of his society. The extreme solitariness of both positions is mitigated as they come to discover a fellowship and camaraderie that exceeds, at least in intellectual force, the kind of bond that binds them to their own kind.[8]

"Winter," or "Gethen," represents a total society with all its accom-panying complexities; conflict, political intrigue, distrust, and suspicion mark the relationships between individuals and between groups.[9] When Genly Ai arrives here, he has more to do than merely understand the multiple dimensions of the Gethenian adaptations: he has to confront the political and social disruption his presence occasions. He must examine his initial inability to accept their ambisexuality and, in doing so, he has the quite humbling experience of seeing himself through their eyes—a pervert. Le Guin thus illustrates the development of cultural relativism by permitting the reader to witness the maturing of the ethnographer. Genly Ai has two dramatic foils in the book—Estraven and the Foretellers—who foster in Ai the rather unpleasant task of self-examination.

Initially Ai is pompous and somewhat hostile. So involved is he in his own psychic and physical discomfort that he scarcely notices the effect his presence has on the events unfolding about him. In the early stages of his visit to Gethen, his boredom is tinged with contempt. He writes: "It doesn't do to be impatient in Karhide. They are anything but a phlegmatic people, yet they are obdurate, they are pertinacious, they finish plastering joints. The crowds on the Sess Embankment are content to watch the king work, but I am bored and hot" (*LHD,* p. 11).

Despite his role as objective observer his early accounts are colored by self-deceiving noblesse oblige: "Power has become so subtle and complex a thing in the ways taken by the Ekumen that only a subtle mind can watch it work; here it is still limited, still visible" (*LHD*, p. 12). Yet it is his own bioform that causes him concern. While the appearance of Karhiders is somewhat revolting to his own sensibilities, Ai is discomfited by the realization that here, on Winter, he is the anomaly. "Of course that was part of my job, but it was a part that got harder not easier as time went on; more and more often I longed for anonymity, for sameness. I craved to be like everybody else" (*LHD*, pp. 13-14). But for all that he claims he wishes to be like the others, he regards the Karhiders at best nervously and prefers to keep them at a distance. Inevitably such a stance leads to misinterpretation. Rather than admitting his confusion at his circumstances, Ai attributes motives to Estraven of which the latter, as we learn later, is incapable: ". . . selling me out to save your skin" (*LHD*, p. 20). At this time Ai not only fails to comprehend the palace intrigue, but he does not recognize his almost complete lack of understanding: "I had no idea what he was driving at, but was sure that he did not mean what he seemed to mean" (*LHD*, p. 24). His pomposity at this early stage of the book contrasts with his later humanity, while his early ignorance becomes apparent only as his wisdom increases.

Estraven, from Ai's point of view, is treacherous. Yet soon after Estraven is banished the complex political maneuverings of the royal entourage convince Ai that perhaps Estraven has not totally misled him. Because of his mission he decides to leave Karhide in search of the Foretellers. There is a crucial difference between Ai's approach and that of the modern anthropological participant-observer: his job is action, for which the gathering of information is no real substitute: "As they say in Ekumenical School, when action grows unprofitable, gather information; when information grows unprofitable, sleep" (*LHD*, p. 45).

Still, he is an egoist. He attains heroic form only when the boundaries, both cultural and psychological, that separate him from the others are broken down. As David Porter has pointed out: "According to Le Guin, to neglect the need for balance, for moderation, for appreciation of the inherent contradictions in individuals and society, is to cause individual and social egoism and all their disastrous consequences."[10] Only when Ai transcends his own discomfort and looks about him, does he turn both inward to examine himself and outward to appreciate the hitherto unnoticed strength of Estraven. As much as xenophobia in all respects is a major subject of this novel, so too is the developing relationship between the two protagonists. Moreover, Ai's sense of himself grows.

This process has its beginnings in his adventures with the Foretellers.

The "introverted" self-sufficient stagnant life of the devotees is a shock to him. But, although the deeper meanings of their commitment prove elusive to Ai, they shed light upon Karhide in general: "Under that nation's politics and parades and passions runs an old darkness, passive, anarchic, silent, the *fecund* darkness of the Handdara" (*LHD*, p. 61— italics added). Before the foretelling actually begins, Ai has recognized that the fertility of the society lies in its private underside as contrasted to the public aspect of snow, coldness, and sterility. Despite the many contraries that separate Ai from Faxe, the Foreteller's sincerity is beyond question, and Ai finds himself slightly cowed in his presence. This in itself is a revelation, for the experience forces Ai to question his previously absolute scale of values. What impresses him about the ceremony is not its result—he learns his mission will ultimately be a success—but the form and substance of the ritual itself. He sees himself through their eyes as the pervert they know him for. Despite his self-conscious distinctiveness, he feels himself, against his will, merging with the Foretellers:

I tried to keep out of contact with the minds of the Foretellers. I was made very uneasy by that silent electric tension, by the sense of being drawn in, of becoming a point or figure in the pattern, in the web. But when I set up a barrier, it was worse: I felt cut off and cowered inside my own mind obsessed by hallucinations of sight and touch, a stew of wild images and notions, abrupt visions and sensations all sexually charged and grotesquely violent, a red-and-black seething or erotic rage. (*LHD*, pp. 66–67)

Quite apart from the power and symbolism of the experience, Ai has come to a very important realization: his solitariness gives him greater terror than his reluctant union with those he considers to be somewhat repulsive hermaphrodites. Moreover, the utter selflessness of Faxe provides a vivid contrast to his own egoism. His ensuing conversation with the Foreteller underscores his arrogance and ignorance. The function of fore-telling, he is told, is "to exhibit the perfect uselessness of knowing the answer to the wrong question" (*LHD*, p. 71).

Ai leaves the Foretellers to go to Orgoreyn, where he encounters a social system quite different from that of Karhide. Unlike the absolute monarchy of Erhenrang, this is instead an authoritarian bureaucracy ruling over a less than benign collectivity. Again he finds his life in danger only to be rescued by Estraven. It is at this juncture that the two heroes are reconciled and one of the major themes of the story takes shape.[11] In Estraven we have yet another solitary being. However, he is marginal both because he transcends the pettiness that surrounds him and because he has a vision for society that is more magnanimous than that of his compatriots. Like many of Le Guin's other heroes (e.g., Shevek), he is motivated less by self-interest than by an overweening sense of good for society. Painfully he has come to realize the consequences of different cultural conditioning. Early in their reunion he tells Ai: "Mr. Ai, we've seen the same events with different eyes; I wrongly thought they'd seem the same to us" (*LHD*, p. 188). He ponders the irony of their early meetings: "It is strange. I am the only man in all Gethen that has trusted you entirely, and I am the only man in Gethen that you have refused to trust" (*LHD*, p. 189). But as the novel unfolds Ai not only comes to trust and love Estraven, he discovers what it is to be a true anthropologist. By overcoming his own egoism, he learns that differences do more than create boundaries; opposition is a means of relating.

Estraven and Ai have several points in common: both stand apart from society, Estraven because of his marked past and his present exile, Ai because of his outworlder alien status; and both wish to see Gethen join the Ekumen. But unlike Ai, Estraven is not naive: he realizes all too clearly the self-seeking motivations of the courtly entourage and the jealous hold which the king retains over his power. More importantly, he recognizes the consequences of actions taken within the context of Gethen culture. What unites the two, then, is not their common purpose but their solitariness. There is an affinity in their aloneness that metaphorically is expressed in their journey over the ice, but which in fact has its roots in the nature of their positions. Without support from their respective societies they achieve equality: with the ice as their world, bereft of social boundaries that emphasize differences and minimize similarities, they seek common points. In such difficult circumstances Ai's humanity comes to the surface. In Estraven's journal we read: "There is no world full of other Gethenians here to explain and support my existence. We are equals at last, equal, alien, alone. He did not laugh, of course. Rather he spoke with a gentleness that I did not know was in him. After a while he too came to speak of isolation, of loneliness" (*LHD*, p. 221). We learn that Ai no longer views Gethen ambisexuality as a repulsive curiosity, but, instead, he is now concerned about the existential aloneness such a biological fact would create. Estraven answers by quoting the Yomeshta: "Man's singularity is his divinity." The conversation turns about wholeness and duality, and we are able to see that they are very closely related. Duality—the distinction of I and thou, of myself and others—is bridged or obliterated by an underlying unity, or, in the words of the Handdara, in "the likenesses, the links, the whole of which living things are a part." Yet wholeness is meaningless unless it appreciates, even celebrates, differences. Theall[12] has written of Le Guin:

The very structure of her works is determined by this theme, for it is a structure of dualities—in *LHD,* of Gethen and the Ekumen, of Karhide and Orgoreyn, of Ai and Estraven. From the bringing together of the dualities and from the understanding that is generated by coming to terms with each of them, the process of discovery by which the meaning of the Ekumen is encompassed comes about. The process is dialectical and complexly critical, for each of the dual ingredients which will end up in creating a wholeness modifies and is modified by the other.

The conflict between duality and wholeness is seen in the dual nature of the Gethenians themselves, who are neither men nor women but both, beings who exhibit simultaneously the characteristics of both sexes without being firmly in either category. For all the sophistication of Le Guin's later books, *LHD* makes the point best and most clearly that there are always underlying similarities whose real meaning is achieved in the expression of differences. Genly Ai comes to see this seeming paradox and in time achieves a deep understanding of and a profound respect for Estraven. Their unity is emphasized when he teaches Estraven mindspeech, but their relationship achieves maturity only in Ai's ultimate recognition of what Estraven is:

And I saw then again, and for good, what I had always been afraid to see, and had pretended not to see in him: that he was a woman as well as a man . . . what I was left with was, at last, acceptance of him as he was. . . . For he was the only one who had entirely accepted me as a human being; who had liked me personally and given me entire personal loyalty: and who therefore had demanded of me an equal degree of recognition, of acceptance. I had not been willing to give it . . . I had not wanted to give my trust, my friendship to a man who was a woman, a woman who was a man. (*LHD,* p. 234)

Involved in Ai's acceptance of Estraven is an equally strong realization of his own limitations. He admits to a love for the being who has shared his exile, but he also accepts the fact that the bond that unites them is one of differences, not of likenesses. In so doing he confronts the troubling paradox that sexual union between them would reaffirm, not obliterate, their separateness. But this puzzle fails to bewilder Ai. On the contrary, he has learned that a recognition of solitariness underlies all unity:

For it seemed to me, and I think to him, that it was from that sexual tension between us, admitted now and understood, but not assuaged, that the great and sudden assurance of friendship between us rose: a friendship so much needed by us both in our exile, and already so well proved in the days and nights of our bitter journey, that it might as well be called, now as later, love. But it was from the difference between us, not from the affinities and likenesses, but from the difference, that that love came: and it was itself the bridge, the only bridge, across what divided us. For us to meet sexually would be for us to meet once more as aliens. (*LHD*, p. 235)

Such a realization forces a reevaluation of his role as envoy: Ai has a sudden insight into the purpose of his solitary mission. It is not merely that a single envoy can in no tangible way pose a threat to a society, but something considerably more complex. He knows now that his relationship with the inhabitants of Winter must be reciprocal:

Alone, I cannot change your world. But I can be changed by it. Alone, I must listen, as well as speak. Alone, the relationship I finally make, if I make one, is not impersonal and not only political: it is individual, it is personal, it is both more and less than political. Not We and They; not I and It; but I and Thou. (*LHD*, p. 245)

The Genly Ai of the early pages, the aloof contemptuous observer, has all but disappeared. He demonstrates his commitment to Estraven not only by offering him friendship and acceptance, but by his pilgrimage to Estraven's home after the latter's death. Yet there is a heavy price exacted for the accommodation to an alien way of life. When other members of the Ekumen arrive, Ai stares at them in disgust; in his eyes they have an incomplete, surreal quality. By affirming his affinity to the Gethenians, he has also underscored the differences between himself and his fellows. Because he can understand and appreciate both cultures, he can not help but increase his own isolation. Despite his existential maturity, or perhaps because of it, he has exchanged one form of marginality for another. Estraven pays far more simply but more drastically— his effort costs him his life. Le Guin thus resolves one paradox—of opposition and unity—only to leave us with another: as differences are overcome, one's sense of isolation deepens and increases.

This point is expressed quite clearly in two of her recent works, *DIS* and *WWF*. Shevek, the protagonist of *DIS*, finds, despite his anarchist ideals, the sameness of Anarres stultifying. In Shevek the insider's and the outsider's points of view are examined as we witness the development of his disenchantment with his native Anarres and his horror as he comes to understand Urras. Rather than presenting us with two individuals who view a similar situation differently, Le Guin now gives us two different situations as seen through the eyes of one individual. In both locales, however, Shevek remains a skeptical freethinker. In this instance, Le Guin examines another aspect of the problem that the individual faces in learning to come to terms with his society, namely, the moral responsibility of the citizen to the social order. Judah Bierman[13] has written:

... the dominant life style [of Anarres] is not permanently set but permits, indeed demands, personal choices to meet inevitable social and environmental changes. Though obviously linked with Le Guin's earlier SF and wizard stories, *The Dispossessed* is a moral allegory that should be read with other contemporary utopian tales. It is a prizeworthy contribution to the debate about the responsibility of knowledge, of the visionary and of the scientist, in a planned society.

But the moral element extends further; the individual has a responsibility to himself and his ideals which often places him in a somewhat paradoxical situation if the two conflict. This is precisely the kind of conflict with which so many of Le Guin's heroes are confronted. They share commitments to at least two ideals and are often unable fully to realize either. Like so many of her other characters, Shevek is a powerful observer because he is an impotent participant. In moving between two worlds, but always keeping them both in his mind (a situation similar to that of Falk-Ramarren), Shevek demonstrates to the reader the complementing strengths and weaknesses of Anarres and Urras.[14]

As a native of Anarres, Shevek realizes that his identity is tied to his anarchistic society. But the society limits him by its petty bureaucracy, its strictures on the import and export of ideas, and ultimately in its inability to support and provide the resources necessary for the development of his abilities. Even as a child, as we learn through flashbacks, Shevek felt stifled and imprisoned. Prison imagery binds the novel together. Le Guin perhaps is suggesting that to see beyond the goals and ideals of any society, to be in a sense above them, is a kind of psychological and mental incarceration. Shevek's dedication to his work places him beyond the reach of political rhetoric, while this lack of commitment to the expressed goals of the social order transforms him into a critical observer, be it on Anarres or on Urras.

After an illness which grows out of his isolation, Shevek comes to a realization about his life on Anarres:

His illness had made him realize that if he tried to go on alone he would break down altogether. He saw this in moral terms, and judged himself ruthlessly. He had been keeping himself for himself, against the ethical imperative of moral brotherhood. Shevek at twenty-one was not a prig, exactly, because his morality was passionate and drastic; but it was still fitted to a rigid mold, the simplistic Odonianism taught to children by mediocre adults, as internalized preaching. (*DIS*, p. 136)

This kind of insight in a sense desocializes him, since the awareness of enculturation and its desired outcomes seldom produces those outcomes. If it was his work that cast him apart before, his new critical awareness of his society is bound to separate him yet further. For Shevek is an anomaly—truly unaware of the effect he has on people. He is surprised and bewildered to discover that others value his company. The tension between his internal compulsion toward his work and the external camaraderie mandated by the society creates problems for Shevek's own personal state of balance.

While he remains loyal to the goals and ideology of anarchist Anarres, he cannot help but regard with increasing skepticism the means of implementing those ideals. As he is separated from his wife and child, as he fails to be allowed to continue his work, and as he learns about a particularly gifted friend who has been committed to an asylum, he begins to question not only the efficiency of this kind of social order but the very moral foundations of the state.

The contrasting lifestyle of capitalist A-Io on Urras offers Shevek little reassurance. Initially surprised and delighted with the beauty and wealth of this new world, he is quickly overwhelmed by its problems. He is caught up in a web of political intrigue which he understands too late. He realizes he is a prisoner manipulated for ends that in his naiveté he did not even begin to suspect. Once again, the importance of his theory of time is seen not for its elegance, but for the social utility that may be derived from it. On Urras he loses his innocence, yet his attempts to become a political being elicit blood and death as a response. As a translator or a commentator he is not successful. Ultimately he sees a practical purpose for his theory of time—it can now define the prison that social life is for him:

Fulfillment, Shevek thought, is a function of time. The search for pleasure is circular, repetitive, atemporal. The variety seeking of the spectator, the thrill hunter, the sexually promiscuous, always ends in the same place. It has an end. It comes to the end and has to start over. It is not a journey and return, but a closed cycle, a locked room, a cell. (*DIS*, p. 291)

The theme of hero as translator and social commentator is more highly developed in *WWF*. But the pessimism evident in *DIS* is to be found here even more dramatically. For although the reader's sympathies are clearly with Lyubov and Selver, it is Davidson's view of the world which will prevail. In fact, Lyubov's protests and demands for a more humane treatment for the Athsheans and their world only reinforce Davidson's prejudice and strengthen his resolve to exterminate the natives.

In Davidson, Lyubov, and Selver, Le Guin presents us with three different views of the same situation—the colonization and brutalization of the Athsheans and their world. Here too she explores in her most explicit manner the consequences of xenophobia. As in *LHD*, her heroes achieve a resolution: they have discovered that difference does not imply opposition, but leads, instead, to a new, more complex, relationship. Her point is more strongly made here, for the humanism of Lyubov is contrasted with the narrow, pedantic self-righteousness of Davidson. The Athsheans live in equilibrium with their world, the forest. It is a balance that is emphasized because the people are themselves in a psychological state of harmony. They practice deliberate dream control, allowing themselves to merge the conscious and unconscious worlds. As Watson points out, they "do not suffer from the divorce that Terrans exemplify between subconscious urges and conscious rationalizations. To the Athsheans the Terrans—deprived of this dream knowledge—seem to be an insane people, their closest approach to self-knowledge being the undisciplined confusion brought on by the hallucinogens they entertain themselves with obsessively. . . ."[15]

Selver and Lyubov strive to instruct one another in the ways of their respective cultures. Although each emerges with a new respect and understanding of the other, they, like Shevek, reach an impasse when they try to communicate this. The balance, a crucial theme in Le Guin's works, is irreparably damaged: Davidson and his cohorts distort and destroy the natural equilibrium, while the Athsheans, in learning to fathom and commit murder, are no longer in psychological harmony.

Lyubov learns not only the ways of the Athsheans, but, more importantly, he comes to terms with the forest. His initial feelings of oppression and uneasiness give way to a sense of comfort. We learn that he was "completely at home under the trees, more so perhaps than anywhere else" (*WWF*, p. 103). But his sense of tranquility in the forest is offset by the difficulties he must face in dealing with his fellow Terrans. Like Shevek, he realizes that his reports have been suppressed, while his sympathies with the Athsheans meet with incomprehension, good-natured or otherwise. It is not surprising that Lyubov suffers from severe headaches. It is an affliction he shares with many Le Guin heroes whose cerebral gifts occasion organic disorders. Lyubov's task of translation is made all the more difficult by the presence of Davidson and all he typifies. Davidson calls the Athsheans "creechies." In so doing he denies them humanness and moral worth: he can thus either ignore them or do with them what he will. His attitude is exemplified quite clearly in the book:

Ben [Davidson's "creechie"] was about a meter high and his back fur was more white than green; he was old, and dumb even for a creechie, but Davidson knew how to handle him . . . he could tame any of them, if it was worth the effort. It wasn't, though. Get enough humans here, build machines and robots, make farms and cities, and nobody would need the creechies any more. And a good thing too. For this world, New Tahiti, was literally made for men. Cleaned up and cleaned out, the dark forests cut down for open fields of grain, the primeval murk and savagery and ignorance wiped out, it would be a paradise, a real Eden. . . . And it would be his world. . . . He knew what he wanted, and how to get it. And he always got it. (*WWF*, p.9)

His intention is myopic and destructive. His lack of vision provides a dramatic contrast with the dreaming capacities of the Athsheans. In dreams they seek and find reality; in the shadow of their forests there is light. Although there are variations in the Forty Lands that the Athsheans comprise, Davidson sees only an inferior uniformity.

By contrast, the initial magnanimity of Selver, who tries to understand these invaders whose purposes are antithetical to his own survival, is underscored. But he has tremendous difficulties to overcome; he cannot understand what it means to lack roots, to destroy, and to conquer as a matter of course. However, he slowly comes to realize that his own culture must change, must take up war against the conquistadors of his world. He becomes Selver *sha 'ab*—a god, a translator of dreams into reality, a change agent—a being alienated by his vision from his own pacifistic kind, and from himself by his hatred of the human Davidson and by his friendship with the human Lyubov:

Certainly they don't see as we do, but they know more and understand more about certain things than we do. Lyubov mostly understood what I told him. Much of what he told me, I couldn't understand. . . . No one can say certainly whether they're men or not men, whether they're sane or insane, but that does not matter. They must be made to leave the forest, because they are dangerous. . . . If they will not go they must be burned out. . . . (*WWF*, p. 53)

The devastation is more than physical. Lyubov is doomed: separated from his fellows, quarantined by the Athsheans, he ultimately is fatally wounded in the foray that results. Selver is transformed in a moral sense: the forest is returned to the Athsheans, but at a price that only Selver can realize. There has been no victory here. Though the humans retreat, we see barely a glimpse of redemption.

In the final analysis, however, Le Guin's anthropologist-outsiders have the edge over their fellows. For all their solitariness, their convictions are strengthened by their ordeals. They are no longer mystified by differences. They can grant humanity to others because they cease to glorify or stigmatize that which is not immediately comprehensible. The irony is that in their realization that opposition does not necessarily imply impenetrable boundaries, they erect barriers between themselves and their society. Because they recognize that the task of understanding is not impossible, they contribute to their own isolation. Their perception of balance is an appreciation of differences. And it is here that the paradox ultimately resides; for if there is an aloneness in the chaos of social life, there is even greater solitariness once order is achieved.

SCIENCE AND RHETORIC IN THE
FICTION OF URSULA LE GUIN

Ursula K. Le Guin's early career suffered, she has suggested, because her fantasy fit no publisher's category. When she did some pieces which were identifiably "science fiction," she broke into print. She describes "April in Paris" (1962) as "the first 'genre' piece—recognizably fantasy or science fiction" (*The Wind's Twelve Quarters*, p. 23)[1] that she had written since childhood. A professor named Pennywither from April, 1961, a sorcerer named Lenoir from April, 1482, a Celtic slave girl named Lutetia from Roman Gaul, a small dog from a contemporary April, and an archeologist named Kislk from an April 7000 years in the future wind up in the same Paris room, compliments of a piece of medieval magic that effectively unites the lonely beings who at times past, present, and future occupy the Island of Saint-Louis in the Seine below Notre Dame. The four improbable lovers constitute a charming and very clever fantasy of a highly romantic sort. There is nothing in it beyond a certain effort at verisimilitude—the slave girl Lutetia speaks "Latin with a thick Celtic brogue" (*WTQ*, p. 33)—which reflects the history of human experience. Science as an item of content is absent and, were the story to be related to Le Guin's later fiction, it would fit most immediately with the Earthsea trilogy.

Le Guin describes "The Masters" (1963) as her "first published genuine authentic real virgin-wool science fiction story" (*WTQ*, p. 37), a partial definition of such being "a story in which or to which the existence and the accomplishments of science are, in some way, essential" (*WTQ*, p. 37). "The Masters" describes a community which labors beneath a "single windingsheet of cloud that had covered earth with its mantle of dust and rain ever since Hellfire fourteen generations ago" (*WTQ*, p. 49).

In this story science is overtly the issue. The Masters are a class of men who are licensed to know the "Mysteries of Machinery" in a culture which as an item of policy has sought to stabilize its technology, to prevent exploration, invention, and development, and, implicitly, to forestall the development of a technology powerful enough to create another Hellfire. The issues in the story are complex. Ganil, the hero, joins a group of heretics who gather to carry on research. His forte is mathematics. As a necromancer, a student of the forbidden arabic numerals, Ganil is in a position which Le Guin carefully parallels with the position of religious heretics hauled before the Inquisition. He is, in a sense, a Galileo. His friend Mede is burned for pointing an instrument at the Sun, "a device, they said, for measuring distances. He had been trying to measure the distance between the earth and God" (*WTQ,* p. 49).

Ganil and Mede are the vehicles for the empathy of the reader of "The Masters." They are heroes because they love knowledge for its own sake and pursue that knowledge at great risks. They are heroes because they are pure scientists in the modern sense of the term, because they are, in the Platonic usage, philosophers. But the culture which oppresses them does so for rational cause. The product of their quests, will, if we extrapolate a scenario similar to that of Walter Miller's *A Canticle for Leibowitz,* produce another Hellfire. Our empathy for Ganil and Mede, for their alienation, their suffering in the face of torture and death, for their deliberate selfhood in a culture which demands the surrender of personality, is qualified by the fact that in the narrative's terms they are plainly dangerous men. Le Guin's characterization of Ganil offers a variation of the Prometheus myth but with a crucial difference. The fire the scientists brought was Hellfire. Ganil's quest will, by implication, lead to another Hellfire.

Science is the issue in "The Masters," not as technology per se, but as a mental outlook both powerfully attractive and dangerous. Its power and danger stem from the status of science as a state of mind and the effect of scientific rhetoric on individual men and their cultures. That the effect of science is the issue in all Le Guin's fiction, both the more orthodox earlier novels like *Rocannon's World,* the innovative later science fiction like *The Left Hand of Darkness,* and the pure fantasy of the Earthsea trilogy, is the thesis of this essay.

In explicating it I would like to do four things. First of all, I would like to examine the ways in which "April in Paris" and "The Masters" illustrate the complex tensions between self, culture, and knowledge which are the basis of Le Guin's work. Second, I would like to explore the way in which rhetorical criticism affects the interpretation of Le Guin's work, using *LHD* as an example. Third, I will describe some characteristics of science as a mode of rhetoric and their consequences for the prototypical scientist. Last, I will survey the major works of Le Guin in an effort to demonstrate the ways in which the dilemmas of their protagonists mirror, in essence, the dilemmas of the scientist and hence of Le Guin's audience, a group of readers nearly all of whom subscribe, in some important ways, to the scientific method.

"The Masters" differs from "April in Paris" because it focuses directly on scientific activity and because its attitude toward the pursuit of knowledge reverses that of "April in Paris." Ganil and Mede love knowledge. Three of the four scholars in "April in Paris" are sick of it. But these differences in characterization are overshadowed by the fact that the major theme of the two stories is the same. They both focus on alienation, and they portray characters in a similar dilemma.

It is a dilemma established by their involvement with science. In "April in Paris" Jehan Lenoir discovers his magic spell after rejecting his life of scholarly inquiry:

There must be some way—some method—so that one could be sure, absolutely sure, of one single fact! . . . What good this life spent in poverty and alone, when he had learned nothing, merely guessed and theorized? He strode about the garret, raging, and then stood still. "All right!" he said to Destiny. "Very good! You've given me nothing, so I'll take what I want!" (*WTQ*, p. 25)

Jehan takes up a book of magic. The spell works. He finds he has summoned a bewildered Pennywither and draws a conclusion: "'Magic works, does it? Then science is a waste of time. Ha!'" He reconsiders in the next breath. "'I wish it hadn't worked'" (*WTQ*, p. 27).

This passage is a brief moment in a story which focuses on loneliness, but it reflects the same ambiguous views of the power of knowledge that are the core of "The Masters." "April in Paris" is a fantasy in which the hero rejects science. "The Masters" is science fiction which celebrates the pleasure of knowing while offering a stark calculus of its effect. Given these differences, the two stories have essentially similar themes. Both Ganil and Lenoir are scientists, seekers of knowledge. Both have found themselves alienated from the cultures which surround them. Both have found knowledge a burden while seeking its power. "April in Paris's" playful resolution of the alienation of its scholars—all three are sick of study, glad to escape—does not contradict the more serious suggestion in "The Masters" that alienation is a permanent condition of the scientist. Master Ganil rejects the love of Lani and seeks exile. Both stories argue that to the extent an individual is a scientist, it is impossible for him to exist as a social being.

Darko Suvin's introduction to the *Science-Fiction Studies* issue devoted to Le Guin's work indicated some disappointment at the absence from that issue of an effort to integrate Le Guin's fantasy and her science fiction. "The Masters" and "April in Paris" suggest, I think, one way in which such a connection might be made. The differences in narrative setting which separate Le Guin's fantasy and her science fiction are tangential. Happy endings are unrealistic and produce comedy like "April in Paris" and fantasy like the Earthsea trilogy. The exile or death of the hero, which is realistic, is the basis of tragedy and of the pressure toward verisimilitude that makes science fiction like "The Masters" or *LHD* seem realistic even though the narratives are governed by far-fetched assumptions. What is essential to Le Guin's work is not detail of setting or the type of action, comic or tragic, which she imitates. What is essential is the argument which runs through most of her major pieces, the way in which explicitly in her science fiction and implicitly in her fantasy, she examines the effects of science on individual personalities.

Several qualifications are in order here. I will hazard the generalization that most science fiction is concerned with the technological consequences of science and hence that when science figures in such work it does so as a source of the setting or of impetus for plot developments. George R. Stewart's *Earth Abides* is a case in point. The themes of the novel do not really involve science. Science, more precisely some hypothetical extensions of current science and technology, provide the furniture of the setting and the impetus of the plot.

In arguing that science is the central focus of Le Guin's fiction, I do not intend to group her with those "hard core" science fiction writers who are in effect trying to predict where science and technology will take us. The quality of Le Guin's fiction is a function of a careful style and of her concern with characterization. She is concerned with science not as technology but as an attitude toward knowledge and as a mode of argument. In saying that her major theme is the effect of science on individual men, I do not mean to suggest that she is concerned about how news of life in outer space will affect us when it comes or what rocket cars will be like. Rather, she is concerned with what the scientific method does to those who try to use it.

What "April in Paris" and "The Masters" have in common, what nearly all Le Guin's fiction has in common, is its status as rhetoric. Le Guin's fiction is a reaction to the rhetoric of science, is itself an argument that science is inherently alienating and an exploration of the process by which alienation is produced and counteracted. Such a claim, as I will try to demonstrate in a moment, seconds rather than contradicts Le Guin's view of her own work and the views of her better critics, from Suvin to

Plank. But it also injects the concepts of rhetorical criticism into a discussion which is usually carried on in literary terms. Before looking at science and its reflection in Le Guin's work, I would like to describe and illustrate the use of the concepts of rhetorical criticism.

Aristotle provides most of these concepts. Rhetoric is "the faculty of discovering in the particular case what are the available means of persuasion."[2] He listed three kinds of discourse—deliberative, epideictic, and forensic—concerned respectively with the future, the present, and the past.[3] Aristotle also described three tools for persuasion available to the speaker: "the character of the speaker," "a certain attitude in the hearer," and "the argument proper."[4] The principal addition to this tradition has been the demonstration by Kenneth Burke that discourse, especially literary discourse, is inherently persuasive.[5] His point of view extends the Aristotelian concern with discourse which persuades using logical means to discourse which induces cooperation by dramatistic means. Poetic in his view is a species of rhetoric, of persuasive discourse, and invokes the questions asked by the traditional Aristotelian rhetorical critic. These questions concern the thesis of an argument (the term Aristotle uses is "enthymene"), the means of persuasion adopted by the speaker, and whether the focus of the argument is on the past, present, or future.

Rhetorical criticism is problematical, but useful. Because it insists upon making inferences about the characters and emotions of writers and their audiences, it willfully risks the intentional and affective fallacies. But, because it does so, it offers richer possibilities than traditional criticism, which under the pressure of the Chicago school, tends to confine itself to one of the three Aristotelian concerns, the argument (i.e., text) proper. Applied to literary forms, rhetorical criticism entails a series of inferences which attempt to elucidate the intention behind and the effect of an author's choices of "act," "action," "agency," and "scene."[6] Having done so, it sees the "fantasy" in a work of literature as an aspect of the content of a work of literature rather than the content itself.

Rhetorical criticism generally evokes more complex and often different readings than does conventional literary criticism. That the message is often quite different from the medium can be demonstrated in Le Guin's work by looking at one of her most acclaimed creations, the androgynous Gethenians of the planet Winter in *LHD*. Suvin finds the "basic novelty" of *LHD* to be "what happens when biology makes it impossible for society to entertain sexual roles, and how does this reflect on everything else in the society such as politics, religion, etc."[7] Robert Scholes finds the novel part of the task of "founding a new morality" and the portrayal of the Gethenians to be central to the process: "Why must we know of any new person what their sex is before we can begin to relate to them? The answer to this involves our realization of how deeply our culture is coded along sexual lines, how much must be undone if a person is to be judged as a person. . . ."[8] Scholes's implication is that it is wrong to think of human beings in sexual terms, that this precludes thinking of them as persons, but his focus is on the content of *LHD*. Another critic of *LHD*, Banks Mebane, extends this concern past the Gethenian androgyne as a topic and adds the second element of the rhetorical triad to his analysis. He describes the effect of Le Guin's portrayal of Genly Ai's relationship to Estraven: "As Genly Ai learns to enter the way of thinking of the Gethenians so does the reader—he has to abandon his usual categories, and she leads him surely to the point where he understands the Gethenians as well as one person can understand another."[9] There is a problem with such critical commentary, if not with Le Guin's portrayal of the Gethenians.

Suvin, Scholes, and Mebane make the same assumption that I am making, that the major source of *LHD*'s power is the sexual tension present in contemporary Western culture. What they do not do is accurately characterize the nature of Le Guin's analysis. As an analysis of the effect of sexuality upon human experience, *LHD* and its androgynes are a nullity.

Human beings are not androgynous. A portrayal of an androgynous being has as much to do with human sexuality as a portrait of a centaur has to do with the runners at a track meet. The mile run would be quite different if men were horses from the waist down. But they are not. Le Guin's portrait of the Gethenians is pure fantasy, fantasy which functions exactly as do the dragons of Earthsea. Mebane characterizes Genly Ai as learning "to enter the way of thinking of the Gethenians" as if this entailed an epistemological advance. But there are no Gethenians. The critic has forgotten for a moment that "the way of thinking of the Gethenians" is Ursula Le Guin's way of thinking. Perhaps he would not write the sentence if it read "to enter the way of thinking of the dragons." The substitution of terms might clarify the commonality of vision behind *LHD*. The "fiction" of the novel describes the encounter of a human being with an alien being. The points of view reflected by the narrative are no more nor less alien than those of Ursula Le Guin. To assume that one contemplates the "other" when one contemplates Estraven is one mistake. To assume that one contemplates himself when he contemplates Estraven is a second mistake. He contemplates in both cases a character in a story by Ursula Le Guin.

What, then, of the Gethenian bisexual as a rhetorical artifact? As an aspect of an argument by Ursula Le Guin? These questions send one not to an analysis of the social implications of androgyny, but to the intentions of Le Guin and the psychological condition of her audience. Two other critics are useful here, although their perspectives are tangential to the one I am trying to develop. Stanislaw Lem finds the portrayal of sexuality in *LHD* a "brilliant idea" but thinks the novel frustrating because it fails to develop this portrayal in a systematic way.[10] He would like to see a portrayal of the existential anxiety inherent in a being which did not know from one month to the next whether it was man or woman, father or mother. His complaint is about the quality of Le Guin's treatment of sexuality as a topic. Properly developed, the Gethenian psychology could be a useful analogy to a neurotic human mind. Here would have been a path "back to Man" rather than "a galactic freak show."[11]

That Le Guin walks by this possibility is surely an act of choice on her part. She has suggested that the subject of *LHD* is "not feminism or sex or gender or anything of the sort."[12] It is rather "a certain unease" about sexuality which she finds in the culture and which is a function of the pressure on sex roles exerted by the women's movement. The argument of the novel is not about sexuality at all. In Robert Plank's terms, its "manifest subject is frustration tolerance." I would describe the subject as anger, not anger about sex roles considered as a topic, but anger in Le Guin and in an audience which has decided that frustration/limitation is an aberration of rather than a condition of existence.

Consider chapter 7 of *LHD*, "The Question of Sex," a report "from field notes of Ong Tot Oppong, Investigator, of the first Ekumenical landing party on Gethen/Winter, Cycle 93 E.Y. 1448" (*LHD*, p. 89). The reporter is describing "Gethenian sexual physiology" and its implications. The culture is matriarchal, descent being reckoned "from the mother." There is no division of labor by sexual criteria; everyone is tied to child rearing, hence no one is "quite so thoroughly 'tied down' here as women, elsewhere, are likely to be (*LHD*, p. 93). There is no family to breed neurosis *à la* Freud. There is no rape. There is no duality of role, relation, or personality. That Mebane and others find this provocative is puzzling. What the investigation reports is nothing new or strange. What it reports is a society "based" upon certain of the clichés of criticism of our own society. The complaint by some that women should not be tied down by child rearing, for example, is a cliché of some contemporary discussions of sex roles. The shared maternity/paternity, the erasing of the distinction between maternity and paternity on Gethen is not a picture of a new and different culture. *LHD* in this crucial dimension is conceived of in familiar terms but abolishes those terms. What the reporter sees is a projection of the hopes of that portion of Le Guin's audience which, in its uncertainty about its sexual identity in contemporary culture, has adopted one of the sets of feminist ideals. The medium of *LHD* is a concern with sexuality which in the case of most of the items on the investigator's checklist is quite familiar. But the concern of Le Guin's audience is not with another world and its differences. It is with their own alienation.

If "topic" is one leg of a rhetorical triangle which, in Aristotle's usage, also involves a "speaker" and an "audience," then a critic may look beyond the topic for the controlling impulse of any discourse. To find the controlling impulses of *LHD* in the speaker-audience leg of the triangle is one result of looking at *LHD* and its portrait of sexuality in rhetorical rather than literary terms. But I share Lem's feeling that this aspect of the novel is a subset of the larger patterns of estrangement for both Estraven and Genly Ai, for the Ekumen and the citizens of Karhide and Orgoreyn, which occupy most of the novel. Particularly, in the long traverse across the ice of Winter, Le Guin returns to her most familiar theme and her most familiar archetype, that of the questing hero/heroine/ heroes. The motif of the quest, which can be traced from Lenoir in "April in Paris" to Ged in the Earthsea trilogy to Shevek in *The Dispossessed,* is the central motif of Le Guin's fiction because it is the archetype which most fully represents the situation of the individual in twentieth-century Western and scientific culture. Science is crucial to Le Guin's fiction not because she is for or against it in any ideological sense in a novel like *LHD,* but because scientific rhetoric, i.e., scientific models of evidence for explanation and persuasion, has created the climate within which Le Guin's work must function. Scientific rhetoric has created, for example, the debate about sex roles which is the source of the anxiety that makes *LHD* a powerful novel.

In this sense, Le Guin's rhetoric is an aspect of, at least a response to, scientific rhetoric, and it is in science *as a rhetoric* that one can locate the sources of the motives which compel her characters. That a commitment to science is a denial of self is a position as close to all of us as the last injunctions we have heard to "be more objective." The position is more clearly visible in the early spokesmen for scientific explanation.

Descartes is one of these spokesmen. The first rule of his method entails radical skepticism and a search for universal propositions: "The first rule was never to accept anything as true unless I recognized it to be evidently such: that is, carefully to avoid precipitation and prejudgment, and to include nothing in my conclusions unless it presented itself so clearly and distinctly to my mind that there was no occasion to doubt it."[13] Items of certain knowledge are rare things in human experience. Descartes's insistence on doubting all propositions which are not self-evidently universal propositions means, for an individual who adopts the position as a model, a kind of paralysis. The areas in which the quality of human life is decided are the areas of opinion and uncertainty, of hope and faith, rather than of doubt and certainty.

It is a characteristic of our culture, to the extent that it has followed the lead of Descartes, to differentiate between fact and opinion in a fashion which excludes the individual and his opinion from a rhetorical climate which values no man's voice for its own sake, which rather values a voice solely for the sake of that part of its content which is objective, i.e., which survives the assault of radical skepticism and emerges as a universal proposition. The formula for this challenge on the personal level is "But that's just your opinion." This popular cliché has the same epistemological origin as does the larger scientific culture's discounting of fantasy as an intellectual activity.

A second spokesman for scientific explanation is Bacon. In the *Novum Organon* he outlines a program for the systematic accumulation of information, the terms of which entail personal alienation. In Book One the natural philosopher is specifically instructed in the ways in which his own personality will falsify his ability to deal with reality:

For it is a false assertion that the sense of man is the measure of all things. On the contrary, all perceptions as well of the sense as of the mind are according to the measure of the individual and not according to the measure of the universe. And the human understanding is like a false mirror, which, receiving rays irregularly, distorts and discolors the nature of things by mingling its own nature with it.[14]

The self is the problem. It selects its perceptions, is influenced by "will and affections,"[15] "gives a substance and reality to things which are fleeting,"[16] and is in love with its past. The remainders of Book One and Book Two are a set of instructions which develop strategies that allow the man who would be a scientist to escape from himself into reality.

The general design of Bacon's method exhibits clearly several of the paradoxical consequences of the epistemology of scientific rhetoric. The aim of science is power, the ability "to generate and superinduce a new nature."[17] Absence of progress does not reflect a condition, it rather reflects error. Bacon is confident that men can know the truth, "that there are still laid up in the womb of nature many secrets of excellent use,"[18] that "there is no difficulty that might not be overcome,"[19] and that the requisite posture of the scientist, who in the moment lacks the universal proposition, is patient waiting. He is confident that eventually, but not immediately, knowledge and power will result from his method. "Neither do I hold out offers or promises of particular works."[20] The culture which would ground its discourse on a Baconian model would be a strikingly silent one. The project of the individual would be an effort to escape those accidents of history and personality, that self, which would cloud his vision, and—once freed—to amass data which would contribute to the edifice of science, The Explanation. The culture itself, refusing to ground itself on error, is left, in the absence of Truth, with a rhetorical vacuum. Silence. The individual is adrift.

A third source of alienation in science is its character as a deliberative mode of rhetoric. Aristotle describes the consequences of this concern with future event, with predication, in terms of "artistic" and "non-artistic" evidence.[21] By "non-artistic proof" he means evidence which exists independent of the skill of the speaker, what we would call empirical data. He was more concerned with "artistic proof," evidence based upon the analytical skill of a given speaker and his arts. Where does one find evidence for persuasion and explanation? Does one turn toward or away from the self? Aristotle saw that there can be no data about the future. It has not happened yet. Deliberative discourse must be based upon artistic proof, but only of a particular sort. No art "has regard to the individual case" since "the individual fact cannot be scientifically known." Deliberative rhetoric must consider instead "what seems probable to a given class."[22] Deliberative discourse cannot, in a cultural context, avoid alienation. It must focus on classes of men and probabilities amongst them rather than upon the individual man himself.

One tradition of science sees it as a "pure" activity, the pursuit of knowledge for its own sake. In the main, science seeks knowledge of causes for the sake of the power available in the successfully deliberative discourse. To the extent that our culture seeks that sort of power, it refuses, as a conscious intellectual project, to consider the character of an individual citizen. This citizen has already been taught, in an extension of Descartes and Bacon, that his own opinions have no legitimate claim, in their own right, to participate in that culture's discourse. The position is untenable.

Men do not keep silent because they do not know anything. Culture exists by virtue of the fact that speaking men live alongside one another. The skepticism proposed by Descartes has not eliminated, although it has radically limited, the effectiveness of the Judeo-Christian underpinnings of Western culture. The quest for impersonal knowledge is oxymoronic, as is the phrase "scientific culture." Culture is made by men, is a personal thing; and a plea for a knowledge which is impersonal is contradictory and ultimately futile.

It is not, however, without consequence. That science does not use Bacon's new method is one thing. That our culture does not operate in the impersonal terms of a scientific formalism is another thing. That masses of our citizenry think it does is a third and consequential thing. The alienated man who is both the hero and the reader of the fiction of Ursula Le Guin is the man whose perceptions of himself and his role in his culture are determined by a bastardized version of the characteristics of scientific rhetoric which I have just reviewed.

The reader of whose consciousness Le Guin's hero is the expression is in an agonizing dilemma. He must grant absolute authority to a series of physical propositions which tell him, in effect, that he is a complex chemical phenomenon, nothing more. This diminution flies in the face of every instinct in his being, instincts which tell him that he is important, capable of pleasure, and should be immortal. The diminution exists alongside a tremendous magnification. This mere bundle of chemicals is capable of absolute knowledge, knowledge which will be forthcoming in time. Scientific man at the same time is everything and nothing, the utterly ignorant, the potentially omniscient, the potentially immortal mere protoplasm. He is man who escapes error only by the denial of self and can encounter self only by denying scientific culture.

Enter science fiction, the rise of which Kenneth Burke sees as directly related to the rise of what I have characterized as scientific rhetoric. To those who feel that rhetoric based upon the personal, upon fantasy, upon what he calls "mystery," is being abolished by the "reign of natural science," Burke points out the "scientific mystery fiction that is vigorously on the rise."[23] While scientific rhetorical stances have attempted to eject personality from the culture, science fiction has been pumping it right back in. Few writers have done this so well as Ursula Le Guin because few have realized quite as consciously as she that the problem which science fiction as a genre addresses is not (1) futurology, (2) a moral evaluation of science, or (3) exploitation or extension of scientific knowledge; it is rather the restoration of personality to those who, in taking seriously scientific rhetoric's celebration of alienation, have found themselves in an emotional cul de sac.

Here is Le Guin on the problem:

I have wondered if there isn't some real connection between a certain kind of scientific-mindedness (the explorative, synthesizing kind) and fantasy-mindedness. Perhaps "science fiction" really isn't such a bad name for our genre after all. Those who dislike fantasy are very often equally bored or repelled by science. They don't like either hobbits, or quasars; they don't feel at home with them; they don't want complexities, remoteness. If there is any such connection, I'll bet that it is basically an esthetic one.[24]

Her comments are striking. I am arguing that "complexities" are not the issue in science fiction but that "remoteness," remoteness from self, certainly is. A certain kind of humanist does not respond to hobbits and quasars because they are the not-me; this sort of intellect is still governed by the classical/neoclassical precept, "Know thyself." The mind which discounts the self for the sake of the quasar or which, discounting quasars, nevertheless finds no legitimization of self in culture, is the mind that needs the hobbit or other projective mechanisms in order to examine its own impulses, most especially its own alienation.

At times Le Guin's descriptions of science fiction are clichés. When she is suggesting that science fiction offers literature "the capacity to face an open universe," she is undertaking an exercise in cant that can be duplicated in dozens of fanzines.[25] *From Elfland to Poughkeepsie* offers better thinking. Her description of fantasy and how it works—it offers "a plane where a person goes by himself, on foot, to get in touch with reality in a special, private, profound fashion"[26] —is precise and careful. It is the element of the personal that is the key to fantasy. It offers "nothing but the writer's vision of the world."[27] The "nothing but" in question is the critical thing, the personal vision, which science excludes from the rhetoric of the larger culture.

Much of Le Guin's criticism is an argument that fantasy matters. As argument, her fiction advocates a similar position. Fantasy, subjectivity, names, mindspeaking, all analogues for personality, are what matter in her writing. That her fiction advocates a set of "collectivist" political positions[28] is incidental. Most centrally, it argues that individual men must undertake quests for personality, for the selves stripped from them by scientific culture. This is the grounding pattern of her fiction, visible at times as its topic, and always in the responses which it invites from her audiences. It is now time to examine Le Guin's major fiction and the permutations of her argument.

Rocannon's World offers the quest for self in a pattern the design of which is a formula. Rocannon is the hero who saves the world from the invaders from Faraday. He does it in an improbable, single-handed way that recalls James Bond. The novel is significant in the Hainish cycle because Rocannon learns telepathy in his travels and because he originates the League of All World's policy of cultural embargo. In terms such as these, the novel is not worth a serious person's time.

But Le Guin's development of the formula plot incorporates a number of nicely archetypal features. Rocannon's isolation is the principal of these. When his survey ship and fellows are destroyed by the Faradayans, he becomes, in effect, a man without a culture. The eight light years between Fomalhaut II and Forrosul cut him off from the support of a community of like-thinking, like-minded men. He is a scientist in a tribal society threatened by evil. The Faradayans are not represented in the book. They are so abstract a presence that they suggest a verbal substitution. For "Faraday" read "evil." To preserve the primitive, personal cultures of Fomalhaut II, Rocannon must confront evil.

But the evil is an offshoot, an aspect of, his own culture. His motives for being on Fomalhaut II are mixed. For his culture, the planet is: "Type AE—Carbon Life. An iron-core planet, diameter 6600 miles, with heavy oxygen-rich atmosphere. Revolution: 800 Earthdays 8 hrs. 11 min. 42 sec. Rotation: 29 hrs. 51 min. 02 sec. Mean distance from sun 3.2 AU, orbital eccentricity slight" (*Rocannon's World*, p. 27). For Rocannon himself it is the home of Semley, the alien whose beauty has haunted his memory. The world which is eventually named for Rocannon is a planet whose cultures are personal, tribal, and which he chooses in preference to that of his origin. "Who are my people?" he says to Ganye. "I am not what I was. I have changed; I have drunk from the well in the mountains. And I wish never to go again where I might hear the voices of my enemies" (*Rocannon's World*, pp. 135-36). Rocannon can not return. He has defeated the Faradayans/Evil/Technology with the power of mind. He wishes to avoid another encounter which will place his personality squarely and inevitably in conflict with scientific culture.

Rocannon's World is not a good novel. It is cluttered with "windsteeds" and other furniture which are transparent plotting devices. The contrast between the power and the powerlessness of Rocannon is not clearly developed. Nor is the precise nature of the enemy whose voice Rocannon does not want to hear. Most of the possibilities for empathy with Rocannon are juvenile.

Planet of Exile does not directly exhibit the quest for alienated self. On Askatevar, Jakob Agat Alterra is a man intact, psychically and socially, although his colony's existence is threatened. The story is space opera. The Indian maiden has become Rolery, daughter of a tribe of natives of Askatevar. The cowboys fight the Gaals, a nomadic horde, read Indians, and Alterra kills a snowghoul, read grizzly bear. The novel reflects the impulse toward fantasy in one characteristic way. Romance—as love, self-sacrifice, courage, and other ideals—is not an objective entity, is rather part of the realm of personality and opinion. As fantasy, romance is increasingly incompatible with realistic settings, whose origins lie in science. Hence, Rolery and Alterra's love story must have a setting on another planet. Everybody knows the girls in New York aren't like that.

When Jakob Agat Alterra's descendant Ramarren crawls out of the clearing and into the sunlight of earth in *City of Illusions*, Le Guin solidly reestablishes the quest motif. Ramarren/Falk has lost his identity; he journeys in quest of it, finds it, and escapes the Shing to return home.

His journey to Es Toch is also space opera. Le Guin's characterization of the enemy, the "mindlying" Shing, is not. In *Rocannon's World* the enemy is left undefined. *City of Illusions* offers a definition of sorts. The Shing are the enemy because they are completely successful liars. "I am a Shing," says Lord Kradgy, when Falk has arrived in Es Toch; "All Shing are liars. Am I, then, a Shing lying to you, in which case of course I am not a Shing, but a non-Shing, lying? Or is it a lie that all Shing lie? But I am a Shing, truly; and truly I lie" (*City of Illusions*, p. 90). Ramarren/Falk has a problem in a sense independent of the split personality which he later unites by an act of will. The illusions of the Shing, which put Spenser's *Faerie Queene* to shame, are an epistemological sink. None of the customary external sources of information, from the walls of his room to the testimony of Estrel, can be relied on as evidence about reality. The Shing can even lie telepathically. The dilemma they pose for the conquered citizens of earth and for Ramarren/Falk is that they have reduced all knowledge to opinion. With the Shing nothing is certain. Falk can recover his identity, and eventually does, only by entering Es Toch, by entering an arena in which his only resource is his own subjectivity. He succeeds because, using solely "artistic" means, he deduces the nature and plans of the Shing: "The delusions and apparitions and hallucinations of his first hours or day in Es Toch had been worked on him, then, only to confuse him and weaken his self-trust: for that was what they were after. They wanted him to distrust himself, his beliefs, his knowledge, his strength" (*City of Illusions*, p. 124). Ramarren holds firm. From the conflicting information given him by Estrel, Orry, Kadgy, Abundibot, and Kenyek, he constructs a personality the expression of which is the formulating of a subjectively derived, but firmly held, opinion: "The Shing were, in truth, the Enemy" (*City of Illusions*, p. 141). Falk stakes all on his opinion, succeeds, and escapes in a stolen spaceship. That is space opera again and incidental to his basic dilemma, that of a man to whom scientific evidence is denied, for whom subjectivity must be a tool.

Falk-Ramarren is a powerful archetype. His dilemma reflects that of the citizen in scientific culture who seeks to operate only in terms of certain knowledge, who rejects the risks of opinion, but finds himself forced to act in contexts in which no certain knowledge is available. Falk is an epistemological hero. His analogue is any man who does not insist that nothing is known simply because everything is now known.

LHD, about which I have already made a number of comments, is an interesting variation of the quest motif. The mechanics of the plot of *LHD* are nicely handled, especially the traverse of the ice of Winter and the struggle to include Winter in the Ekumen. The sociology of the novel, in Lem's term, is "caricature." The rhetorical power of the novel comes from Genly Ai's situation, rather than from any specific action. The hero is, again, isolated. He is in the midst of a culture that is alien, and the issue here is not only epistemological; it is also sexual. Genly Ai's identity is intact. His problem is to determine how his own sense of himself as a sexual being relates to the conglomerates around him. As I suggested earlier, much of the description of his encounter is simply projection. Here are Estraven and Genly in a tent on the ice:

And I saw then again, and for good, what I had always been afraid to see, and had pretended not to see in him: that he was a woman as well as a man. Any need to explain the sources of that fear vanished with the fear; what I was left with was, at last, acceptance of him as he was. Until then I had rejected him, refused him his own reality. (*LHD*, p. 234)

The last sentence of this passage, especially, is not effective. The line is a cliché from a T-group transported to space. But the outline of Genly Ai's encounter delineates quite properly the sexual self-consciousness of contemporary culture.

Most people encounter their own personalities far more powerfully as sexual entities than as intellectual entities. *LHD* is, correspondingly, a more powerful experience for most readers than *City of Illusions* because the isolation of the hero is couched in sexual rather than intellectual terms. The pressure of his sexually ambiguous surroundings on Genly Ai is a mirror of the pressure which our culture's plethora of sexual roles and liberation movements places upon the sense of identity of its members.

The way in which Genly Ai's posture functions as a model for Le Guin's readers is interesting. What does one do with androgynous Gethenians? How does one react to a pair of homosexuals kissing, flamboyantly, on a street corner? How does one remain open to the "other" without dulling the edges of one's own identity? Here, in terms of sexual identity, is an analogue to the problem of intellectual identity posed by science. One is to remain open (read "skeptical"), but knowledge is, inherently, closure.

City of Illusions and *LHD* deal with selfhood in sexual and intellectual terms. *The Lathe of Heaven* is typical Le Guin because the issue in the novel is, again, subjectivity. It is an especially interesting novel because *LOH*'s plot turns on a device which neatly allegorizes one of the aspects of self in the face of science that I described earlier.

George Orr, an otherwise unremarkable draftsman for the Bonneville-Umatilla Power District, has dreams which are "effective." They change reality. He is in the office of Dr. Haber, a well-intentioned but increasingly demonic psychiatrist, because he finds that all is not well with his realization of the infantile dream of omnipotence. He has power, but no conscious control over its use.

A plot device gives Haber control over Orr, and the psychiatrist (read mad scientist) begins to use hypnosis to suggest dreams to Orr. Orr's argument with Haber is emblematic of our culture. Attacked by Orr for playing God, Haber paraphrases Bacon: "But in fact, isn't that man's very purpose on earth—to do things, change things, run things, make a better world?" (LOH, p. 82). George's answer is no. It is wrong to "force the pattern of things." His dreaming is a trap. He dreams aliens onto Mars. Instructed by Haber, ambiguously, to get the alien threat off Mars, he awakes to find the aliens in Portland. Each change requires a change: "The end justifies the means. But what if there never is an end? All we have is means" (LOH, p. 83). George is simultaneously the most powerful, the most helpless, the most dangerous, and the most fragmented man in creation. George is the archetype of the man of science.

What he has is a mind that, as does science, makes him powerful. But this same ability alters the world and completely shatters, as does science, his own place in that world. George produces one world after another, just as science produces one theory after another, but he is no closer to improving the world than science is to providing any kind of certain knowledge. The quest in LOH is internalized. George's desire to stop dreaming, to escape the power of self so that he can stabilize his sense of self, is a marvelously precise analogy to the paradoxical magnification of intellect and diminution of spirit that is characteristic of scientific rhetoric.

DIS returns the pattern of alienation and quest to a setting characteristic of Le Guin and, in a fashion which I find more successful than that of LHD, adds an overlay of political implication. Politically, the dispossessed are the Odonian settlers of Anarres. They constitute a nicely imagined collectivist and anarchist utopia which has successfully de-emphasized, if not obliterated, the competitive and materialistic mores of the parent culture on Urras. The rubric of the novel in these terms hinges on the word "progress." If that concept is injected into human culture, it must be in moral terms. The progress of Urras has been technological/scientific. Its basis is a massive inequality in the distribution of resources. Anarres is a model, in spite of the harshness of the life it offers, because it has developed a large-scale cooperative culture. Prima facie, DIS is a piece of utopian political fiction; and it is satisfying, as such. The harsh conditions of Anarres, as much as the Odonian ideology, maintain the cooperative basis of the culture. Anarresti must cooperate to survive. There is little sentimentalism, as well, in the portraits of childhood in such a culture. Shevek, as one who "just can't take life easy," as a genius, is estranged even as a child, admonished by a generation of teachers to stop "egoizing."

Egoizing—exhibiting behavior which is in some way self-assertive— is the target of Anarresti socialization. Shevek is dispossessed of his native culture, not because he rejects its ideology—he does not, he serves it willingly—but because his pursuit of science alienates him from the emotional climate of his culture: "He looked inward, inward to the calm patterns. If a book were written all in numbers, it would be true. It would be just. Nothing said in words ever came out quite even" (*DIS*, p. 25). He pursues physics and in doing so encounters the boundaries of Anarresti morality. In the face of the demands of Sabul, a caricature of the ruthless scientist, cooperation becomes cowardice. His need for independent information from the more advanced scientists of Urras is instrumental to Shevek's involvement in the Syndicate of Initiative and to his voyage to Urras.

As his need for information increases, he learns that the wall around the rocket pad is not the only wall on Anarres. Public opinion is also a wall, and he is forced into a new definition of his role. "I'm going to go fulfill my proper function in the social organism," he tells Takver. "I'm going to go unbuild walls" (*DIS*, p. 267). The tension in Shevek between political and scientific motives is one he can resolve by journeying, as the first man from the moon, to Urras.

He does so, and finds his dilemma intensified. Among other things, he achieves his scientific epiphany, the description of which occupies Le Guin for a number of pages of hocus pocus. In the midst of this, "The difference between this planet and that one, between Urras and Anarres, was no more significant to him than the difference between two grains of sand on the shore of the sea" (*DIS*, p. 226). But Shevek quickly discovers that his problem is intensified rather than solved, for his hosts wish to use his science for base purposes. He must choose between science, the easy but morally corrupt life of the research institute, and the sphere of political action. Shevek does not hesitate. No sooner does he have his physics than he flees to join the descendants of the old Odonian movement. He chooses, finally, words instead of "calm patterns."

As a vehicle for fantasy, the distinguishing characteristic of Shevek is his personal power: "Uninfluenced by others, he never knew he influenced them; he had no idea they liked him" (*DIS*, p. 47). He is again the man alone, unsupported by culture, who labors to save. His return to Anarres reiterates his acceptance of that culture, which had trouble accepting him. His rebellion is against Urras, which, as an allegory of Western culture, is distinguished by its refusal to respect the being of its humans. Shevek is the man who will restore community to a culture crippled by walls; as such he carries considerable psychological force for any reader who counts himself, consciously or unconsciously, dispossessed of significance in the scheme of things.

Shevek, as an archetype, is not so clearly a creature of the alienation bred by science as are Falk-Ramarren and George Orr. His quest is a quest by a man with a solidly established personality for community. It is in the pure fantasy of the Earthsea trilogy that Le Guin offers her clearest representation of the task of the psyche in a scientific age. She has said that *The Tombs of Atuan* is about sex. Why there is a man in the tomb is an interesting question. The story is also about alienation from culture, but I share her feeling that the novel's dynamic differentiates it from her other works and will not consider it here. *The Farthest Shore* repeats the archetype of *DIS*. The man with personality saves the community. Before discussing that novel, I would like to comment on science and sorcery in *A Wizard of Earthsea,* which is the high watermark of Le Guin's fiction.

WOE is a novel of initiation. There is nothing in it that I would call allegory. But Le Guin's use of the plot establishes a set of parallels to the situation of the disestablished self in scientific culture that is stunning. Ged is, or will be, the most powerful. He is also the most threatened. Offered an apprenticeship of silence and the pursuit of wisdom by Ogion, he rejects it. He goes to Roke and to power. The crucial aspect of his magical power in rhetorical terms is its analogy to scientific activity. The reader of the novel, generally uneducated, stands in relation to Ged's magic exactly as he does to the power of modern science. The things one says to a computer are the emotional equivalent of a magic spell for the vast majority of men in our culture. Ged, as the man of power, is the scientist. That science is not magic goes without saying. That it generates a set of images which, as possessed by the popular imagination, supply the loss of priest and sorcerer is the major testimony of the canon of science fiction.

Ged is power. But he is also the victim of his power; he has loosed the shadow. As is the "enemy" of *Planet of Exile,* the shadow is insubstantial. It is "something," "a shapeless clot" (*WOE*, p. 22), "a clot of black shadow" (*WOE*, p. 61). His spell has loosed this indistinct but horrible thing. It waits for him. The most powerful of magicians is the least free of men. Ged's liberation is portrayed as an education. He learns that he must pursue the shadow, must call it by its true name, must account for the fact the shadow looks like him. And then he learns the truth. The shadow *is* he: "Aloud and clearly, breaking that old silence, Ged spoke the shadow's name and in the same moment the shadow spoke without lips or tongue, saying the same word: 'Ged.' And the two voices were one voice" (*WOE*, p. 179).

On one level, *WOE* is a sophomoric book, full of pretentious ambiguity and climaxed by a resolution that lacks analytical content. How does one learn what one is, after all? But the paradigm of the plot is a powerful vehicle for the expression of alienation precisely because of its ambiguity. The cult of objectivity, as the celebrant of the universe of rational cause, is singularly ill equipped to deal with the unconscious core of personality. Those whose concepts of self are articulated in rational terms are indeed pursued by a shadow. As a metaphor, the term represents precisely the force of the sorts of undifferentiated anxiety which are the result of completely buried psychological impulses. The more scientific one's conceptual schema, then the more total one's exclusion of personal knowledge from the realm of cultural significance and the more powerful the catharsis of Ged's quest for his own shadow.

The better critics of the history of science and of its epistemology give copious documentation of a glorious tradition of which all of us are a part.[29] The man who looks at the world and tries to explain the causes of its workings is a scientist. But the characteristics of science as a formal method which our textbooks have inherited from Bacon, Descartes, and Locke are the vehicles of a reduction which has had powerful consequences. Science as a formalism is not a formula for knowledge, a continuing and glorious encounter with the nature of things. As a formalism, science is a rhetorical charade which foists upon the popular consciousness of culture a formula for neurosis. It offers the George Orrs of the world a means but no end, a "Catch-22" in which knowledge can be achieved if self can be denied but in which the self is escaped only in death. The power of the quest in *TFS* stems from Le Guin's recognition that recovery of self, the essential task of her fiction, means acceptance of death.

Tangential versions of this reaction to science are visible in Le Guin's more important short fiction. "The Word for World Is Forest" is a nicely imagined exploration of the thesis that "Progress" is not always progress. The story is ideologically antiscientific. Its fantasy power comes from two sources. The characterizations of Captain Davidson, a snowmobiler transported to space, and Lyubov, the well-meaning man overwhelmed by cultural pressures, provide black and white hats for the plot. Its thesis is one that could be easily documented in realistic narrative, but, as is the case with *Planet of Exile,* Le Guin and her audience do not seek to cultivate information about reality. They cultivate rather a fantasy, in this case an ideological one.

"Vaster Than Empires and More Slow" is less interesting as fiction, more interesting as rhetoric because, along with "The Ones Who Walk Away from Omelas," it centers on a sacrificial motif. The ten volunteers of the "Extreme Survey" crew are crazy and getting crazier. The attention of the nonsentient but conscious vegetation of World 4470 triggers the paranoia of the crew. They know they lack an essential connection to the world around them. They achieve it when the "Sensor" Osden engages in an ambiguous, empathic self-sacrifice. The motif of *VTE* is not quest. It is sacrifice. But the sense of personal alienation and of the necessity of using personal resources to heal the alienation which are the thematic features of *VTE* link it with Le Guin's other work.

The sacrificial motif is developed with more complexity in *OWW*. The town is a paradise, described again in terms of reversed clichés. It has the good things we do not: "One thing I know there is none of in Omelas is guilt" (*WTQ*, p. 255). But the paradise is based upon a paradigmatic scapegoating. The price of the paradise is the abuse of one child, locked in a basement in the town. What is the relative value of an individual human personality when viewed in terms of the "liberation" promised by modern scientific culture? That is the question of the short treatise. Most citizens of the town willingly accept the sacrifice of an individual human being for the brave new world. Some few reject it and walk away. The demand of science is that self be sacrificed. In *OWW* it finds expression in an archetype which is as striking as is the quest archetype in Le Guin's longer fiction.

Le Guin's characters tend to be scientists, especially anthropologists, but range from the wizard Ged to the citizen George Orr. Her settings range from fairylands to other planets to Salem, Oregon. Her themes involve topics as diverse as sexual equality, ecological consciousness, political repression, and romantic love. The mechanisms of her plots range from windsteeds to telepathic plants to scientific genius to ice fields. There is much variety, if not of technique then of invention, in her work. But it is inherently unified. This is axiomatic in one sense. It is all the product of one personality and its impulses. That her work is unified in its effects on her audience is a more complex proposition but one which is axiomatic in a related way. Le Guin's audience is her culture, and this culture is, in a primary way, a rhetorical artifact, a complex of explanations based on a science which conditions the sensibilities of every individual in it. Hence my suspicion that it is science considered abstractly, as a theory of explanation and not as technology, which is the paradigmatic and unifying element in her work.

Scientific rhetoric demands of its adherents a psychological suicide which generates what Wayne Booth calls "motivism."[30] The dominant intellectual posture of American culture accepts the terms of scientific formalism. Subjectivity is devalued. Objective knowledge is valued. But as Booth has observed, many, while agreeing that only the objective is knowledge, simply choose the subjective, perceived as ignorance, rather than surrender their sense of self. Le Guin's primary point of contact with her audience is at this juncture. Her fiction's limitations, particularly the way in which one character and one theme dominate nearly all her work, stem from the fact that it caters to a neurotic impulse in the psyche of scientific man. The power of her fiction stems from the force with which it reaffirms the beleaguered self in the face of the challenge of science.

PART 3

THE EARTHSEA VOYAGE

Only in silence the word,
only in dark the light,
only in dying life:
bright the hawk's flight
on the empty sky.

A Wizard of Earthsea

ROLLIN A. LASSETER

FOUR LETTERS ABOUT LE GUIN

I

Friend and challenger:

You should know that each time I sit down to write something, as you asked, on "religious, moral, or ethical themes" in Le Guin's fiction, my mind starts drawing pictures of dandelion plants. So I conclude that I should rather write you this letter, not about "religious themes" in Le Guin, though I'm sure there must be some, but about what Le Guin's tales illumine in the workings of the human spirit.

For instance, I thought I understood what Le Guin meant by the shadow, when several years ago I read *A Wizard of Earthsea*.[1] I still thought I understood it when I first read the last of the Earthsea trilogy, *The Farthest Shore*. The shadow was, it appeared, the other side of one's self, the opposite of our conscious image of ourselves, the unknown complex of motives and appetites that seems to have a life, a personality, of its own, and which lives in the other world of the unconscious unless loosed on this conscious world by our acts of hubris. It is that part of us that is unknown, unloved, and hence, unredeemed. And that's not a wrong understanding of her symbol, but it *is* too neat, too clean and rational. I recall a teacher I met, who had a talent for exposition of symbols. He said one day, "And why are we afraid of the giant in Jack and the Beanstalk?" I didn't answer. He said, "I know what you were going to say; that is, that the intrusion of God in our lives, giant-like and destructive, is always frightening." And I had to say, "No, I was just going to say that we are afraid of him because he's so big."

I then read *The Lathe of Heaven, The Dispossessed,* and then "The

New Atlantis," "The Ones Who Walk Away from Omelas," and just recently "The Diary of the Rose." And I think I understand more about the shadow; indeed, I understand *TFS* in a new and more unsettling way. For in the later works there is "a hole in the world, and the light is running out of it" (*TFS*, p. 92). For the world they describe, all these tales, is the shadow's kingdom. The people who must live in that world are like the dyers of Lorbannery that Prince Arren describes: "It's as if they had no lines and distinctions and colours clear in their heads. Everything's the same to them, everything's grey" (*TFS*, p. 95). And I realized that though these people are set in future worlds, or distant, in totalitarian polities that we of the U.S.A. have known only secondhand, or in nightmares, these people are we; and that the grayness is our grayness; the loss of color, our tiring imaginations; and the nightmares, our nightmares. The shadow of Earthsea is the shadow of Western, European, mankind; and even more pressingly the shadow of each and every one of us individually as well as collectively. It is my shadow. It is the backside, the mocking opposite of the meaningful and ordered cosmos we inherited from the Ages of Faith. It is the inane world of Joyce's *Ulysses*. And the creeping gray comes from it to remove the colors, the lines and distinctions, and leaves life, as the narrator of "The Diary of the Rose" puts it, "bean soup with a pair of shoes in it" (p. 3).

This nightmare, it may or may not come to pass, but the fear of it is the shadow's hold on us, and leads us, like the boy Arren, to see "at the depths of the dream and of the sea . . . nothing—a gap, a void. There were no depths" (*TFS*, p. 118). And the political solutions, the struggles that have engulfed us collectively for the past two hundred years, how much do they but externalize the struggle within, the struggle each man wages against his own shadow, against his own duality, to achieve the balance within that is the source of true authority in a man or a *polis?*

Robert Louis Stevenson almost a century ago, in his autobiography *Across the Plains,* spoke of how much he suffered from "a strong sense of man's double being which must at times come in upon and overwhelm the mind of every living creature." I think of Stevenson because he wrote the classic tale of the shadow, and of the tragedy of surrender to the shadow, itself a work of early "science fiction." I mean of course, *Dr. Jekyll and Mr. Hyde,* where he writes that "man is not truly one, but truly two," and that those two are severed into "provinces of good and ill which divide and compound man's dual nature." And like Stevenson, Le Guin has been fascinated with "the dual nature of man," returning to it either as man and shadow, as in the Earthsea trilogy and the political tales of recent years, or as male-female in the "Winter" stories, *The Left Hand of Darkness* and "Winter's King."

The problem that duality poses, its potential power to tear the fabric of life by opposing the power of one to the other and insisting on the conquest and domination of one by the other, is the most "religious" theme I have ever found in Le Guin's tales. And she suggests a further solution to that opposition beyond conquest or domination, beyond all exercise of the mastering will or all use of power against power. It is a solution that has little currency among the nightmares, and she herself disclaims it now and then, but not, if we are to believe the inner logic of the tales, whole-heartedly. The solution is, for want of a better name, and it has no good name among us these days: suffering. We might perhaps call it, in "psychologist-speak," bearing the shadow. It used to be called bearing one's cross. But it is still suffering. It is knowing and feeling that the shadow is named by your own name. That you and he/she are one *I*. And it is embracing that otherness without capitulation or domination.

In the words of Ged, "There is only one power worth having. And that is the power not to take, but to accept. Not to have, but to give" (*TFS*, p. 147). And rejecting that one power for any other, we fall into the possession of the shadow and become its prisoners or its agents, like the evil mage Cob of *TFS*, seeking to draw the world to us, all that light and life we lost to fill up our nothingness. Then, only with the word that will not be spoken until time's end, can the hole be closed and the nothingness filled, the word of greatest suffering and total cost, as those who have said it know, the word, "Go Free" (*TFS*, p. 193).

I see that since I keep coming back to the Earthsea books as paradigmatic, I had best try to tell you how I read them before I say any more about the other tales. Anyway, the Earthsea books seem to be a kind of watershed in her fiction so far. The earlier works, including *LHD,* with their elements of exotic locale and adventure and isolated archetypal symbols, seem to work toward Earthsea; the later works, even *DIS,* written in the influence of the shadow's gray nightmare, as is to some extent *TFS,* are working away from or out of that gray spell, defining it and delineating it, naming as they do the collective shadow we all bear.

2

First, *A Wizard of Earthsea:*

That a goatherd, Duny of Ten Alders village in upper Gont, should become the Archmage and dragonlord remembered in many songs, he must endure all the failures and humiliations that lead to those magic sands of World's End, where light and darkness, "met, and joined, and were one" (*WOE*, p. 187). The action of the tale's pursuit-quest is the humiliation of Duny, the self-reliant and proud, into Ged, whose wound is healed, who is "whole," "free." Ged the mage must learn how to name the shadow of his death with his own name and make himself whole. He must become, as his friend Vetch says, "a man: who, knowing his whole true self, cannot be used or possessed by any power other than himself" (*WOE*, p. 189). Ged must learn what Stevenson's Dr. Jekyll refused— *to suffer*. He must learn defeat.

We don't like that word, "defeat"; along with "humiliation" and "suffering" it has become one of the great names we of the modern West have bent all our magic to erase from the realities of creation, both by our manipulation of political programs and by massive charitable institutions and schemes. We make war on poverty and define our four freedoms as the negation of want. But despite our best efforts, we know somewhere within that peoples achieve their real greatness in their response to defeat and before they are glutted with success; even the "causes" know that they can best win adherents through the numinous examples of martyrs and those who lose everything in the service of the cause.

Defeat is the loss of all consciously held expectations, self-definitions, and personal congratulation. It is humiliation of illusion. The response a man makes to defeat is the key to his eventual greatness or final degradation.

To refuse to suffer, to bear as a consciously known fact of reality the will's limitation and weakness and the vanity of self-improvement through willed effort, is the mistake and the tragedy of Stevenson's Dr. Jekyll. It is an unwillingness to suffer the burden of his dual nature, of his "unacceptable" and "improper" desires for gross sensuality and cruelty, that brings Jekyll "to dwell with pleasure, as a beloved daydream," on escaping this suffering by separating his two natures into two identities, so that "the unjust might go his way, delivered from the aspirations and remorse of his more upright twin; and the just could walk steadfastly and securely on his upward path, doing the good things in which he found his pleasure, and no longer exposed to disgrace and penitence by the hands of this extraneous evil."

Le Guin's Ged responds to his first major defeat, the release into this world of the shadow from beyond, with acceptance of his own failure, of his responsibility for the evil he has let loose on the world. So opens his way to World's End. He wills suffering, and gains his freedom.

For that in Ged which must learn defeat is what the Archmage Gensher calls Ged's "arrogance." His natural power strains against his youth and humble origins, and in the young boy there was "the wish for glory, the will to act" (*WOE*, p. 35), a craving that led him to try to impress the daughter of the Lord of Re Albi by his summoning powers. In the lore books of his master Ogion, he reads the spell of spirit-summoning; and the darkness beside the door begins to heave into shape. Only the arrival and intervention of Ogion saves him this first time. But he does not yet know his danger or his fault, so the incident causes Ogion to send him to Roke to study with the great mages. For Ogion knows the boy's power, and his wish for glory, knows his nature and destiny, having first named his name, Ged.

The boy who craves glory and wills to act finds the taunts of school-boys as irresistible as those of the princess of Re Albi—too young! too ignorant!—and challenging a rival to a duel of magic, Ged performs the spell of summoning remembered from the earlier incident at Ogion's hut. The fabric of the world is torn. The beast-thing that in this world embodies his shadow is set loose.

This is, of course, not just an exciting moment in an adventure tale, or a stock figure of occult romances about Blech the Barbarian. It is exactly what happens when the will to act chooses action for the wrong reason—for any reason of self-aggrandizement.

One can not help but think of the three temptations of Jesus in this regard, especially the third: all the kingdoms of the world, if *only*. Action taken to fulfill some other demand than itself alone; things done "for good reasons"; perhaps, even the demand at all, have about them the unmistakable aura of insidious self-aggrandizement. See Me! See Me do it! See Me do it *my* way! And in the demand-fulfilling act the fabric of the world is torn apart. The unspoken craving, the unnamed and unloved beast of the shadow world is waiting and leaps upon us, as upon Ged, and is loosed into this world to taint every successive and related act with the poison of its craving. The means is corrupted by the motive and corrupts the end. It is in this respect that power tends to corrupt, as Lord Acton put it, and may be close to what the Christians mean by the taint of original sin. And the lack of real authority in their acts is obvious in those who act loose their shadow every time they respond to the world with "good intentions."

Ged is nearly killed. The power of the shadow is too much for him. Only the self-sacrifice of the old Archmage Nemmerle in closing the hole in the world drives away Ged's embodied shadow, embodied with the true shape of his act—almost formless, without a head, taloned with Ged's hatred and rage. And the ordered and balanced enclave of Roke Island, its steady and wise life, keeps that shadow away from Ged until he is healed. Nemmerle is killed, having spent his power in the act of setting the world in order. His sacrifice prefigures Ged's great act in *TFS*.

Ged's attempt to impress his fellows with his power has only proved his hubris, his foolishness, his weakness. In response to this defeat, Ged makes a choice, an inner choice, that sets his destiny and distinguishes his greatness: he chooses responsibility for his shadow.

He could have, like Stevenson's Jekyll, chosen to dissociate himself from his shadow, attempted to deny that the beast set loose was his beast, the evil his evil. The new Archmage asks him, "What do you want?" He replies, "To stay. To learn. To undo . . . the evil . . ." (*WOE*, p. 75). To undo is beyond him or anyone. We can't take back our actions. Gensher knows that premature confrontations with what was loosed would be worse than deadly, it would be possession, "a *gebbeth*, a puppet doing the will of that evil shadow" (*WOE*, p. 75). All good intentions to control one's self-demand, to undo the evil, are themselves further hubris, further demands. And we are, you and I, all too familiar with acquaintances from our past who are filled with the craving to "do good" whatever the cost and who have become the opposite of what they claim to crave, *gebbeths* in the service of their own self-importance, and insistent on the submission of everyone else to their own notion of how this "good" is to be brought about. Gensher keeps the young Ged on Roke where in the ordered routine and the company of the wise he may heal the hurt of his defeat and learn to defend himself against the shadow of his will. He says, "They tell me you were clever. Go on and do your work. Do it well. It is all you can do" (*WOE*, p. 76).

That is, of course, all anyone can ever do: the work in front of us, the job we have. But to do it without thought to the end, without congratulation as to its great importance. To do the job because it's the job to be done, that's the hard part. Ged learns how to do the job and only the job by his continued study at Roke, his conscientious attention to his assignment at Low Torning, his facing and resisting the Dragon of Pendor, and finally by his resistance of the tempting promises of the Terrenon and its servants.

In the incidents of his first assignment, among the fishermen of the isles, Ged learns the limits of his power and the way to do his job. His attempt to bring back Pechvarry's son from death is well meant but nevertheless wrong. He meets the shadow, who was, of course, present in his reasons for the attempt, on the borders of death and he is nearly overcome. Ged had left Roke for the unimportant post in Low Torning because, as Le Guin tells us, "his desire had turned as much against fame and display as once it had been set on them. Always now he doubted his strength and dreaded the trial of his power" (*WOE*, p. 87). Ged had swung from the hubris of self-importance to the hubris of self-disparagement. The job on Low Torning, then, had been as much an escape from doing his job, a place to hide and not be challenged, as it had been a recognition of his limitations and acceptance of a dangerous and little appreciated task.

Troubled by dreams of his shadow, he would defend himself with spells. But he knows that he can not defend himself against his beast and defend the fisherfolk against dragons at one and the same time. The job is the dragons; he must put aside his inner troubles for the sake of the job. So he will face the dragons. Nor is the dragon incident irrelevant to the shadow-pursuit, though it may seem so to Ged. In defending his fisherfolk against the dragons' attack, he is also taking true and right action to bring these primeval powers under control in himself, thus facing, without fully realizing it, the formless and tearing beast-nature of his shadow. Attending to his appointed task and duty, he is attending to his personal, inner danger.

Further, the temptations of the Terrenon and his successful resistance of them, of the promises to fame and power, of evils older and deeper than any personal shadow, the evil of occultism and Satanism, deepen his self-knowledge and his strength. The price of his victory, which includes the loss of his friend the little *otak,* corresponds to the loss of spontaneity that attends all contact with the suprapersonal evils, with the occult in all its forms. Only by giving up feeling and humanity, and becoming fierce, intellectual rationality, the hawk of his public name, can he escape the occult power of the Terrenon. And as a Hawk, as dehumanized, aggressive intellect, he returns to the one place where he knows he can regain what is lost, to the one model he can trust—Ogion the Silent. It strikes me as not unintentional on Le Guin's part that Ogion is translated "fir-cone." The pineal, the fir-cone in the brain, is long associated with clarity of mind and wisdom.

There, to Ogion, he says, at last recovered from his hawk-mood, "I have come back to you as I left: a fool" (*WOE,* p. 135). But he is not a fool in stupidity, only in the humility of his self-knowledge.

When Ogion questions him about the shadow beast that pursues him, Ged says, "I have no strength against the thing" (*WOE,* p. 135). Ogion sees otherwise, and reminds him of the strength he had "to outspell a sorcerer in his own domain, there in Osskil" (*WOE,* p. 135) and at Pendor the strength to stand up to a dragon. Ged still draws back; he has not yet the humility, the courage, to admit all the facts. "Luck" he says of Osskil; "chance" of Pendor where he "happened" to know the dragon's name.

Ogion is not fooled: "*All* things have a name" (*WOE,* p. 136), he says. And he advises Ged actively to pursue the shadow-beast now. The time to turn and pursue has come, as it had not before, when rightly Ged kept to the refuge of Roke. "You must turn around," Ogion says: "If you go ahead, if you keep running, wherever you run you will meet danger and evil, for it drives you, it chooses the way you go. You must choose. You must seek what seeks you. You must hunt the hunter" (*WOE*, pp. 136-37).

Ogion advises a willed confrontation with the shadow because only by finding, holding, naming the unnamed and unloved in us can we redeem it, can we make whole the rent fabric of life which our demands of others, and of ourselves, have left us. We must know what it is we demand and the little insidious ways we go about demanding. And we must know what part that demanding has in darkness greater than our own personal psyche —what thing from *unlife* it corresponds to and belongs to. We must *name* the shadow. All things have a name. And that is no mere intellectual examination of sin. To try it too soon, before we have power within us, the deep *will* beyond mere good intentions, is to face almost certain defeat, and a Nemmerle may not be around. As Ged says, "If it defeats me wholly, it will take my knowledge and my power, and use them. It threatens only me, now. But if it enters into me and possesses me, it will work great evil through me" (*WOE*, p. 137). But Ged understands that danger and still chooses, with the same inner choice that was made on Roke as he recovered from his first defeat. He chooses Ogion's wisdom: "Master, I go hunting," he says (*WOE*, p. 138).

The pursuit of the shadow takes the form of a long chase over the wilderness of the empty sea. One is reminded, certainly, of the chase over the ice that ends Mary Shelley's *Frankenstein*. Le Guin likes these wilderness-scapes. The landscape becomes harsh, empty, hostile, even as the inner landscape of the traveler becomes increasingly "emptied" of its distractions and excuses and concentrates more and more on the job of locating or defining its wholeness.

Along the way Ged, tricked to shipwreck by the shadow, receives "by chance" a half of the lost Ring of Erreth-Akbe that will involve him later in the incidents of the second book, *The Tombs of Atuan*, of the trilogy. For so stories seem to work in reality, don't they? One story beginning before another has quite ended, and everything overlapping very disconcertingly. No classical unities, unfortunately, outside of art.

Though the symbol perhaps demands it and the story clearly does, I wonder if, in our own inner journey, we ought to say without qualifying it that the shadow is named with our name? It is a part of our name, surely, for it is part of us. But there are other parts. Moreover, as here in the story we are told, the shadow is also from beyond us, one of the *old* things. Our name is more than the shadow, and also less; and it may be one of its better tricks to call itself by our name. The illusion that one is utterly depraved is not of much help in growing toward authority of choice and act, and is only a further refusal of suffering. But this part of Le Guin's symbol is, I think, balanced out and qualified by the event that completes the symbolic moment. The shadow and Ged move toward each other, and merge. And the form that remains is Ged. The active will, masculine choice, when it has confronted its shadow and been able to accept that the shadow is part of the whole self, not "somebody else's fault," does receive, must receive into itself the knowledge of evil and bear it, suffer it, in all action. Then, I think, a man or a woman would have the right to say, "The wound is healed, I am whole, I am free" (*WOE*, p. 188).

Likewise, the form or shape of the shadow has been transformed through Ged's years of chosen responsibility for it. The blank, shapeless thing with no head and four taloned paws that first leaped upon him through the hole in the world was a parody, an inversion of four-square wholeness. Like Ged's own spirit, it had no head, no governing intelligence. It was formless and bestial and ravenous with hate and craving as he himself. But though that formless beast haunted his dreams, it did not appear to him again in that form. When it appears in his trance at Low Torning, it is still shapeless, neither man nor beast. But it doesn't leap mindlessly at him; it whispers to him, though there are no words in its whispering; and it reaches out towards him. It is growing more human, more formed, trying to speak and hesitant to rush to an attack. Ged's hard work at Roke, without pretensions or hurt feelings, and his newfound compassion for the weak and pained, for Pechvarry and his people, have begun to humanize his spirit, too. Ged's Ged-ness can now whisper, though it has yet no words, and it can reach out to others.

When next he meets the shadow, it is as a false human, a *gebbeth,* the sailor Skiorh. On Osskil the *gebbeth* casts aside its appearance of humanity and turns on Ged, a shadow, a nothing in a cloak, and speaks his name—Ged. As it chases him through the night and snow, it whispers, mumbles, calls to him. His courage and steadfastness at Pendor before dragons has given the shadow its seeming human form and given it words for its tongue. That is, Ged knows more about his own shadow, his "good intentions" and his real desires. He knows he does not desire wealth—no dragon hoard. He knows he does not desire killing or death for its own sake—the dragon goes free. Nor does he desire a quick and easy end to his own internal struggle—the name of his shadow, at the cost of others' lives. He will not sell his fisherfolk to the dragons for the shadow's name. Now, as he runs before the whispering shadow, Le Guin says: "He knew that all his life that whispering had been in his ears, just under the threshold of hearing, but now he could hear it . . ." (*WOE*, p. 117).

The shadow who comes to his summons across the waves when Ged has turned to pursue it, at last has "some likeness to a man," a shape now, even in daylight. It has drawn power from him through the struggle on the moors of Osskil, Le Guin says. But it has also been shaped *by* him, his "power" being his apprehension of the thing that drew on him. Still, it is not yet a true shape—"a dim ill-made thing pacing uneasy on the waves," "half-blinded by day" (*WOE*, p. 143).

But "the dim ill-made thing" grows steadily more manlike, that is, grows more recognizable and *namable,* as Ged takes active pursuit of it, *tries* to name it. When Ged reaches Ismay, the home of his old friend Vetch, his friend's greeting is dampened and troubled by Vetch's sighting three days earlier of what he had then thought to be Ged himself. That is, the shadow has now grown form enough to be mistaken for its original. And on Ismay, Ged's attraction to Vetch's younger sister Yarrow completes Ged's own humanization. It awakens his feeling for woman, as the cold witch-beauty of Osskil could not, and allows him to trust her with his spontaneous jests and gentleness.

Thus, at last, the shadow has shape on the sands of World's End, the several shapes of all those on whom Ged had projected his own shadow, who had through his life embodied his hates and fears, his father the smith, Jasper, Pechvarry, Skiorh, a dragon, and then: "a pair of clouded, staring eyes, and then suddenly a fearful face he did not know, man or monster, with writhing lips and eyes that were like pits going back into black emptiness" (*WOE*, p. 187).

In the light of Ged's staff, of his true self-knowledge, the monster-face must give way; and the thing falls back into its first form, "crawling on four short taloned legs upon the sand," "lifting up to him a blind unformed snout without lips or ears or eyes" (*WOE*, p. 187). Ged has seen it in all the disguises and projections it has taken in his life, all the spoiled or self-demanding relationships that littered his past, and now in the clear light of self-vision he sees it in its only true shape, no longer terrible and paralyzing but almost pathetic and pitiable. He reaches out and takes hold of his shadow, of the "black self" that reached out to him.

"Light and darkness met, and joined, and were one" (*WOE*, p. 187).

3

The Tombs of Atuan, the second of the trilogy, holds a special place in this discussion—and in fantasy fiction. Still, there is reason to hesitate in talking about *TOA*. The pattern in this tale, the subject of the story, is a pattern of the feminine spirit, a woman's story. To say anything about the way of a woman, even about "the feminine" or "the masculine" these days, is to arouse controversy, hostility, before anything further has been said. Also, Le Guin herself has not dealt with the matter of the feminine way often in her tales. There is the early work, *Planet of Exile,* and the tale of "Semley's Necklace" in *Rocannon's World,* and there is lately "The Diary of the Rose" and the splendid "The Day before the Revolution." But the greater number of the tales are about the masculine way, the pattern of the masculine spirit.

In an interview Le Guin said that for her, writing women characters was too easy to be fun.[2] But writing about the feminine way, finding the "story" of the feminine can hardly be "easy," as it has so seldom been done. What great works of literature tell the "feminine" soul-journey before the last century and the creation of the gothic romance? Only in the great treasure-store of fairytales, which is but recently unlocked for us and still little known to most readers, is there a "literature" of the feminine way.

If writing about the feminine way becomes any "easier" after our times, this tale of Le Guin's, both fairytale and gothic romance, should make it so.

Three sentences, three symbols, strike me as characterizing the situation and the meaning of this tale:

"She is eaten! She is eaten!" (*TOA,* p. 15)

"*You are Arha.* There is nothing left. It was all eaten." (*TOA,* p. 32)

"You have set us both free," he said. (*TOA,* p. 128)

To be eaten. Nothing left. To have no name, no being who you are. All the feminine side of a human being, the feelings, the natural and spontaneous responses to the world around us, to other people, eaten up and dark and cold and poisonous, locked underground in moldering treasure-rooms where no one will ever find or enjoy them again. To be shut up, and buried, and denied acknowledgment in the world of day— that is real horror, that is the effect of the shadow's control of the feelings.

Le Guin's second Earthsea tale takes up the story of the liberation of the feminine from the shadow, as the first followed the liberation of the masculine. It is, on the literal level, a woman's story, as it recounts what is, probably, more the way a living woman would experience the liberating movement within her than a man would. But it is also a man's story, and as such can't be dismissed as merely a sexist division of labor. As a woman must also liberate the masculine within her by the same journey as Ged's pursuit of his shadow, so a man must liberate the feminine in him from the powers of inner darkness that would eat up his responsiveness and feeling and use it as a vessel of evil. The two tales are complementary. Ged's life is not complete without Tenar, nor does she find her name again without Ged.

The feminine that must be released in this tale is that deep feeling-response that allows us to reach out to others in love, and to sense the depth of things, the reality of the powers greater than our ego, and to hold in love and kindness the self-identity that is our name. It is the interior liveliness of experience that we name Joy.

And in most people, the feminine feelings are held tightly by the darkness, undifferentiated, unawakened, through the power of fear and self-doubt. "There is nothing left! It was all eaten" (*TOA*, p. 32). Who am I? There is no me. Only the massive weight of the unforgiving past, the inmost center of night that has always been there and always will, duties and rituals that no longer mean anything but must be performed. "Over and over they chanted the empty word" (*TOA*, p. 16).

Too many women in our time are saying that they find themselves thinking, "There is no me, only the chanting of the empty word," for us to deny that this tale of Tenar become Arha represents symbolically a woman's problem of this era—how to break free from the weight of the past, of the accumulated demands and expectations of mothers and grandmothers and great grandmothers as far back as can be imagined. As Tenar in this book thinks, "All human beings were forever reborn— but only she, Arha, was reborn forever as herself" (*TOA*, p. 58).

There is a certain mean glee in that—to be the only one, to be always yourself, never changing or undergoing the viccissitudes of change. But it is more horrible than happy. Never changing, always the same, not even escaping through death, over and over the empty word. The same dull round.

But we must not dismiss it as only a woman's problem. There may not be any purely women's problems or purely men's problems. The problem here is the imprisonment of feeling and that is a man's problem, too, though he may meet it later than does a woman. Le Guin jokes that she writes most often about men because she likes to write about "aliens."[3] But men and women are not, on the level of the inner life, "alien." Their roads are at least parallel.

To free the feminine responses from the power of the ancient dark, from heritage, guilt, security, the Bell Jar, they must be brought to affirmation of their own existence; the feminine must have a name. Then must follow an abjuration of the darkness that held them. And to reach either of these great acts, the only power that can call the feminine forth from its imprisonment, is *eros*, love for another, for a man, for an "alien."

That is why *TOA* must resemble the form of the gothic romance. It must be a love story, because the liberation of feeling *is* the story of love. Tenar has, at least, known the love of her parents. Her first five years were happy in the full freedom of childhood, jealously guarded for her by her mother, who knew she would soon lose the child to the priestesses. That knowledge of impending loss made the mother's love more intense, and the father's as well, though he tried to suppress his feeling and dreaded the pain of giving her up.

But from her fifth year she has lived in The Place of the Tombs, among the black-robed girls and priestesses, the eunuchs, and the slaves. She has learned the rites and dances of the Nameless Ones, has danced before the Empty Throne. But chiefly she has spent her childhood and girlhood performing the routine chores of life in the Place, spinning, washing, sweeping, cooking, and being bored.

She is alone, the only priestess of the most ancient shrine, tutored and controlled by the two high priestesses of the God-King's temple. Her loneliness is broken only by the kindliness of the elder high priestess, and by the adoring affection of her personal eunuch, old Manan. Significantly, it is only from Manan, a male, that she receives tenderness and warmth, and from him that she learns how to respond with feeling.

In this desert locale of the Tombs, also a desert of feeling and vitality, she must place all her natural feeling on the only object that permits her to love, the "cause" of her Dark Gods, whose ancient worship is ignored by the parvenu cult of the God-Kings, and whose temple falls into ruin by the God-King's neglect. These dark and evil spirits of the Tombs take all her love, and she devotes herself to learning all that she can about them, their shrine, the former glories of their cult, the labyrinth of tunnels that twist everywhere beneath the Place. The labyrinth's twists and traps guard the treasures accumulated by the cult in former days, before the power of the God-Kings ended the influence of the cult worship of the Nameless Ones.

These dark powers, to whom she gives her fierce love in default of any other object for that feeling, belong to that company of which Ged's shadow-beast was one. They are the ancient evils of the Earth, the suprapersonal powers of darkness that work in this world through the loosing of the personal shadow. They remain nameless and bodiless until, wrestling with the personal shadow, we find their names and master them in our own bodies.

Because their power is over the will and feeling, they eat up those who give up will and feeling to them. As their "body" in this world, their priestess has herself no name. She is the vessel only, the *gebbeth*, of the insatiable cravings. She is the Eaten, *Arha.*

But Tenar can not be the Eaten. She has too much of herself, of natural and spontaneous feeling, to be consumed by the darkness. She resists the loss of her selfhood even by the gift of her loyalty and love to these powers she is supposed to serve. We can not love and be eaten at the same time.

It is the younger of the God-King's two high priestesses, Kossil, who is in truth the Eaten One of the nameless darkness. A woman "heavy-footed, heavy-faced," she has no more natural feeling, no loves. She fears, resents, gloats, grudges, but she does not love.

Tenar notices about her that she holds nothing sacred but power, and therefore upholds the God-King's cult, because the God-King is powerful, and scorns the Nameless Ones because their cult is in decay and weak. She can not discern the sacred nor admit of powers beyond her own, but she can fear them, as she fears the dark in the cavern beneath the Tombs. She is made cruel and stupid, and finds pleasure in the whipping of a truant priestess, the torment of dying prisoners. Tenar says, "All she knew was cold waiting and death at the end of it" (*TOA*, p. 80). And Ged says of her that it is she who has really been eaten by the dark powers, *because* she will not acknowledge their existence—"and now she cannot see the daylight any more" (*TOA*, p. 119).

The appearance of Ged in Tenar's bored and desperate existence forces the opening of all her imprisoned feeling. Taught to think all the dark-skinned folk of the inner islands soulless, and the mages, especially, to be evil and frightening enemies, to be truly "aliens," she reacts to finding him in the cavern below the tombs with a mixed excitement of curiosity and fear. She knows he is a mage and that he has come for one of the treasures in the labyrinth, the half of Erreth-Akbe's ring, for she has heard tales from the two high priestesses of all the dark-skinned mages who have come to Atuan for that "trinket" and died in the labyrinth without finding it. She locks Ged in the labyrinth and runs away, struggling with conflicting feelings she cannot understand.

At one point she tells herself, "She would not give him any water. She would give him death, death, death, death, death" (*TOA*, p. 85). But she remembers the horror of her one killing, the decision she made, at Kossil's prodding, for the execution of three befouled and tortured prisoners sent to Atuan by the God-King as sacrifices to the Nameless Ones. She had ordered they should die lingeringly, in darkness, by thirst and starvation. That decision, made to impress Kossil and assert her own importance and power as Arha, has haunted her dreams ever since. She cannot do this again, not to this man. Further, her curiosity is aroused about a man, the only man she has ever seen. She chooses compassion, and that begins her liberation and selfhood.

As she cares for her prisoner, Ged, with the help of old Manan, secretly feeding Ged with her own rations, she finds compassion and curiosity becoming something greater. What that new feeling is she cannot name, but she fears it and tries to suppress it. On the excuse that she must save the prisoner from Kossil, who now knows about him and about her feeding him, she has Manan take him to the innermost rooms he seeks and which only she, not Kossil, can find. Even in this she tries to protect herself from acknowledging her feeling and tells herself and Kossil that she has taken him there to die at last, locked in the cold and dark.

But she cannot do it. She is not, like Kossil, eaten. She thinks of the labyrinth now not as shrine but "nothing, in the end, but a great trap" (*TOA*, p. 66). "There was no centre, no heart of the maze" (*TOA*, p. 77). The labyrinth represents physically what her life at the Tombs of Atuan is spiritually. It has no center, no heart. It is nothing in the end but a trap. And she must escape the trap or perish. She must find the center, the heart that is real, and take back herself from all the shadow forces that would eat her up.

Ged has told her who these Nameless Ones are, and that he has met them before; that they are strong, and real, but not gods, not worth the worship of any human soul. But more importantly, he has told her her true name, called her Tenar, the name unspoken since childhood. Hearing it again, she has found her selfhood again and with it can find the right objects of her affections. Struggling within herself, she resolves the quarrel and her confusion. "I am Tenar," she says to herself, "I have my name back. I am Tenar!" (*TOA*, p. 109).

Ged has found in the treasure room the half of Erreth-Akbe's ring. But she has the other half, Ged's half, which she took from him in mockery soon after imprisoning him, not knowing what it was. Together they rejoin the ring, giving to each the other's half. And as it rests on her open palm, Ged's hand covers it in a spell of patterning. She has given him a treasure greater than any other in the world, the ring that holds the lost rune of dominion. But she has given him a greater treasure—his own feeling in response to hers, his love. Seeking one treasure, he has found a greater. And while still in the labyrinth, holding off both the attacks on his will by the Dark Ones and the earthquake of their wrath, he is able to say, "You have set us both free" (*TOA*, p. 128).

Their escape from the tunnels and cavern, the death of loyal Manan who thinks he is defending her, the earthquake and the fall of the temple above them, are the climax but not the conclusion of Tenar's liberation, of her story. The feminine is not free of the shadow when it stands against the upper world of consciousness, though it may be safe from the labyrinth of meanness. The habit of bondage, of labyrinthine feeling must be named and refused tunnel by tunnel, root by root, before the feelings can stand free and authoritative.

But Tenar finds in their trip over the green mountains away from the desert of the Place of the Tombs, a joy she had never exepcted and an image of the life she really desires. "Living, being in the world, was a much greater and stranger thing than she had ever dreamed" (*TOA*, p. 139). That joy and peace remembered allow her to face the final attacks of the darkness within and refuse their lures and illusions.

As she thinks about the strangeness of the world Ged is taking her to, about cities and tongues she has never known, about dark skins rejecting her white one and manners she will not match, she becomes terrified. All that she knew she has left behind.

"Now he didn't need her" (*TOA*, p. 152), she thinks; he would leave her behind, desolate, fooled. She is caught by the dark powers still, by the clutching that masquerades as love, demanding proofs of love returned. She draws her dagger to kill him while he sleeps, sacrifice him to the Powers she has abjured. But as she would strike he wakes and speaks to her, and touches the Ring she now wears on her wrist, the Ring of Peace and of their bond, their gift to each other. "At the sound of his voice the fury left her" (*TOA*, p. 153).

Le Guin says of her: "What she had begun to learn was the weight of liberty. Freedom is a heavy load, a great and strange burden for the spirit to undertake. It is not easy. It is not a gift given, but a choice made, and the choice may be a hard one" (*TOA*, p. 154).

Last, she is hit by a false remorse, "I have done a very evil thing," that is a mask for her fear of a new life. "What evil have you done, Tenar?" asks Ged (*TOA*, p. 157). The memory of the three prisoners and the death of Manan, and last her unkindnesses to the old eunuch are all she can name. "The evil must be paid for. I am *not* free," she says (*TOA*, p. 158).

Ged silences the remorse, "The evil is poured out. It is done. It is buried in its own tomb" (*TOA*, p. 158). And then he reminds her of what great and good things she has done, of the old evil brought to nothing, of his own release, and of the broken made whole. When she protests, he goes on, "quietly" describing the place he will bring her to, his own center, the home of Ogion on Gont among the silent forests and the strong mountains.

Not only in romances, but in every man and woman, in both men and women, the quiet masculine voice of clear intellect and strong decisiveness must silence fears and straighten out the feelings, disentangling feeling from fear and fear from fact, disclosing objects among illusions and allowing the feelings to move on with the flow of life to their proper loyalties and objects. The masculine intellect, by its clarity, must make possible the feminine trust in which hope, joy, grows; and life moves on.

So, in the spirit of all good romances, and of the best and happiest weddings where everybody cries and knows a marvelous thing is taking place, Ged and Tenar come to Havnor and triumph. Two free spirits, male and female, entrust themselves to the third thing that is their mutual completion: "Gravely she walked beside him up the white streets of Havnor, holding his hand, like a child coming home" (*TOA,* p. 160).

4

We come, finally, to the third tale, *The Farthest Shore.*

"There is a hole in the world, and the light is running out of it" (*TFS,* p. 92). And in our world, too, isn't there? That grayness like a spider's web over Enlad and the outer isles, we've all been seeing over everything these days. And for so long we've almost grown used to it, as the normal and real state of things. And one knows that there is something uncanny, spooky, unnatural, about that burdening oppression of gray, and about the future-terror, the waking nightmares, that grow in it. The creeping grayness that eats up the will in our time, where does it come from? Le Guin's tale tells us, symbolically at least, if we can read it.

The nightmares, and the gray web growing daily, come upon us from the shadow-land even as a shadow-inspired-and-fed wrong craving eats up the true and proper light of day.

I can not help thinking of Le Guin's more recent stories "The New Atlantis" and "The Diary of the Rose."

Setting these stories as she does in *our* country and in *our* more immediate future, makes even more clear than the fantasy setting of *TFS* that the problem in the Earthsea tale, "the hole in the world," is a hole in *our* world. That we respond to the nightmare vision of "The New Atlantis" with no effort of belief—we *know* it could happen here, and fear it will—is proof enough that we share the shadow problem of Earthsea, and that that shadow is not just personal or peculiar but collective, the shadow of the whole culture and of our era.

Under the tyranny of the shadow, imaginative perception becomes reduced to a polarized "me" vs. the great faceless "them." The particularity of things is steadily lost to a meaningless round of struggling, grasping, clutching at the necessities of life with no satisfaction in the attainment. Life becomes "the same dull round." Julia de Beausobre says, in the autobiography of her imprisonment in the Stalinist slave camps, *The Woman Who Could Not Die,* that the greatest danger to keeping one's spirit free was the constant temptation to think of her guards and the men they served as "them."[4] For then prison had you, cut off, at "their" mercy, in real slavery. And the daily struggle for the necessities, for warmth, for food, became insatiable and neither warmth nor food enlivened. Only when every guard had a name, only when a hut or a scarf had its own warmth or when the swill of that day its own taste, only then was one "free" though in prison.

In *TFS* Arren says of the folk of Lorbanerry:

They're strange here. It's that way with everything, they don't know the difference. . . . They complain about bad times, but they don't know when the bad times began; they say the work is shoddy, but they don't improve it; they don't even know the difference between an artisan and a spell-worker; between handcraft and art magic. It's as if they had no lines and distinctions and colours clear in their heads. Everything's the same to them, everything's grey. (*TFS*, p. 95)

And the mage then asks the boy: "What is it they're missing?" Arren said without hesitation, "Joy in life!" (*TFS*, p. 96). How is the joy lost? Where does the shadow insinuate its power into our feeling for life? The collective shadow, at least, creeps in through the whispering of the individual shadow. It plays on the craving for power, the demands, of the individual shadow, magnifying it and empowering it through doubts about the value or reality of individual goals and the denigration of the job at hand as inferior to the promised reward. It demands that we give up "the names" in return for future immortality.

Earlier that same day Arren had experienced the joy in life he now says is lost to Lorbanerry: "Earlier, the day had seemed dreary and insipid to Arren, as if infected by his dream; now he took pleasure in the bite of the sunlight and the relief of shade, and enjoyed walking without brooding about their destination" (*TFS*, p. 95). This "pleasure in the bite of the sunlight and the relief of shade," the awareness of distinctions and boundaries, is so simple, so obvious, so commonplace. But so hard to achieve, to release a single bite of bread from all the schemes and resentments and fears and notions and demands that hide it away from us. The narrator of "The Diary of the Rose," a young woman who operates an "autopsychoscope," a machine that projects the innermost thoughts onto a screen in pictures, says of the minds she has screened that all they can manage to picture is an undifferentiated mass with an occasional dim object—"bean soup with a pair of shoes" (p. 3).

In *TFS* the loss of names and distinctions, the loss of mage-powers, comes over the world through a great and fallen mage, a man Ged once met and in a fit of temper humiliated beyond right measure. The advance of the shadow over Earthsea is collective, for it takes the collective shape and affects everyone, but it has been released in some way by Ged. It is Ged's own shadow as much as the collective. How much is the present collective shadow derived from the unrealized shadow of some one man? How much of its spread and power in our own life is due to a "shadowed" act we committed and forgot? Ged says of his mistake with Cob: "His fear made me sick and angry. I should have known by that that I did wrong. I was possessed by anger and vanity. He was strong, and I was eager to prove that I was stronger" (*TFS*, p. 84).

Now Cob has learned how to live on both sides of death at once, neither alive nor dead. And in his wretched fear of death he has convinced himself that it is immortality he has discovered, life unending and unchanging. In fear of death, of change, and of suffering, he has deluded himself with desire for fixity and stasis; and in revenge on Ged and all mages lures with promised immortality people all over the world into his death-in-life, into the joyless shadow-land where the thirsty drink dust. Of that immortality, the safety of unending life, Ged says to Arren:

"Life without end. Life without death. Immortality. Every soul desires it, and its health is the strength of its desire. But be careful, Arren. You are one who might achieve your desire."
"And then?"
"And then—this. This blight upon the lands. The arts of man forgotten. The singer tongueless. The eye blind. And then? A false kind ruling. Ruling forever. And over the same subjects forever. No births; no new lives. No children. Only what is mortal bears life, Arren. Only in death is there rebirth. The balance is not a stillness. It is a movement—an eternal becoming." (*TFS*, p. 145)

Ged knows the temptation, to power even over death. He too once opened a hole in the world. But he now knows more about himself and about the world than he did then. He tells Arren that Cob calls to the living through the shadow-craving in each of them that desires, as Cob desires, the powers of self-importance. Ged hears the voice, but wills not to hear it. He says, "I know that there is only one power worth having. And that is the power not to take, but to accept. Not to have, but to give" (*TFS*, p. 147). Having met and borne his personal shadow, Ged can resist and see through the blandishments of the collective shadow.

What, then, is the collective shadow, in this book and in our age? Le Guin does not openly name it until near the end of the book, in the dark land, as Cob is questioned by Ged.

"What is life, Cob?"
"Power."

"What is love?"
"Power," the blind man repeated heavily, hunching up his shoulders.
"What is light?"
"Darkness!" (*TFS*, p. 188)

The collective shadow of our age is despair: the loss of hope that the movement of life from one moment to the next will bring to us anything "good," anything lovely. It is more dreadful perhaps than any loss of faith, i.e., loss of the trust that the movement of life is indeed "good" and meaningful. For hope, unlike faith, is substantial, both in the old sense and the new of "substance." Hope contains the personal reality, "the substance of things looked for." And when hope is lost, the "essence" of life, of everything, changes. Despair is the shadow of the Age of Anti-Faith. That can't be avoided. We can't have it both ways. And power, the craving for power, which is the inner form of the craving for safety, will be the externalized symptom of the sickness.

There is, in each of us, a little Stalin, full of "good intentions" and for whom the end justifies the means, who can not tell light from darkness. In the collective of the culture, that little social reformer becomes the great urge to achieve "safety," control over life, an end to the necessity of suffering.

And those who would wield the power of the shadow, as well as those who succumb through fear to its description of life, become like Cob as Ged names him: "You exist, without name, without form. You cannot see the light of day; you cannot see the dark. You sold the green earth and the sun and stars to save yourself. But you have no self. All that which you sold, that is yourself. You have given everything for nothing" (*TFS*, p. 189).

To escape the collective shadow's fear of death and desire for safety, a twofold effort is required: first, of identifying the source of the shadow effect and naming its error, and second, of restoring the true king—educating and empowering the governing will. Le Guin's story is in this sense a mystery-puzzle as well as a hero tale: as detective, Ged must find the criminal and know for certain the nature of the crime; as hero-king, Arren must learn true values and the limits, great and small, of his will and courage. Both tales are told at once and are intertwined.

Unless the king that comes to that throne be the one prophesied, unless he has "crossed the dark land living and come to the far shores of the day" (*TFS*, p. 25), he will be no king but anti-king. To cross the dark land living, to experience imaginatively the full nature of the world as it is described for us by the shadow—a land without light or change or meaning, a land where the stars do not move and the thirsty drink dust—

to cross that land experiencing it fully, and to get out of it again—that is the real test of maturity. And one must not get out by a trick, an illusion, or a regression to the way one got in, as if being there had never happened. It is only by crossing the place and suffering the mountains of pain that one comes at last to the far shores of the day, to a new and transformed experience of the daylight of life, to a resurrected vision. This is the experience and initiation of the real king. I think it is Shevek's failure in *DIS* to conceive of the possibility of such a transformational change *in himself* that makes him seem to me such an awful schlemiel. He imagines, and finds, the key to transformation in the external world, the simultaneity of space-time. But he never sees that there is a simultaneity of inner space-time to which his mathematics corresponds. And though his heart is in the right place, and he has the best of intentions, he still wets his pants for a female cat in gauzy silks. And the crucial thing is that one man's choice makes all the difference. The one man being you, me, anybody—the Shevek or the Ged within—nobody else can do for us this work, make this individual choice. Ged says to Arren, "One man may as easily destroy, as govern; be king, or anti-king" (*TFS*, p. 144).

To cross the dark land—I have already said how I read that symbol of the dark land in these books. I know several critics take it at face value as Le Guin's representation of the land of the dead, the afterlife. It seems to me the dark land is not the land of the dead but the land of the shadow —the world as it looks when the perverse illusion of the shadow has replaced reality and the light of day with its meaningless despair. Not death itself, for death is part of the balance; "Only in death is there rebirth" (*TFS*, p. 145), Ged says, and later, to Cob in the shadow-land, "All who ever died, live; they are reborn, and have no end, nor will there ever be an end" (*TFS*, p. 189). But in the shadow-land there is nothing but endless unchanging existence, the dreadful certainty that the craving for safety demands.

The characters of "The New Atlantis" are all caught in that shadowed fixity. Burdened with resentment and fear and "demands," they find nothing wonderful, nothing remarkable—not even the convulsion of the earth itself and the sinking of the outworn continents beneath the sea. Admittedly, the totalitarian prison of a U.S.A. polluted and used up, short of all the luxuries-thought-to-be-necessities of technological affluence, and deprived of privacy as well as liberty, is hardly a pleasant place to live in. But the substance of the situation has invaded the character and imagination of those who live in it. They are as trapped by the rule of anti-king and his servants within themselves—"the self that cries *I want to live, let the world rot so long as I can live*" (*TFS*, p. 144), as

Ged describes it—as they are trapped by the circumstances of the corrupt polis in which they live.

The king that is to rule, the mature judgment, must have his attachments, his values, directed toward the right goals and worthiest models. In his long voyage with Ged, Arren is prepared for the goal by the steady stripping away of illusions from his expectations of life and the uncovering of spontaneous feeling responses. While Ged unravels a puzzle, using the boy's innocence and natural nobility as guide and lure to the criminal, Arren goes through what can only be compared to a purgation, a dark night, first of the senses and then of the soul.

First, Arren is deprived of the physical comforts he had been used to, learns they don't really matter to him, that they are distractions. Also, he is deprived of the illusion that there is civil order everywhere as in his well-ordered and comfortable little island home. Hort, with its poverty, its drug addicts, its thieves, its fraudulent traders, its slavers, is the existence of evil which he must learn. His capture and night on a slave ship, expecting to be sold on the block, brings to him in a most personal way the reality of evil in the world. His failure to save Ged from what he thinks are mere thieves, deprives him of the twofold illusion of his own power or mastery: he can not save Ged or outwit evil, nor can good intentions, "meaning well," achieve safety or defeat evil.

Further, though Arren is not yet aware of it, the thing desired can come out of failure, out of weakness and error. His failure to maintain guard while Ged questions the mad and broken sorcerer Hare results from his being drawn into trance by the call of him Ged seeks—the source of the shadow invasion of Earthsea. And what he can tell Ged about that trance and its call is the clue, the evidence, Ged needs to unravel the puzzle. It leads Ged, by association, to his own memory of having drawn another into the shadow-land; and that memory reveals to Ged the possible identity of the criminal.

On Lorbanerry, Arren discovers the importance of names, and of distinctions. More especially, he learns the importance, though he can not yet comprehend it, of compassion. Ged's treatment of the old madwoman Akaren and of her murderously insane son Sopli strike him with bewilderment but remain as facts about his model that he must accommodate.

But sailing away from Lorbanerry, listening to the insinuations of Sopli, Arren comes to doubt his model: Ged leads them to their death; Ged would deprive them of the promised immortality for the sake of his pride, and so on. This betrayal of his deepest and truest love is a necessary deprivation of illusion and false images. It is a dark night of the soul, as even the most treasured images of what is valuable, what is real, what is trustworthy, are stripped away. Arren finds himself drifting in a little boat alone with a dying friend, and utterly paralyzed to take even the least action of moving the oars. He must learn what it means to be shadow-bound, as he learned what it means to be chain-bound: "He watched dawn come over the quiet sea, where low, great swells ran coloured like pale amethyst, and it was all like a dream, pallid, with no grip or vigour of reality. And at the depths of the dream and of the sea, there was nothing— a gap, a void. There were no depths" (*TFS,* pp. 117–18).

It would not be wrong to recall John of the Cross, again, describing the deepest point of the dark night: "The soul not only suffers the void and suspension of natural supports and apprehension, which is a terrible anguish, like hanging in midair, unable to breathe, *but it is also purged* by this experience" (*The Dark Night of the Soul,* 2.6.5). And again: "Added to this, because of the solitude and desolation this night causes, a person in this state finds neither consolation nor support in any doctrine or spiritual director. . . . He resembles one who is imprisoned in a dark dungeon, bound hands and feet, and able neither to move, nor see, nor feel any favor from heaven or earth" (2.7.3).

The relief of their stay with the raft-folk, the healing of body and spirit both Ged and Arren find there, allows Arren to assimilate what has happened to him. And though he will not be free of all doubt or moments of despair, he has passed his personal nadir, his greatest test of will and courage, and has done it in the simplest and most obvious way—he has acted out of habit and unthought response. Unable to *act,* to will himself to aid Ged, he has left the little remaining water for his friend to reach. "It never occurred to him to drink from that water. He had set out fishing lines, having learned since they left Lorbanerry that raw fish fulfills both thirst and hunger" (*TFS,* p. 120).

Among the raft-folk that spontaneity is bolstered and fed. For, as Ged says, though "in innocence there is no strength against evil . . . there is strength in it for good" (*TFS,* p. 133). Arren swims and dives and learns to play in the open and calm water with the children of the raft-folk, "'like an eel,' 'like a dolphin,' 'like me!' squeaked the three-year-old, bobbing like a bottle" (*TFS,* p. 127). The homing instinct of a man carries him along out of the paralysis of despair as long as he moves spontaneously, like an eel, like a dolphin, like a three-year-old bobbing like a bottle. The despair has been necessary for the burning up of the intellect's habitual way of understanding, that a better might take its place.

For Arren this illumination comes in the long conversation he has with Ged, when he admits his betrayal of the mage, of his love, in the previous week's drifting. Ged knows better than to take that darkness at its face value as the substantiality it purports to be, and reads it rightly as: a stage of the way, a necessary purgation, even a "felix culpa." The acceptance of it, however, the suffering of one's failure and humiliation, is crucial. From Ged's own rending of the world's fabric has come his mature mastery. Ged says, "Lebannen," calling Arren by his secret name, "Lebannen, this is. And thou art. There is no safety. There is no end. The word must be heard in silence. There must be darkness to see the stars. The dance is always danced above the hollow place, above the terrible abyss" (*TFS*, p. 130).

Because he does accept and suffers, Arren begins to free himself from the power of the shadow, to act despite despair, and, like Ged, to will not to hear. When, on midsummer's night in the Long Dance, the raft-folk's singers suddenly are overcome and falter—"'I do not know the words,' the chanter said, and his voice rose high as if in terror. 'I cannot sing. I have forgotten the song'" (*TFS*, p. 136)—it is Arren who makes himself sing, and sings, indeed, the song of the creation, the oldest song, of "the balancing of the dark and the light, and the making of green lands by him who spoke the first word . . ." (*TFS*, p. 137).

It is then that a dragon, Orm Embar of the primal age, can come and lead them to the confrontation with the shadow itself, as manifest in the sorcerer Cob. The terror has reached even to the depths of the dragons and they are crazed with it and deprived of speech.

And Ged must struggle still with the infection of the shadow that would pervert the job to other ends than its own. He looks at the sleeping Arren one night as the little boat speeds toward Selidor, the farthest island, and thinks: "I have found none to follow in my way. None but thee. And thou must go thy way, not mine. Yet will thy kingship be, in part, my own. For I knew thee first. I knew thee first! They will praise me more for that in afterdays than for anything I did of magery . . ." (*TFS*, pp. 164-65). But Ged recovers, through humor and self-irony, and the shadow passes: "A goatherd to set the heir of Morred on his throne! Will I never learn?" (*TFS*, p. 165).

That little victory frees Ged to work the last and greatest act of his magery, when at last they have followed Cob across his shadow-kingdom to where Cob's hole in the world sucks up the light of the living world. There Ged gives up all magery, all power, all demands, and speaks the rune of ending, which closes roads and is drawn on coffin lids, the word that was spoken at the making of things and will not be spoken until time's end: Go free!

It is the end of all magery even while it makes the world whole, for it adjures all compulsion, all summoning, all domination. Go free! I make no more demands on you.

There remains only the one last great act, not of wizardry, of the spiritual power, but of will, of physical endurance and steadfastness: the act of a king. Arren must carry himself and the failing Ged, who has spent himself in the great sacrifice. He must cross the Mountains of Pain and reach the far shore of day.

Then the pattern will be complete; the crowning in Havnor inevitable, and the right king, not an anti-king, in control of life.

Arren carries the half-dead wizard over the stones of the mountains, following only his instincts for a guide, and comes out where they entered the Dry Land, on Selidor, beside the body of Orm Embar, fallen in his attack on his enemy Cob. He is free, the world is free, but he doesn't yet know it. To be back is not yet real to him. But he goes about the necessary tasks of the moment: finding water, fishing for food. "And that was all there was left to do. Beyond that he could not see; the mist was all about him" (*TFS*, p. 199). Then he finds in his pocket a small black stone from the mountains he has just come through. "And he smiled then, a smile both sombre and joyous, knowing, for the first time in his life, and alone, and unpraised, and at the end of the world, victory" (*TFS*, p. 200).

He does not fear, not even the old dragon Kalessin, parent of Orm Embar, who crawls into view over the ridge. Ged and Arren climb up the dragon's leg to its neck and it leaps into the air, toward Roke, at Ged's request.

The raw emotional force, primeval and reptilian, at once both destructive and helpful, either foe or friend, turns friend to the man who has mastered the shadow and willingly suffered the pain of its dry rocks and desert. The dragon Kalessin, oldest of dragons living, "turned and looked at them sidelong; the ancient laughter was in its eye. Whether Kalessin was male or female, there was no telling; what Kalessin thought, there was no knowing" (*TFS*, pp. 202-3).

And it is on that beast of the ancient laughter that Ged, having brought Arren back to Roke and knelt before his lord in homage to one greater than himself, having in his own eyes "something like that laughter in the eyes of Kalessin," mounts again into the air from Roke Knoll and flies off "north and eastward, towards that quarter of Earthsea where stands the mountain isle of Gont" (*TFS*, p. 205).

Well, this is how I read these little books, big tales. Not the way Le Guin reads them, perhaps, though not too distant from her, if the texts themselves are to be trusted. And not the religious, moral, and ethical themes you may have wanted me to isolate and explicate. But it may illumine some of what I feel she has been defining for us by binding her imagination, her narrators, within the power of the shadow for the sake of the later tales. It is unfair to ask of any writer that she herself be always saying the rune of ending. And if it were truly said, would there be any more writing? I prefer instead the loveliness of that little companion story to *DIS*, "The Day before the Revolution," where Odo the revolutionary is herself at last dispossessed of her lifelong possession: "Tomorrow? Oh, I won't be here tomorrow" (p. 246). There is no tomorrow, only the job today, the silence, the truest wizardry, and above all, the myriad myriads of names of things:

[Odo] started up the second flight of stairs one by one, one leg at a time, like a small child. She was dizzy, but she was no longer afraid to fall. On ahead, on there, the dry white flowers nodded and whispered in the open fields of evening. Seventy-two years and she had never had time to learn what they were called. (P. 246)

Will we finally come to know their names?

Yours, and Ursula Le Guin's respectfully.

JOHN R. PFEIFFER

"BUT DRAGONS HAVE KEEN EARS"
On Hearing "Earthsea" with Recollections of "Beowulf"

> In the old silence all voices and all names would be
> lost.
> All sounds of water, wind, wood, sail, were gone,
> lost in a huge profound silence that might have been
> unbroken forever.
> But magic, true magic, is worked only by those beings
> who speak the Hardic tongue of Earthsea, or the Old
> Speech from which it grew.
> And the mage's long listening silence would fill the
> room, and fill Ged's mind, until sometimes it seemed
> he had forgotten what words sounded like: and
> when Ogion spoke at last it was as if he had, just then
> and for the first time, invented speech.
>
> *A Wizard of Earthsea*

In a world of only words and memories we recite, embellish, and repeat
the statements we are afraid to forget. We give them oral form. Taken
from Le Guin's *A Wizard of Earthsea*, the lines above, as well as the lines
with which each section of this essay begins, discuss and illustrate such a
process. In fact, they underscore the principal statement of *WOE*: words
and speech—the genesis, discipline, and creative power of language—make
the world. The first of all wisdoms is to know this thoroughly. *WOE*
itself is a story told in the old oral way, a telling both childish and primitive as well as mature and modern. In it words are physical. Speech is the
stone with which intuition works and imagination is erected. No written
word is real unless spoken before and after the writing. Mankind's brief
history of literacy and printing reveals this by dramatic contrast with

the ages when people neither read nor wrote but only heard and spoke; and by dramatic contrast with the eons before speech was made. This last is the greater drama, whereby we are witnesses of the awesome evolutionary event marked by voices and words breaking a primordial silence.

The Earthsea trilogy *(A Wizard of Earthsea; The Tombs of Atuan; The Farthest Shore)* is everything that heroic fantasy in English should be. Its themes are archetypal and Germanic. Its milieu presents events, customs, and a climate rooted in a planetary temperate zone. Its language, poetics, and scale are elemental and oral. Even as we read Earthsea, we become increasingly aware of its preliterate narrative character. Reading it is not at all enough. It was made to be heard. It was made to be heard very much in the way the Anglo-Saxon heroic epic *Beowulf* was made to be heard. Moreover, the special purpose of *WOE* is to tell us that speech and language, especially the Old Speech, act much as metaphysics. Once the processes of speaking and the Old Speech are explained in *WOE*, we are provided with a theory and practice for hearing and interpreting the whole of the Earthsea trilogy. So I have limited my analysis to *WOE* with only occasional digressions to *TOA* and *TFS*.

1. EARTHSEA AND *BEOWULF*

Only in silence the word, . . . bright the hawk's flight.—p. vi

"To hear, one must be silent."—p. 18

"To hear, one must be silent. . . ."—p. 171

"Only in silence the word . . . bright the hawk's flight."—p. 181

A Wizard of Earthsea

Knowledge of at least four features of *Beowulf* can enrich the appreciation of *WOE* and the Earthsea trilogy. The Anglo-Saxon word beorht, "bright," appears with special prominence in both compositions. Both provide elementally life-affirming cosmologies. Subjects, events, and scenes belong to a common epic and mythic tradition. Finally, and of immense importance, *Beowulf* is the product of a tradition of oral composition, of a storytelling poetics, many of the parts of which are preserved in the fine narrative of all modern prose fantasy. The Earthsea trilogy is such a fantasy.

I think the high frequency of the use of "bright" in the *WOE* narrative triggered my recollection of *Beowulf*. The root "bright" appears at least thirty-six times in *WOE*, in such phrases as "bright the hawk's flight," "bright road," "bright autumn," "spring . . . quick and bright," "bright days," "bright eyes," "bright rip in the world's darkness," "bright water," "bright stones," "bright danger," "earth's bright hearth."[1] To the English-speaking ear it seems a common enough word because it is. It belongs to the primary Germanic *wordhord* that supplies the strong vocabulary of modern English. It predates that enormous infusion of Greco-Roman words that came with the Roman and southern European invasions of the British Isles. Moreover, "bright," as the Anglo-Saxon "beorht," appears in the eleventh-century *Beowulf* manuscript at least nineteen times—most sensationally, perhaps, in brego Beorht-Dena, "prince of the Bright Danes," an epithet for Beowulf himself.[2] This relatively conservative distribution of the word in the 3182 lines of the old poem suggests that it was reserved for descriptions of special power. It is not surprising for a word whose translations include "splendid," "stunning," and "beautiful," among others. However, the total vocabulary of *Beowulf* consists of only a few hundred root words: each root is precious. The poet or *scop*, would distribute them judiciously. On the other hand, Ursula Le Guin in composing *WOE* had thousands of words available. I believe she could have found thirty-six different (many of them effective) adjectives to substitute for her use of "bright." Why did she not? Without elaborating, I can offer a hypothesis. When you wish to compose fantasy, with all its emphasis on elemental clarity of thought, mood, and place, you employ the elementary vocabulary of the language in which you are telling your tale. You use the words that have meant what they mean for the longest time. The message you seek to communicate is most stable in them. I think Le Guin has done this in narrating *WOE*. At best, the *Beowulf* poet had fewer choices.

When I finished *TFS*, and was still heady with the gentlest of all the versions of the case against immortality I have ever encountered, I understood fully, for the first time, the force of *wyrd* in Germanic cosmology—in the universe of para-Greco, para-Christian *Beowulf*. *Wyrd* does not mean "fate," in spite of the perfunctory glosses that say it does. Fate is effete and degenerate in the way it evokes the essential resignation of the Greek psyche. It also encourages a perverse interest in the possibility of a spiritual residue. *Wyrd*, on the other hand, is a hammer on the anvil of the world. It orders that no man escapes death except in the quick memory of those who will live. At the same time, the will is free. The individual has a significant control over the events of his life. Moreover, great quests are, therefore, profoundly personal. They may sometimes be inspirational or emblematic. They are never messianic. Each life may be negotiated only by its owner. Fate is a doom. *Wyrd* is an achievement.[3] The triumphs over Grendel, Grendel's Dam, and the Fire-Dragon belong to

Beowulf alone. The defeats of the shadow-self *(WOE)*, and Cob-who-said-that-men-need-not-die *(TFS)*, are Ged's alone. These victories are achievements in the spirit of *wyrd*, the Germanic affirmation of a single man's power in the world.

The settings, subjects, and events of *Beowulf* and Earthsea seem stock matters from a common lore. Both present island worlds with the sea always nearby, and with weather varied in the shocking polarity of the high summers and deep winters of a temperate zone climate. Both settings reveal civilizations of only primitive technology, fragile in an ecology largely in its natural state. In each world there are dragons. Beowulf kills one and dies from it. Ged kills a few, almost casually by contrast with Beowulf, and survives to learn from dragons without always killing them. In both cases, there exists a story of a dragon-killing exploit. For the Anglo-Saxon hero it is the actual *Beowulf* composition. For Ged it is the hearsay one in the Earthsea trilogy called "Deed of Ged." Both are recited or sung in the preliterate manner with which orally transmitted cultures preserve and convey their personalities and histories. Other similarities in the content of *Beowulf* and Earthsea might be enumerated, but what interests me more is that the works exhibit similar features of storytelling style. They employ to a remarkable degree a common poetics, an oral poetics evolved and refined long before literacy happened. *Beowulf* is well known as the principal composition in the English language in which this poetics is exhibited. Therefore, I shall point out directly several compositional strategies employed in *Beowulf* that I think I can show are present as well in *WOE*. "If a practical word of advice may be added for the benefit of the student, it is the obvious one, that in order to appreciate . . . [Beowulf] fully, we must by all means read it aloud with due regard for scansion and expression. Nor should we be afraid of shouting at the proper time" (Fr. Klaeber).[4]

> Hwaet, Wē Gār-Dena in géardagum
> theodcyninga thrym gefrūnon,
> hū tha áethelingas éllen fremedon.
> *Beowulf*, lines 1-3

Most memories work best when the thing to be remembered is repeated. This simple procedure is used boldly and effectively in *WOE* with the repetition of the logo, "Only in silence the word, . . . bright the hawk's flight" (pp. iv, 181) and "To hear, one must be silent" (pp. 18, 171) from the interior narrative. These carefully shaped statements are designed to be easily said and easily heard and remembered—the more so because they are practiced by repetition. Effective narrative employs no less effective if somewhat diluted strategies of repetition. One of these is alliteration.

The basic poetic vehicle of *Beowulf* is the Anglo-Saxon alliterative line in which two or three of its normally four stressed syllables begin with the same sound. The famous first three lines of the poem printed above, illustrate this with the stresses on the alliterating syllables. The rules for this effect are relatively strict and simple.[5] The use of the alliterative line and alliteration in general is the interesting thing. Alliteration is a proto-form of rhyme, yet easier to make and less restricting than rhyme, especially end rhyme. With it the poet, reciting as he composes, manages the dual process of remembering lines he has already made or heard, and making new lines of his story with relative ease. Like rhyme, alliteration is fundamentally a mnemonic device, and well serves the poet and his audience in that it preserves with the concreteness of repeated sound the verbalized form of the oral work. Therefore, when we encounter the wholesale alliteration in the narrative of *WOE*, with due regard for the diluting alterations it will undergo in prose discourse, we can recognize it as the survival of an oral storytelling technique. The effect is not accidental. The following examples should be persuasive.

"... *i*sle to *i*sle *o*f *a*ll *E*arthsea" (vocalic alliteration as in line 3 of *Beowulf* above; p. 1).

"The *b*easts *b*egan to *b*leat and *b*rowse ..." (p. 3).

"*S*he had tried not only to gain control of his *s*peech and *s*ilence, but to bind him at the *s*ame time to her *s*ervice in the craft of *s*orcery" (pp. 4–5).

"They *f*ound only the *f*og about them, *f*ull of *v*oices" (p. 11).

"... *b*ack down to the *b*eaches ..., where they found their ships *b*urnt; so they fought with their *b*acks to the sea ..., and the sands of Armouth were *b*rown with *b*lood" (p. 12).

"He lay thus *d*ark and *d*umb" (p. 13).

"... *s*way the *w*inds with his *w*ord" (p. 16).

"... *w*aded *b*arefoot in the *b*oggy grass, pulling the heavy *w*hite hallow-*b*looms" (b/w alliteration; p. 21).

"... *convers*ing quietly ..., the fishermen unload*ing* their catch, coopers pound*ing* and shipmakers hammer*ing* and clam *s*ellers *s*ing*ing* and *s*hipmasters *b*ellow*ing* and *b*eyond all the *s*ilent *s*hin*ing* *b*ay" ("ing" terminal rhyme, with s/b alliteration; p. 26).

"You *w*itless *w*oodenhead! ..., you *s*pineless *s*lave-*s*ons!" (p. 32).

"... drums *s*ilent and only the flutes playing *s*oft and *s*hrill" (p. 55).

"He *d*oubted his strength and *d*readed the trial" (p. 77).

"... hear*ing* the autumn wind finger*ing* at the thatch roof and whin*ing*" (p. 84).

"*S*mall white peaks *s*tood *s*harp against the blue, and *s*outhward one could guess the *s*hining of the *s*ea" (p. 111).

"... *l*istened to the *l*ong *s*oft *s*inging of *s*pells" (p. 129).

". . . silk brocade stiff with seed-pearls, stained with salt" (p. 142).
"No Deeds are sung, nor swords nor edge-tools sharpened, nor oaths sworn" (p. 170).

Beyond its own ubiquitous alliteration *Beowulf* presents an almost equally ubiquitous repertoire of "formulas"—set lines or parts of lines, used repetitively by the poet to move his composition along without much creative effort. Furthermore, they can signal a certain kind of content to come. The *gefraegn* formulas in *Beowulf* are a particularly appropriate example.[6] They translate variously as, "It is said;" "They say;" "It has been heard from ancient times," and so on. This formula is a signal to the listeners that familiar old lore is coming, even as it gives them a momentary rest to prepare their attention. In addition, the meaning of "gefraegn" implies the existence of and reference to a compendium of orally preserved and transmitted cultural history and wisdom. The *WOE* narrative provides precisely this formula at least twelve times, beginning in its first paragraph: "Of these some say . . ." (p. 1); "Ged had heard . . ." (p. 25); "For he had heard . . ." (p. 31); "They say . . . that a man . . ." (p. 49); "'They say Gontish wizards . . .'" (p. 72).[7]

A staple of *Beowulf*'s Anglo-Saxon poetics is the kenning, a compact figure combining the elements of a riddle and a metaphor. In *Beowulf* the sea is a hronrād, "whaleroad;" a warrior is a helmberend, "helmet-bearer;" a ship is a wundenstefna, "curved prow;" and a man's body is a bānhūs, "bone house." It is a brilliantly conceived device to provide variation within a composition otherwise repetitive by design and by the necessity imposed by a limited vocabulary. It is also a circumlocution that subtly retards narrative to give a listening audience another momentary rest in attention. In *WOE* Le Guin provides only a single obvious kenning—without calling it so. But there is no mistaking it, even as we are made aware that if we could hear the tale told perhaps in the Hardic tongue of Earthsea, the discourse would be rich with kennings. Le Guin rather explores the mechanism to illustrate the levels of power governed by the way things are named: "We call the foam on waves *sukien:* that word is made from two words of the Old Speech, *suk,* feather, and *inien,* the sea. Feather of the sea, is foam. But you cannot charm the foam calling it *sukien;* you must use its own true name in the Old Speech, which is *essa*" (p. 47).

Beowulf is "gnomic." A gnome is elementally useful advice or knowledge memorably stated—very much like an aphorism or a proverb. In function it is like the more nuclear oral devices of alliteration, rhyme, and meter (which it may often incorporate) in that it aids an oral culture in packaging, remembering exactly, and transmitting its wisdom and lore.

For what it is worth, all poetry of serious content, in deploying its mnemonic devices, is gnomic. Certainly *Beowulf* can be so described. But of more immediate interest are examples of the gnome in its special form. *Beowulf* is studded with them. As the poet recites his poem, he integrates gnomic formulas that both retard his narrative, giving his audience a reflective pause, and expound his story in terms of the wisdom his audience should appreciate:

> Wà bith thãem the sceal
> thurh slĩth nith sãwle bescũfan
> in fȳres faethm
> [Woe be he who shall through terrible
> rancor his soul shove into the fire's
> arms.] *Beowulf,* lines 183–85

> Wyrd oft nereth
> unfãegne eorl, thonne his ellen dẽah!
> [Wyrd often saves the undoomed man,
> when his courage is strong] *Beowulf,*
> lines 572–73

> "Ne sorga, snotor guma! Selve bith ãeghwãem,
> thaet hẽ his frẽond wrece, thonne hẽ fela murne."
> ["Sorrow not, wise man! Better is it for everyone
> that he his friend revenge, than he him mourn."]
> *Beowulf,* lines 1384–85

Listening for gnome and proverb in *WOE* will not go unrewarded.

"The wise don't need to ask, the fool asks in vain" (p. 33).
To light a candle is to cast a shadow (p. 44).
"He who would be Seamaster must know the true names of every drop of water in the sea" (p. 46).
"A man favored by a wild beast is a man to whom the Old Powers of stone and spring will speak in human voice" (pp. 49–50).
"Rain on Roke may be drouth in Osskil" (p. 54).
"Envy eats you like a worm in an apple" (p. 58).
Who knows a man's name, holds that man's life in his keeping (p. 69).
"Tired is stupid" (p. 70).
"And the truth is that as a man's real power grows and his knowledge widens, ever the way he can follow grows narrower: until at last he chooses nothing, but does only and wholly what he *must* do" (p. 71).
The hunger of a dragon is slow to wake, but hard to sate (p. 77).
Heal the wound and cure the illness, but let the dying spirit go (p. 80).

"But it is very common," said the dragon, "for cats to play with mice before they kill them" (p. 91).

"Two staffs in one town must come to blows" (p. 153).

"Infinite are the arguments of mages" (p. 161).

In these sayings *WOE* belongs with *Beowulf* in a tradition of conversation, debate, and storytelling that now seems timeless and is certainly oral.

Another device of the oral storyteller is the inventory, a list of objects, generally, designed to put furniture and detail into the usually generalized macro-setting in which the events of his tale take place. Elaborate description might retard the action too much. More likely, however, it is difficult for the oral narrator to create description at a level of brilliance to compete in interest with heroic character and tumultuous event. Moreover, detailed description tends to specify, individuate, and risk idiosyncrasy in stories that wish to emphasize the universal significance of the events they relate. With few exceptions, epic and fantasy try to be universal. The inventory is, then, a sparingly employed compromise. *Beowulf* includes lists of the armor and weapons of the hero and his men (lines 1442–64), and, predictably, a description of the Fire-Dragon's hoard (lines 2755–71). *WOE* includes lists of herbs, "mint and moly and thyme, yarrow and rushwash and paramal, kingsfoil, clovenfoot, tansy and bay" (p. 3); the "lore of herbals and healing, . . . the crafts of finding, binding, mending, unsealing and revealing" (p. 6); the activities at the seaport of Gont, "merchants conversing, . . . fishermen unloading their catch, coopers pounding and shipmakers hammering and clamsellers singing and shipmasters bellowing" (p. 26); the analysis of a locale, "cape, point, bay, sound, inlet, channel, harbor, shallows, reef and rock" (p. 46); and of energies and forces, "light, and heat, and the force that draws the magnet, and those forces men perceive as weight, form, color, sound" (p. 53). These details appear and are gone in the elementally general progress of the narrative. Yet the very efficiency with which they can be rattled off allows a listener to remember them intermittently and use them as concrete referents to balance the abstract profundity and grandeur of the tale.

Perhaps the most significant accommodation that a preliterate composition like *Beowulf* makes to the requirements and opportunities of oral presentation is in the fact that a solid one-third of all *Beowulf*'s lines (about 1300) are devoted to dialogue and speeches. The importance of this quantity of speeches can hardly be overestimated. The *Iliad* is nearly 46 percent dialogue and speeches. The *Aeneid* is 46.8 percent, and the *Odyssey* is an impressive 68 percent.[8] We are certain that these epics, like *Beowulf*, were composed for oral delivery. With all this direct discourse, the recitation of the tale could approach a dramatic effect only a step or so away from choral performance, or even a staged performance with individual parts. Meanwhile, it is well worth noting that, in the case of *Beowulf* at least, when speeches and dialogue invest the narrative, plot action comes nearly to a halt. When there is much talking, there is little doing. The great fights with Grendel, Grendel's Dam, and the Fire-Dragon are reported in narrative with very little speechmaking.

I searched for these elements in *WOE*, with some interesting results. Over 20 percent of its narrative is in speeches and dialogue. By chapters the breakdown is: I-7.6%; II-19.02%; III-24.4%; IV-26.32%; V-15.8%; VI-11.62%; VII-28.3%; VIII-1.3%; IX-47.4%; X-18.34%; and the epilogue is 0%. In *WOE*, as in *Beowulf*, when there is very much talk, there is little action. In chapter 8, "Hunting," Ged begins his sustained pursuit of the "shadow." There is virtually no dialogue or speech in the episode (1.3 percent), even as it marks the point in the tale when Ged's prospects, through a fantastic physical effort, begin to improve. The next chapter, "Iffish," is full of conversation among Ged, Vetch, and Yarrow, during which Ged gathers his strength for the victory expedition of chapter 10. The "Iffish" chapter is nearly half talk (47.7 percent). Within these extremes the talk is present in proportions only somewhat less than those of the older epics. Thus, making allowances for *WOE*'s genesis in a literate milieu, as prose, with the certain constraint that it will, after all, be most often read silently, the incorporation of its speeches and dialogue is remarkable—and certainly proper for those who will hear the story told aloud.

2. WIZARDS AND DRAGONS

"For a word to be spoken," Ged answered slowly, "there must be silence. Before and after."

It seemed to him that he himself was a word spoken by the sunlight.

"My name, and yours, and the true name of the Sun, or a spring of water, or an unborn child, all are syllables of the great word that is slowly spoken by the shining of the stars."

Speaking it aloud word after word, . . . he saw the markings of how the spell must be woven with the sound of his voice and the motion of body and hand.

. . . but dragons have keen ears.

The oral elements of the style of *WOE* are a superb vehicle for what I regard as its major subject. Telling once again, as most fantasy works do, an "initiation" tale, the story of the youth and maturation of Duny/ Sparrowhawk/Ged is explicitly interpreted in terms of his growing command of speech and language. Put another way, the message of *WOE* is that the achievement of the fully human experience requires the mastery of speech as the means for creating that experience. I might even claim that with this message in *WOE* Le Guin has wonderfully discovered the perfect message for the formal vehicle of fantasy narrative. What could be more fitting to the decidedly oral conventions of fantasy discourse than a theme that asserts the importance of the making and discipline of speech?

Whether or not we are prepared to appreciate *WOE* as an epitome of the orally told fantasy narrative, its fairly common manipulation of light and darkness, sound and silence, and its extraordinary and elaborate discussion of the nature and use of the "Old Speech," the "True Speech," combine to dramatize the importance of the concrete linguistic act, speaking. Moreover, as I try to unravel the terms of the existence of the Old Speech, and try to explain the character of people like Ged who want to learn it, I am intrigued with the prospect that the hostility between people and dragons need not be permanent. Dragons are not as alien as they seem, or perhaps a fully enriched human experience will appear more alien than is often thought. Perhaps only wizards can endure it.

The Earthsea of *WOE* is often a dark world: "The darkness of the hut" (p. 4); "the lightless coasts of death's kingdom" (p. 5); the magic mist Duny (Ged) uses to save his home village (ch. 1); the reading of the Lore-Book in the dark (p. 22); the darkness of the Great House of Roke (p. 41); Ged's "shadow" was "bodiless, blind to sunlight, a creature of a lightless, placeless, timeless realm. It must grope after him through the days and across the seas of the sunlit world, and could take visible shape only in dream and darkness" (p. 98); Ged's "thoughts went on dark paths to imagine how the shadow would appear to him next" (p. 132); the whole of the "Hunting" (ch. 8) is dotted with reminders of darkness: "dark paths" (p. 132), "dark land" (p. 133), "darkness of the deep sea" (p. 134), "dark mists" (p. 135), "darkening ... day" (p. 136), "a featureless pallor ... deadened light and sight" (p. 137), "black night" (p. 138), "the hollows of the waves were full of darkness" (p. 144). All this darkness is both functional and symbolic. It colors Ged's world and it emblems his existential confusion. Moreover, the darkness of *WOE* is a proper conditioning for a person who must also face the sustained darkness of the labyrinth in *TOA* and the moral darkness of the underworld in *TFS*. Whatever the case, darkness makes speaking very important, since sight for seeing faces and reading (if you can) is useless when there is no light. In the dark the voice and the sense of hearing guide people. One must learn to listen carefully to the sounds ... and the quality of silences.

WOE's narrative reminds us of this on nearly every page: "[Duny] heard his aunt crying out words [magic words that require a perfect ear for proper reproduction] to a goat" (p. 2); "She had tried ... to gain control of his speech and silence" (p. 4); "Ogion the Silent" (p. 123) was Ged's first mage mentor; "To hear, one must be silent" (p. 18); "Ged ... hearing the rush of rain ... or the silence of snowfall" (p. 19); "And the mage's long, listening silence would fill the room, and fill Ged's mind, until sometimes it seemed he had forgotten what words sounded like: and when Ogion spoke at last it was as if he had, just then and for the first time, invented speech" (p. 19); "Only in silence the word" (p. 181). Over and over Ged is caught in an attitude of listening, hearing, keeping silent, for this is the way to learn. Moreover, the things to be learned are the words and language that create the world—the Old Speech.

The passages and lines which begin each section of this discussion leap from the story like a coda. They are the laws and codicils of True Speech. They explain how existence and human consciousness operate in the world. I have them in mind as I turn finally to the most important subject of *WOE*, the Old Speech—and its makers, the dragons.

The nature of the Old Speech may be explained somewhat if we think of it as a metaphysics. It is a "given"; it is axiomatic in the Aristotelian sense. With it the physical world is founded and made to work. The countless younger languages are reflections of the Old Speech, but they are not it. The younger languages are no more than any of the other furnitures of the world called into existence by the Old Speech. They operate in the world just as the world's weather operates, but they do not change the world. They make no new laws; they don't create; they do not adjust "balances" or modify "patterns." Only the Old Speech does this, as "syllables of the great word that is slowly spoken by the shining of the stars" (p. 164). I think it is extremely important that we recognize that this last statement is an axiom; it is not an explanation. We find explanations in a "physics," which function as evidence that axioms, the content of a "metaphysics," are true. The axioms are the Old Speech.

But who speaks the Old Speech? From whom and how does one learn it? What finally are the consequences of knowing it? The narrative informs us that the stars speak it. But we are also told, much more often, that it is the only language of the dragons. Pell-mell! Are dragons of the same stuff as stars? They seem to be. The recognition of this possible identity is, after all, not shocking. It is satisfying. Stars and dragons are elemental. Both are ancient. The behavior of both is what men, for most of their history, have called magical. Both are beings of energy and fire. Both are, if we unite the visions of the mythic imagination and modern physics, the makers of worlds. Meanwhile, the disarming reports of the personalities of various dragons are the storyteller's license. Dragons are not human. Furthermore, a person who would speak to dragons (or stars) and understand dragons (or stars) must exceed the conventional limits of human knowledge. Such a person, for example, is the Ged of *WOE* who will live to discover the company of dragons to be more and more compatible.

For their part, dragons are not only the users of the Old Speech, but also its makers. This follows in keeping with the universal phenomenon that the speaker of any language is a maker of that language, a maker in a sense that we can never really distinguish from "creative." The Old Speech creates the world. It must be that the dragons, then, create the world. What wonder then that conversations with dragons should be so perilous! They are silent and lonely beings for endless centuries. And the world is changeless. Then some extraordinary person gets a dragon to talking. A casual greeting (none on record) is worth at least a typhoon. A bravely negotiated bargain (like the one between Ged and Yevaud) will stabilize a climate for at least an age. One can only imagine the effects of a violent argument in which a dragon's temper is lost. So, too, would go the "temper" of the world: The ocean would rise in smoke while the mountains and land began to flow—the end of the Eden of that person's race. Such is the power of the Old Speech. People call it magic.

For the most part, Ged learns it by listening, with what amounts to a more and more awesome and lonely intensity. First he learns the discipline through the example of Ogion the Silent: "To hear, one must be silent" (pp. 18, 171). Then he studies the True Names of things from the old books with the Master Namer. Then there is the dangerous experiment which a person does not always survive (Ged's release of and reunion with his "shadow"-self—the beginning and end of psychotic pride). Eventually there is an epiphany: "For a word to be spoken, ... there must be silence. Before, and after" (p. 165). Of course, there could be no valid apprenticeship without discussions with the makers and masters of the Old Speech, the dragons themselves.

Above all, the learning of the Old Speech emphasizes its concretely oral character. It is a heard discourse—by speaker as well as by hearer. And one must be a master listener. Dragons are. Twice in *TFS* Ged speaks in the Old Speech to dragons high in the air a great distance away from him. The dragons hear and come to him (pp. 125, 146). They have a magnificent ability to hear. Nevertheless, so far as I can tell, this revelation is provided explicitly only once in *WOE* (perhaps because an elemental fact is too dramatically solitary to require repetition), happily nearly exactly at the center in the length of *WOE*'s telling: "[Ged's] voice fell short in the sound of breakers beating on the ashen shore; but dragons have keen ears" (p. 87).

Dragons must be master listeners by nature. But Ged, extraordinary person that he is, has come to know this art as well. "He listened [to Yevaud] with an untrustful ear, all his doubts ready" (p. 90), exercising the terrific discipline, now with more wisdom, that came upon him instinctively when he released the "shadow." With an illuminated detachment the narrative tells us of that urgent moment, as if the story itself were striving to tell us just how it tells itself: "Speaking it aloud word after word, and he [Ged] saw the markings of how the spell must be woven with the sound of his voice and the motion of body and hand" (p. 60). Spells, like stories, tell themselves.[9] The words must be heard, if only by the maker of the spell. Written in books, they have no power until they are spoken.

In some of the last words of *TFS*, the final book of Earthsea, we are told, Ged's "face was quiet, and in his eyes there was something like that laughter in the eyes of Kalessin" (p. 196). Ged is a wizard and Kalessin is a dragon. In learning all that he has about language and speaking, Ged becomes more and more lonely and dragon-like. He learns that only a life of silence and listening leads to mastery of True Speech, the speaking that makes spells of discourse that otherwise would be merely common saying. Were Ged to describe a world, we come to see, it would be a true world and therefore it would exist because, at last, there is very little difference between a wizard and a dragon.

A proper experience of *WOE* and Earthsea is to hear it told because it uses oral elements that make it easy to hear. The ancient and famous *Beowulf* narrative exhibits similar oral elements. These same elements and much more concerning the nature of language and how a person creates his consciousness and power through a disciplined knowledge of words and speech are the principal subject of *WOE*. The story is told with the narrative conventions typical of the finest fantasy. Its account of the Old Speech could not be more fitting.

FRANCIS J. MOLSON

THE EARTHSEA TRILOGY
Ethical Fantasy for Children

The 1972 National Book Award for Children's Literature notwithstanding, Ursula K. Le Guin in her public statements has yet to be completely reconciled to the fact that in the United States the Earthsea trilogy[1] has been classified as children's literature. Witness, for instance, the testy remarks in her essay "Dreams Must Explain Themselves," written to discuss the genesis of the trilogy:[2]

> The real problem isn't the money, it's the adult chauvinist piggery.
> "You're a juvenile writer, aren't you?"
> Yeth, mummy.
> "I love your books—the real ones, I mean, I haven't read the ones for children, of course!"
> Of courthe not, daddy.
> "It must be relaxing to write *simple* things for a change."
> Sure it's simple, writing for kids. Just as simple as bringing them up.
> All you do is take all the sex out, and use little short words, and little dumb ideas, and don't be too scary, and be sure there's a happy ending. Right? Nothing to it. Write down. Right on.

Le Guin's irritation is understandable once it is perceived as deriving not from any dissatisfaction with children's literature—these comments and others in the essay attest just the contrary!—but from her impatience and frustration over readers, commentators, and critics who, manifesting "adult chauvinist piggery" in one form or another, tend to denigrate the trilogy. First are those who, biased against what they are inclined to call "kiddy-lit," deny the trilogy critical scrutiny because it is, after all, only a work intended for children and, as such, scarcely worthy of such scrutiny. Then there are those who, explicitly acknowledging the existence of children's literature as authentic literature, refuse to permit this acknowledgment to temper their critical stance toward the trilogy and, hence, are blind to the latter's special merits as a juvenile. Finally, there are those who, ignorant of children's literature, do not know what to say about the trilogy beyond the obvious and banal and who, hence, omit extended critical commentary and scrutiny. However, for anyone who cares for the quality of reading available to children and, at the same time, respects their intelligence and taste, labeling a work as children's literature is a culmination of the critical process and is meant to be laudatory. Indeed, the Earthsea trilogy *is* children's literature which ranks among the best written in recent times.

1

As the author of the Earthsea trilogy, Ursula K. Le Guin belongs to a group of authors—prominent among whom are C. S. Lewis, Lloyd Alexander, Madeleine L'Engle, Susan Cooper, and, possibly, J. R. R. Tolkien—who have written outstanding fantasy of a kind whose special appropriateness for the contemporary child is becoming increasingly manifest. Sometimes this kind of fantasy is termed heroic fantasy or romance because it utilizes traditional heroic or mythic conventions and material. The world of heroic fantasy is, according to Northrop Frye, the "world of heroes and gods and titans . . . a world of powers and passions and moments of ecstasy far greater than anything we meet outside the imagination."[3] At other times this fantasy is called high fantasy, perhaps because its makers are not content just to refashion traditional material in order to update old stories that may still be interesting, but design them for a purpose "higher" than entertainment. Eleanor Cameron, the well-known critic and author of children's books, says of high fantasy that it reveals "a striking attitude regarding the human condition and our relationships with one another. For within these tales lies the essence of their creators, the philosophy of their lives subtly woven through the pages of a story that children love and remember, and which may, quite unbeknown to the children themselves, become a lasting influence."[4]

Despite the currency of the terms "heroic fantasy" and "high fantasy," this essay proposes the term "ethical fantasy" to designate the kind of fantasy Le Guin and the other authors, mentioned above, have written. Like the other two terms, "ethical fantasy" recognizes that fantasy for children is purposeful; but, unlike the former terms, "ethical fantasy" refuses to restrict itself to traditional notions of heroism and eschews any possible invidious comparisons between so-called "high" or "low" purposes. Moreover, "ethical" fantasy specifies more openly than either "heroic" or "high" fantasy the fundamental purpose of this kind of fantasy: to teach and instruct as well as to please. In other words, "ethical fantasy" acknowledges that for most readers a book's capacity to "teach" and the kind of "message" it delivers continue to be, as they have been from the origin of children's literature, important criteria (although often unexpressed or unavowed) for evaluating its merits as a children's book. Finally, because its own phraseology avoids the connotation of tedious moralizing and simplistic thinking often associated with the word "didactic," "ethical fantasy" is, by far, preferable to yet a fourth possible designation, "didactic fantasy."

Ethical fantasy, as it has emerged in contemporary children's literature, dramatizes several interrelated propositions whose continuing validity is taken for granted: making ethical choices, whether deliberate or not, is central in the lives of young people; actions do bear consequences not only for oneself but for society, and sometimes apparently insignificant actions can bring about momentous consequences; maturity involves accepting responsibility for one's actions; and character bespeaks destiny. Ethical fantasy, moreover, is a symbolization of these propositions which does not usually endorse or reflect explicitly any particular religion, sect, or ideology. At the same time, generally speaking, ethical fantasy presupposes a world either enmeshed in a vast struggle between Right and Wrong, Good and Evil, or grievously periled by an unexpected shift in equilibrium between Light and Dark, Balance and Imbalance. One typical scenario may place several children in a situation where, in spite of being told that any untoward actions on their part may influence for the worse an ongoing war between Good and Evil, they disregard the warning, do something "small" but forbidden, and reap more than they bargain for. Thus, in C. S. Lewis's *The Magician's Nephew* Digory, just to spite Polly, taps the golden bell, and the reverberated sound precipitates the destruction of the vast palace and restores to life Jadis, Queen of Charn and evil witch, who plots to destroy Narnia. Another scenario may situate a youth in circumstances where the carrying out of seemingly trivial tasks initiates a sequence of events that culminate in an outcome beyond the youth's wildest fancies. Thus, Taran, in Lloyd Alexander's chronicles of Prydain, discovers that faithfully discharging the duties of Assistant Pig-Keeper eventuates in his becoming the High King.

Ethical fantasy, then, is didactic but not exclusively or simplistically so: it does not moralize. The fantasies of the authors mentioned above, in addition to being didactic, are also exemplary literary entertainment because the authors are skilled fabulists who never allow theme or subject matter to overwhelm or distort other narrative elements—plot, characterization, pace, and so on. In other words, the didactic element has not been allegorized as a foul-tasting pill is sugarcoated to make it palatable; nor is the didactic unassimilated into the narrative whole as raisins and nuts may be poked into a pudding after it has been cooked. In short, these fantasies have not been trivialized and reduced to some banal message. These writers, furthermore, know their putative audience and, as a consequence, take advantage of two salient characteristics of young readers—their need to identify with a story's protagonist and their seeking the assurance of the familiar.

Accordingly, it is not surprising that virtually all the protagonists of juvenile ethical fantasy are youthful. Just on that basis alone the stories are readily attractive to children. But the appeal of ethical fantasy goes deeper. Most of today's youth are denied any meaningful participation in matters that concern society as a whole. It is quite possible that a good number of these youngsters would be willing to identify with a young protagonist whose actions are essential to the successful outcome of an important event, and immerse themselves in his or her story, if a narrative offering such a situation would be made available. Ethical fantasy provides such situations. For example, in Madeleine L'Engle's *A Wrinkle in Time*, Murry, the famous scientist, and his genius son Charles Wallace can be released from the control of the evil It and, far more importantly, the entire earth spared the encroachment of the sinister Black Thing only if Meg Murry can bring herself willingly and unselfishly to chance all on her capacity to love and to sacrifice. Meg's decision is also the young reader's decision.

Additionally, young readers may find ethical fantasy appealing because it is an unusual blend of the new and the old which reassures as it surprises. To achieve this blend the writer of ethical fantasy makes use of what Lloyd Alexander calls the "pot of story:"

Among the most nourishing bits and pieces we can scoop out of the pot are whole assortments of characters, events, and situations that occur again and again in one form or another throughout much of the world's mythology: heroes and villains, fairy godmothers and wicked stepmothers, princesses and pig-keepers, prisoners and rescuers; ordeals and temptations, the quest for the magical object, the set of tasks to be accomplished. And a whole arsenal of cognominal swords, enchanted weapons; a wardrobe of cloaks of invisibility, seven-league boots; a whole zoo of dragons, helpful animals, birds, and fish.[5]

What the fantasist dips out of the pot is the old, whose familiarity reassures readers. What surprises them is the new, which the fantasist adds to what has been dipped out. How the fantasist blends the old and new in the final state is what sustains interest and, ultimately, pleases readers. Whether a particular writer of ethical fantasy can utilize the "pot of story" effectively is, naturally, determined by the writer's skill. Interestingly, despite its very recent emergence as an identifiable subgroup of children's literature, ethical fantasy already boasts a relatively large number of outstanding writers. The explanation for this is uncertain and, perhaps, best attributable to chance.

What appears not to be fortuitous, however, is the actual emergence of ethical fantasy, for there is reason to believe that it may have developed, to some extent, as a result of an attempt by critics, educators, and even writers to solve a problem peculiar to contemporary children's literature. It is commonplace to point out that there is no longer a core of religious and moral values acceptable to almost everyone. In spite of this, society remains, understandably, quite concerned for the development of ethical discernment in youth. As it seeks whatever assistance it can find, society looks, as it was accustomed to in the past, upon juvenile literature as an essential means of socializing children and instructing them in morality. Unfortunately, one result of the disappearance of a common core of values is that traditional didactic children's literature, which once could assume its readers' knowledge of biblical and religious history and culture and could build on that knowledge, can do so no longer. Consequently, this literature has lost a considerable amount of both its effectiveness as a means of moral instruction and its appeal as story.

As an alternative to, if not a substitute for, much traditional didactic literature, ethical fantasy has a lot to offer. On account of its tendency to espouse no one religion or ideology, ethical fantasy has considerable potential for engaging young readers who may be indifferent to or repelled by overt references to a particular sect or group. With its stress on the centrality of ethical choice in the lives of youth and the interrelation of accepting responsibility and maturing, moreover, ethical fantasy champions a morality similar to that which contemporary cognitive, developmental, and humanistically oriented approaches to ethical growth argue for.[6] Traditional literature, on the other hand, has championed, by and large, an absolute code of morality buttressed by originally supernatural sanctions. Finally, because it is contemporary, ethical fantasy cannot help but reflect or incorporate psychoanalytic understanding of human consciousness. In his recent *The Uses of Enchantment: The Meaning and Importance of Fairy Tales,* Bruno Bettelheim points out the superiority of fairytales over biblical stories in the moral development of children. His remarks can apply to ethical fantasy just as well, suggesting the latter's superiority over traditional didactic literature:

As long as parents fully believed that Biblical stories solved the riddle of our existence and its purpose, it was easy to make a child feel secure. The Bible was felt to contain the answers to all pressing questions: the Bible told man all he needed to know to understand the world, how it came into being, and how to behave in it. In the Western world the Bible also provided prototypes for man's imagination. But rich as the Bible is in stories, not even during the most religious of times were these stories sufficient for meeting all the psychic needs of man.

Part of the reason for this is that while the Old and New Testaments and the histories of the saints provided answers to the crucial questions of how to live the good life, they did not offer solutions for the problems posed by the dark sides of our personalities. The Biblical stories suggest essentially only one solution for the asocial aspects of the unconscious: repression of these (unacceptable) strivings. But children, not having their ids in conscious control, need stories which permit at least fantasy satisfaction of these "bad" tendencies, and specific models for their sublimation.[7]

Already there is evidence that adults have begun to experiment with ethical fantasy as they search out material that can be utilized in discussions structured, in part, to help youngsters establish their values. For instance, a group of British teachers and their pupils were brought together to discuss various approaches to presenting *A Wizard of Earthsea* in the classroom. Some of the teachers' remarks clearly reveal an awareness of the novel's didactic utility: "We talk about the stress on learning a craft, achieving self knowledge, the morality of the book, the importance of fantasy in the development of the child. Someone talks about the book as a personal challenge and argues the need for individual reading and response rather than communal class reading and discussion."[8] Of even greater interest are the children's comments because they demonstrate that *WOE* did affect their ethical speculation:

Must have been terrible for him because he'd have to think—it was me who let this Shadow loose and this Shadow's taken over bodies, it's killing people as soon as it comes out of this body and it was because of him the Master Mage died. One slip-up that the woman makes, she says only black or only dark evil may fight dark evil and then he comes out with the suggestion that only light can defeat dark.[9]

Obviously, Le Guin did not just sit down to write "ethical fantasy" when she began *WOE,* for the simple reason that the former had not yet been identified as a discrete subgroup of fantasy. On the other hand, while she was composing the trilogy, she was aware that she was writing fantasy especially relevant to young people. Both the degree of her awareness and the suitability of the trilogy's subject matter to youngsters Le Guin acknowledges in "Dreams Must Explain Themselves":

> The most childish thing about *A Wizard of Earthsea,* I expect, is its subject: coming of age.
> Coming of age is a process that took me many years; I finished it, so far as I ever will, at about age 31; and so I feel rather deeply about it. So do most adolescents. It's their main occupation, in fact.
> The subject of *The Tombs of Atuan* is, if I had to put it in one word, sex. There's a lot of symbolism in the book, most of which I did not, of course, analyze consciously while writing; the symbols can all be read as sexual. More exactly, you could call it a feminine coming of age. Birth, rebirth, destruction, freedom are the themes.
> *The Farthest Shore* is about death. . . . It seemed an absolutely suitable subject to me for young readers, since in a way one can say that the hour when a child realizes, not that death exists—children are intensely aware of death—but that he/she, personally, is mortal, will die, is the hour when childhood ends, and the new life begins. Coming of age again, but in a larger context.[10]

Le Guin focuses her study of coming of age and maturation on Ged, the famous Archmage of Earthsea. In *WOE* Ged can step across the line dividing adolescence from adulthood only after he confronts the dark, terrifying shadow his youthful vanity and lust for power have allowed to enter Earthsea. At the end of the novel as the young mage and the shadow embrace, they recognize themselves in each other, call each other by the same name, Ged, and merge into one person. Before that integration can occur, however, Ged has had to acknowledge his weaknesses and shoulder his responsibility for tilting the fundamental equilibrium of Earthsea. He has had, also, to admit his dependence on others, going as far as staking his very life on Ogion, his old teacher, and Vetch, his only friend. Ultimately, what Ged must accept is that Ged, the same name as the dark shadow's, is his true name and not Sparrowhawk, the use name which suggests the self-sufficient hero.

In *The Tombs of Atuan* Ged, already a famous mage, decides to retrieve from the tombs the ring of Erreth-Akbe. To do this Ged steals into the tombs and is trapped and captured. His captor is Arha, the first priestess of the Dark Powers, who, recently turned fourteen, has presumably come of age. Instead of growing into her maturity, however, Arha actually teeters on the brink of becoming permanently stunted emotionally and psychologically by her unhealthy worshipping of the Dark Powers. Thus, in a way she too is trapped. To escape their respective traps, Arha and Ged find there is only one way—mutual dependence and help; learning to trust each other, they manage to escape. Arha, freed of the unwholesome cult of the Dark Powers which deprived her of her real name, Tenar, regains the latter and begins anew the process of coming of age. For his part, Ged never again thinks of himself as Sparrowhawk and is reminded once more of the necessity of mutuality.

In *The Farthest Shore* Ged, acclaimed in middle age as the greatest mage, confronts his most challenging task—the restoration of death to its rightful place in the universe. Ged sets out on this task accompanied only by the young and inexperienced Prince Arren whose presence and assistance the older man senses he will need. Arren becomes the not always comprehending audience for Ged's doubts concerning the appropriateness of his profession, and his speculation about the necessity of death. Arren also provides invaluable help, aiding the mage's successful crossing of the Dark Land of the Underworld. In return, Arren finds that his journey into the underworld is his rite of passage, and the successful crossing not only heralds Arren's becoming a man but fulfills the prophecy of the coming of a great king whose reign restores peace and equilibrium to Earthsea.

Interpreting the Earthsea trilogy as ethical fantasy does not exhaust the meaning of the work. Indeed, other interpretations can be presented and themes distinguished; but of these only one directly relates to a reading of the trilogy as ethical fantasy. This is the trilogy's investigation of the nature of the hero; in particular, the mage as hero. Wizards have been heroes before; consider Merlin and Gandalf, whose deeds are stupendous and conventionally heroic. Ged, as celebrated hero, is a bit unusual. He too can perform conventionally heroic deeds such as conquering the dragons of Pendor Island, and traveling into the Kingdom of the Dead and coming out alive. But the deeds Le Guin singles out for extended treatment are anything but traditionally heroic. Accepting oneself as a finite creature made up of good and evil, and assisting a fifteen-year-old adolescent girl to shed an unnatural lifestyle and opt for genuine freedom are not the actions usually celebrated in heroic romance. That Le Guin chooses to stress this side of her hero underscores her intent to point out to her readers that coming of age is important for youngsters and that it consists mainly of accepting responsibility for oneself, one's actions, and one's relationship with others.

2

When Ged first appears in *WOE*, it is as seven-year-old Duny, "a tall, quick boy, loud and proud and full of temper" (*WOE*, p. 12). By accident

Duny learns of the power he can have over an object once he knows its true name. A quick learner, Duny soon masters several spells, one of which enables him to call down fog upon the invading Kargs so that his village is spared—a deed that gives the boy a modest reputation and brings him to the attention of the mage Ogion the Silent. Realizing Duny's great potential, Ogion invites him to become his apprentice. At the public ceremony marking Duny's selection of wizardry as his trade and the beginning of his passage into adulthood, the boy receives from the mage his true name, Ged. Previously the villagers had begun referring to Duny as Sparrowhawk because of his mage prowess. As the first chapter ends, the reader suspects that crucial to Duny's maturation may be his deciding which of the two names he prefers to live under: the public and use name, Sparrowhawk, which suggests an aggressive, self-sufficient user of power, or the private and true name, Ged, whose significance the boy has no inkling of save that it has to do with wizardry.

When Ged complains to Ogion about the dullness of learning the names of many objects, and wants instead to know their use, the mage responds: "When you know the fourfoil in all its seasons root and leaf and flower, by sight and scent and seed, then you may learn its true name, knowing its being: which is more than its use. What, after all, is the use of you? or of myself? Is Gont Mountain useful, or the Open Sea?" (*WOE,* p. 29). Refusing to take the time and effort to understand, Ged persists in his desire to acquire power. Shortly after, the first signs of conflict between a desire for power and a disinterested love of learning appear within the boy. His vanity stung by the taunt that he can not perform some really great deed, Ged consults a forbidden book of lore and happens upon a spell of summoning spirits from the dead. Almost against his will he finds himself reading the spell even without understanding the words. As he reads, an ominous darkness enters the room and seems to solidify. Fortunately, Ogion returns, disperses the form, and cautions the boy that mage actions are always fraught with ethical import. "'Think of this: that every word, every act of our Art is said and is done either for good, or for evil. Before you speak or do you must know the price that is to pay!'" (*WOE,* p. 35). When Ogion decides to release his apprentice and send him to the School for Mages at Roke, Ged realizes belatedly that he has come to love the mage, but the wish for glory and a predilection for action outweigh his love.

Ged's first years at the school are marked by the development of the two sides of his personality represented by his use and true names. (That the two sides will eventually separate, so to speak, into discrete entities is strongly hinted at in the incident before the gate. When Ged responds to the Doorkeeper's invitation to enter by walking into the School, a shadow accompanies the boy.) However, the development is one-sided. Ged's knowledge of magic expands rapidly, and soon he is one of the most skilled students. His moral and ethical growth, unfortunately, is less extensive. His pride and vanity continuing, he takes an instant dislike to Jasper, an older student, and wishes to overtake him in mage knowledge. More significantly, Ged refuses to apply the law of Equilibrium to himself. In his arrogance he even imagines he may one day control the Balance that should exist between light and darkness: "But surely a wizard, one who had gone past these childish tricks of illusion to the true arts of Summoning and Change, was powerful enough to do what he pleased, and balance the world as seemed best to him, and drive back darkness with his own light" (*WOE*, p. 57). Ged does become friendly with Vetch, another student, and is able to tame an otak for a pet: evidence of the fact that the boy is not completely turned in upon himself and consumed with ambition.

Ged's envy of Jasper festers until the inevitable challenge to determine who is really the more powerful apprentice occurs during the festival of the Long Dance. As the two rivals step up their show of power, Vetch attempts to intervene. His words to his friend—"Sparrowhawk, will you be a man and drop this now—come with me" (*WOE*, p. 72)—indicate what the challenge really is: the climactic moment when a show of restraint and humility on Ged's part will signify his actual coming of age. Sparrowhawk cannot rise, however, to the ethical challenge and sinks to a display of naked power as he boasts—"By my name"—that he will summon a spirit from the dead.

Le Guin's handling of the summoning is most provocative. Imagery of brightness and darkness, sometimes in balance, more often contrasting or blended harmoniously or wildly, suggests the inextricability of good and evil motives in Sparrowhawk and the consequent moral ambiguity of his actions. For instance, as Ged speaks the rune of summoning, he falls forward on the earth and rises holding something dark and heavy in his arms. The dark mass splits apart, and light, the form of Elfarran, emerges from between his arms. Then a breech in the "fabric of the world" opens and a "terrible brightness" appears; out of it springs a "clot of black shadow." The tantalizing, submerged metaphor of violent birth hints, further, Ged's aborting of the opportunity to complete his rite of passage. Ironically, instead of the integrated personality that accompanies maturity, he has produced a monstrous symbol of the childishness he persists in. (Subsequently, as the shadow-monster and Ged engage in their pursuit-flight ritual, the former will grow considerably—paralleling a growth in Ged's ethical character).

Moreover, it is fitting that the shadow leap upon Sparrowhawk, seeking to cleave to him, and then, meeting resistance from "Ged," viciously claw his face and wound him almost fatally before taking off into the darkness. For the shadow, embodying arrogance and immaturity, wishes to return to what it assumes is its origin and master, Sparrowhawk. When it encounters resistance, however, it senses the presence of Ged and not "Sparrowhawk" and attempts to destroy its enemy. Unsuccessful, the shadow is forced to retreat, but not before it leaves on Ged's face a mark of their close kinship and enmity.

Two other points must be made. Obviously, the shadow is an intrinsic part of Ged since it knows his true name. This point, incidentally, Ged does not begin to grasp until Ogion will ask why it is that the shadow in the form of Skiorh spoke to him his true name. The second point concerns a further role of the shadow. As has been remarked, the shadow represents the "Sparrowhawk" within Ged. At the same time, the shadow also constitutes the best evidence that Ged may be the greatest of all mages inasmuch as he did successfully summon Elfarran from the dead. If this is so, then the shadow must be joined ultimately to Ged both to signal the young man's full acceptance of his responsibility for doing wrong and to seal his status as a great wizard.

Surviving the shadow's attack, Ged determines to stay at Roke and undo the evil he has perpetrated. Daunted by what he perceives as a formidable task, he begins to lose faith in himself and his capabilities: his survival as Ged becomes problematic. What restores his faith is Vetch's unexpected revelation of his true name to Ged. This offering of friendship and trust so moves him that immediately Ged divulges his true name to Vetch. This action, because it involves a willingness to entrust one's survival to a second party, is convincing evidence that at last "Ged" has attained dominance over "Sparrowhawk." Hence, the action marks the real beginning of Ged's coming of age. Le Guin underscores the importance of the exchange of true names by having it take place on the anniversary of Ged's public Passage four years earlier when Ogion bestowed upon him his true name:

He had not thought of these things for a long time. Now they came back to him, on this night he was seventeen years old. All the years and places of his brief broken life came within mind's reach and made a whole again. He knew once more, at last, after this long, bitter, wasted time, who he was and where he was. (*WOE*, p. 85)

"Ged," the young man realizes, is his true name while "Sparrowhawk" is only a use name. From this point in the narrative, then, Ged's destiny involves finding out and accepting all that is implied in his true name.

Reluctantly concluding that he is the only one who can ever discover the identity of the shadow he loosed, Ged returns to his mage studies and prospers. Paralleling his intellectual growth is a deepening of his ethical sense, so that finally Ged grasps the Archmage's point about the limitations and responsibilities of mages:

> You thought, as a boy, that a mage is one who can do anything. So I thought, once. So did we all. And the truth is that as a man's real power grows and his knowledge widens, every the way he can follow grows narrower: until at last he chooses nothing, but does only and wholly what he *must* do. (*WOE*, pp. 86–87)

Before he can depart Roke, furthermore, Ged is put to an unexpected test. Returning to the Great House, he is challenged at the door to give the Doorkeeper's name. After pondering for a while and dismissing the use of power and ruse, Ged decides to own up to his ignorance and asks the Doorkeeper his name. By this simple request in which he acknowledges his limitations, Ged demonstrates clearly that he has at last internalized what his teachers had to offer. His formal training as a wizard thus concluded, Ged departs Roke to begin work as a mage. More importantly, he commences the final stage in his search for his identity.

A bit more than half of *WOE* is given over to Ged's adventures as a wizard and his several confrontations with the shadow. Roughly half the adventures have Ged fleeing the shadow; the other half, Ged playing Sparrowhawk and aggressively pursuing the shadow. Interesting as the adventures are, their real purpose is to reveal the permanence of the changes within Ged. His unsuccessful attempt to save the life of Pechvarry's son indicates a generous, caring person. His rejection of Yevaud's offer to divulge the name of the shadow in return for allowing the dragons to continue raiding signifies a man who will not swerve from his duty. His immunity to Serret's sexual blandishments reveals a young man who can control his emotions. Exhausted by the ordeal of escaping from Terrenon, Ged returns to Gont and home. There Ogion heals the young man's physical hurt and attempts to do the same for his soul by reminding Ged that the shadow knows his true name. Hinting at the final outcome, he recommends that Ged become, as his use name indicates, a hunter. The fact that "Sparrowhawk" is a use name does not preclude Ged's ever again being aggressive or resourceful. At the same time, however, adopting one or two of the characteristics of "Sparrowhawk" need not entail internalizing all the latter represents, in particular, "Sparrowhawk's" self-sufficiency. Nevertheless, Ged does not yet understand this and sets out alone to track down the shadow. Not unexpectedly, failure dogs his endeavors, and the only success he enjoys is to comprehend, belatedly, the true nature of his quest: "never . . . to undo what he had done, but to finish what he had begun" (*WOE*, p. 168).

The final chase and confrontation chapters are rich in thematic implications. His quest, for instance, takes Ged beyond the farthest island in the East Reach where there is no land or sea, only earthsea. Here, in the uttermost east, the mythic place of origins and beginnings, he learns all he is and what he is capable of. Also appropriate is that this breakthrough occurs after days spent in silence; in this way Ged comes to appreciate the very first lesson Ogion ever gave him: "To hear, one must be silent" (*WOE*, p. 29). Except for the last, the various forms the shadow takes as Ged approaches it—his father, Pechvarry, Jasper, Skiorh—are of people who contributed in one way or another to his ethical development. However, the shadow's final form is unknown, even unrecognizable, neither human nor monster—perhaps suggesting the potential for good or evil which still exists within Ged. Undaunted, Ged lifts up his staff and in view of its brilliance "all form of man sloughed off the thing . . ." (*WOE*, p. 201). That is, when the young mage irreversibly determines to be Ged, the shadow is revealed not as an independent entity but as the ugliness each person is capable of doing and can control only when both its evil and its source are acknowledged and accepted. Finally, the shadow can do nothing but return to its origin. Face to face, they call each other the same name, embrace, and become one. At this moment Ged becomes whole, of age, and free—free of the tyranny of impulse and external force, free to choose to act or not.

3

Since Ged does not appear until one-third of the novel is over, initially *TOA* may disappoint the reader coming to it directly after *WOE* and eagerly anticipating the further adventures of the young mage. Moreover, Ged must share center stage with Arha, the fifteen-year-old priestess. This way, Le Guin makes sure that the second part of her trilogy is not read merely for whatever new information it may provide concerning Ged's career. By dividing her focus between Arha and Ged, Le Guin underscores what she may believe is too often overlooked: girls, as well as boys, come of age, make ethical choices, and become free. In designing the plot of *TOA* around two protagonists whose survival depends upon each other, moreover, Le Guin again intends to dramatize for her young readers both the inadequacy of the solitary, self-sufficient hero as a model, and the necessity of social interdependence.

TOA opens with a prologue that introduces little Tenar as a healthy, normal girl whose parents respond differently to the knowledge that their daughter will soon be taken from them so that she can become priestess of the Tombs. Her mother wants to hug and love her as much as she can, pretending that nothing has really happened. Her father is bitter, feeling that for all practical purposes she is already buried and dead to them. Thus, at the very beginning is sounded the dominant note of the novel—the disruption of the natural, organic development of a girl and its deleterious effects upon her maturation.

The first chapter describes the installation of five-year-old Tenar as an apprentice priestess. The ceremony, whose ritual reflects the cult's obsession with darkness, cold, and dust, initiates the process whereby the vitality of the young girl is slowly sucked out. The climax of the ceremony is the stripping away of Tenar's name and substituting for it not a true name, or any name for that matter, but an honorific that signifies the cult's use of the little girl—Arha, the eaten one, the one sacrificed to the dark powers of the underworld who themselves are Nameless. Arha's installation ceremony, then, is no true naming ritual. Nor is it her rite of passage, for this will occur when she reaches fourteen. Clearly, the event should be momentous since it will celebrate both her leaving girlhood behind and becoming an adult, and her initiation into the full power of her priestly office. However, Le Guin does not describe the rite but makes just passing reference to it, thus indicating, in all probability, that Arha has matured very little in the intervening years. Accordingly, her public rite of passage marks only the community's recognition of her chronological aging and the imminence of her becoming all "eaten up." The community, it would appear, prefers Arha this way, for she continues to be treated more like a child than an adult. She is subject to outside forces and authority; she lacks power; she is unable to show initiative or encouraged to do so. In short, her training and conditioning have been intended to stunt and distort her psychological and emotional development. Under such circumstances, it is not surprising that little of Arha's womanhood has been actualized. Yet what growth has materialized is real because, under the surface acquiescence and obedience, Arha, sensing that something fundamental is lacking in her life, has become restive, bored, and resentful of her monotonous routine.

At the age of fifteen, therefore, Arha has entered the most critical period of her life even though she does not realize it. The temple community, as mentioned, expects her complete submission to the destiny implied in her use name—to be eaten up. How close she actually is to this submission is indicated when she orders the sacrificial death of the several prisoners sent by the God-King. But she does so under the influence of a deeper descent than any before into the "very home of darkness, the inmost center of the night" (*TOA*, p. 30), and under the prompting of the evil Kossil, who has pointed out that it is Arha's duty to sacrifice humans to the Dark Powers. These extenuating circumstances lessen Arha's guilt, as Ged will argue later, since she, less a person and more a receptacle into which evil has been poured, has not acted on her own volition. Furthermore, Arha's fainting spell upon returning from the underground after ordering the prisoners' death, and her subsequent illness and nightmares, seem reactions to being forced to do something contrary to her nature. Thus, in spite of the public's belief that Arha is ready to enter into her majority as high priestess and meet her destiny, "Tenar" is not yet eaten up.

There are other signs that Tenar is still alive. The boredom and frustration Arha feels after her public coming of age reflect her suspicion, more felt than expressed, that something is amiss in her life and environment. Also, her dreams of eating, the mouth-watering that instinctively starts when she sees Penthe eating apples, and even her looking upon her friend as "round and full of life and juice as one of her golden apples" (*TOA*, p. 40) prove Arha's failure to eradicate a wholesome appetite for food. Penthe's role, incidentally, goes beyond representing the "vital juices" Arha is being forced to squeeze out of her own life. Penthe is responsible for implanting the first seeds of explicit disbelief in her friend's mind. Penthe tells the funny story of Kossil's being bucked by a goat and Arha cannot help giggling. More importantly, Penthe complains about temple life and its repression of fun and life. Arha's reaction indicates that her own faith and commitment are not as solid as one might expect: "She felt as if she had looked up and suddenly seen a whole new planet hanging huge and populous right outside the window, an entirely strange world, one in which the gods did not matter. She was scared by the solidity of Penthe's unfaith" (*TOA*, p. 41). Beneath Arha's conditioned behavior and unreflective obedience, therefore, still exist the "juices" of life, but they are dammed and in peril of drying up. Some profound and unexpected shock, one suspects, would go a long way in breaking down the dam of repression and release these "juices" to flow once more and eventually restore Tenar to full vitality.

Ged's entrance into the Tombs of Atuan provides this shock. That her Masters did not instantaneously strike dead the intruder troubles Arha, renewing the erosion of her faith that Penthe began. She views, for the first time, and is exhilarated by the splendor of the caves revealed by Ged's mage light, an aspect of the underworld she had never known. The "smell of the wild sage that grew on the desert hills, overhead, under the open sky" (*TOA*, p. 60), brought into the underground by Ged, quickens her atrophied sense of smell. The presence of another human being, although clearly a profanation of sacred ground, is inexplicably exciting. All this is shocking, and all will permeate Arha's consciousness, eventually forcing open her mind to accept Ged's description of the world and his explanation of the Equilibrium that should exist in everything, including herself. In the short run, however, Arha perceives these shocks as a challenge to her Masters and, by extension, to her own raison d'être, and her first conscious response is defensive. To prove her power she will give the intruder what she believes she is undeniably mistress of— death. Yet Arha cannot bring herself to kill the stranger. Clearly, the erosion of her faith and the shocks to her sensibility have begun to have an effect. Perhaps more than anything else, it is Arha's wanting contact with some human other than the stunted priestesses and half-men around her that continues the revitalization and brings about the eventual restoration of balance and orderly development in her life.

The importance Le Guin attaches to Arha's wanting human contact can be inferred from the fact that she devotes nearly half of *TOA* to depicting painstakingly and with a heavy reliance on dialogue the relationship between Arha and Ged. Some readers may consider this part of the novel too long, too slow, and too talky, especially for young readers. Even granting that some of the latter might be turned off, still Le Guin's decision to spend so much time on the trust that developed between Arha and Ged is sound.

Arha's hesitation over what to do with Ged reflects her keen awareness that her decision involves more than summary judgment and punishment: her own life, as well as the interloper's, is in jeopardy. To kill the latter would be, for all practical purposes, to make permanent her acquiescence in the rites of the Masters, thus sealing her own psychological and moral death. On the other hand, not to kill Ged represents an opportunity, at the least, to defy Kossil and, at the most, to claim independence of action with the promise of more in the future. In short, Arha's decision is fraught with ethical implications. To make Arha's decision convincing, then, Le Guin must take sufficient time and space to show all that went into her making it: her defense of her vocation; her faith in the Masters and their power; her panic that there will be nothing to replace her faith if she abandons it; her wanting to believe Ged, who knows her real name; her eagerness to learn more about the world above; and Ged's argument that the Nameless Ones are real and deserving of her respect but not worship.

The longer Arha speaks with Ged, the more likely it is that she will not have him killed. What this also means is that the more she speaks with Ged, the less likely it is that "Arha" is her true name. Thus, the probability that what "Tenar" represents will become dominant depends upon the length of the exchanges between Ged and Arha. To put it still another way, the lengthy conversations in toto constitute a verbal matrix within which a valid naming ceremony can take place. Gradually divesting herself of her use name, the young priestess is more and more ready either to receive a true name or to regain her real name. Ged, sensing what is happening and hoping to assist the young woman in her struggle, decides to reveal her real name. It is true that Ged's revelation of Arha's real name may not be totally disinterested; obviously, he knows that as long as the priestess thinks of herself as Arha his chances of living are slim. It is even possible that Ged's original plan to steal the ring smacked too much of the heroic Sparrowhawk. But a genuine sympathy for Arha's plight, along with his altered circumstances, induces him to put aside his initial, morally ambiguous plan. The lengthy dialogue is, then, necessary since it shows Ged broadening his concerns to include Tenar as he maneuvers and pleads to save the young woman's soul from evil. In this way Le Guin demonstrates the characteristic behavior of the ethical hero.

The heavy emphasis on dialogue serves one other important function: it is essential for the development of an authentic human relationship between Arha and Ged. Unable to see each other clearly in the dark, and physically separated from one another, the two have just one means of relating—speech. The extensive dialogue leaves Arha the option to break off whenever she wants to. It also allows her to mask the shock of discovering the intruder and learning that he is not as wizards have been described. Indirect, slow, and tentative talking also enables Arha to begin establishing the grounds for friendship and trust, whereas direct, immediate, and physical contact might prove harmful to a young woman who is repressed and knows no other relationship with a male than that of mistress toward a slave. For his part, Ged realizes that the young priestess needs gentle and sympathetic handling; and his role vis-à-vis Arha becomes that of an older brother. (Such a role, incidentally, precludes any romantic or sexual involvement between Tenar and Ged. Further, the absence of any hint of such an involvement in the section describing Tenar's unfolding self-awareness as a female is a sign of Le Guin's tact and sensitivity.) Like a brother, Ged suspects Tenar may need a parent. Since he knows of no better surrogate parent than Ogion, who has been like a father to him, he determines to take Tenar to Gont and Ogion. His performing the role of an older brother watching over a young and inexperienced sister accounts, in part, for the touching relationship that ensues after the two young people escape from the tombs. It also gives context to the last sentence of the novel: "Gravely she walked beside him up the white streets of Havnor, holding his hand, like a child coming home" (TOA, p. 146).

By her decision to assist Ged to steal the ring and escape from the tombs, Tenar rejects the sovereignty of the Nameless Ones. In doing so, she is released from the trap the unbalanced and unwholesome worship of these elemental powers forced her into. But genuine freedom is not hers. Regardless of her age, Tenar is not yet a woman. Her decision to escape is clearly ethical and admirable, granted; but it has been fundamentally a decision not to be Arha. What she is to become, whether she is really Tenar, or whether she is to have another name, her true name, are questions only the future holds answers to. This is even more reason why at the end of the novel Tenar has become a child eager for real living, eager to begin anew the process of coming of age.

4

What *TFS* directly says concerning coming of age involves young Arren. When first introduced, he is clearly of princely rank; as a prince, he suffers no identity crisis. He is generous, blessed with good fortune, inexperienced, and untried. As soon as he meets Ged, boyishly, enthusiastically he loves the great mage and thereby takes his "first step out of childhood" (*TFS*, p. 8). Subsequent steps—in fact, Arren's entire rite of passage—are also a test of the depth and permanence of his devotion to Ged. These steps comprise an ordeal of pain—the heartfelt pain of suspecting that Ged is not his hero and is unworthy of love, the intellectual pain of doubting whether Ged knows what their goal is, and the physical and spiritual pain of the journey through the Kingdom of the Dead—which Arren must undergo to reach the glorious end that has been prophesied for him, King of All the Isles. Furthermore, the very last steps out of childhood are the arduous ones Arren forces himself to take back to the beach where the initial journey into death's kingdom commenced. In successfully traversing the underworld Arren wins through to his adulthood and enjoys the keen sense of victory and accomplishment each youngster, regardless of circumstances, requires and is too often denied or has postponed needlessly: "And he smiled then, a smile both somber and joyous, knowing, for the first time in his life, alone, unpraised, and at the end of the world, victory" (*TFS*, p. 191).

There are other indications that Arren's coming of age, unlike Ged's and Tenar's which necessitated a fundamental rebirth before their passage could be completed, is more traditional in that it stresses what the boy is to become in the end. That is, Arren's end is contained within him: character bespeaks destiny. One is the hint implied in Orm Embar's salutation to the prince, "Agni Lebannen." Since in Old Speech "agni" appears to be a variant of Agnen, the Rune of Ending, the crafty dragon recognizes not just the youth's role in bringing to an end Ged's quest but the fact that the prince's becoming king is the end the quest has always pointed at. Another is that Arren's ordeal culminates in the uttermost west where, mythically, destinies are manifested and endings consummated. Moreover, Arren tends to think of himself as the hero in the olden stories who, although unrecognized initially, enjoys the prospect of a glorious destiny at the end of his ordeal or struggle. Exhausted by his ordeal, however, Arren cannot help ruefully comparing his reality with that of the olden-time hero in the stories: "He was the prince. But in the old stories, that was the beginning: and this seemed to be the end" (*TFS*, p. 190). Seconds later, as the realization hits home of what his immediate end actually implies, to wit, his victory into adulthood, he begins to sense that his more remote "end" may be glorious.

What *TFS* indirectly says concerning coming of age is part of the novel's overarching concern for death. Surely, the sense of accomplishment and victory Arren savors on the beach encompasses the realization that he has conquered fear of his own dying, not by denying its actuality and taking refuge in the childish sense of being immortal, but by facing death courageously and honestly. Because he has internalized at last what hitherto had been only Earthsea gnome—one must do only what one must do—Arren perceives the truth of what Ged had pointed out to him earlier: "You enter your manhood at the gate of death" (*TFS*, p. 164). Moreover, Arren's acceptance of death is neither stoic nor existentialist, for he does not just endure life until its inevitable end. On the contrary, he is prepared to live to the fullest since he has ample reason to assume the validity of the other insights into death's meaning and value Ged (here also spokesman for Le Guin's acceptance of Taoism) has shared with him.

Death and life are the same thing—like the two sides of my hand, the palm and the back. And still the palm and the back are not the same.... They can be neither separated, nor mixed. (*TFS*, p. 74)

Lebannen, this is. And thou art. There is no safety, and there is no end. The word must be heard in silence; there must be darkness to see the stars. The dance is always danced above the hollow place, above the terrible abyss. (*TFS*, p. 121)

Look at this land; look about you. This is your kingdom, the kingdom of life. This is your immortality. Look at the hills, the mortal hills. They do not endure forever. The hills with the living grass on them, and the streams of water running. ... In all the world, in all the worlds, in all the immensity of time, there is no other like each of these streams, rising cold out of the earth where no eye sees it, running through the sunlight and the darkness to the sea. (*TFS*, p. 165)

Ged's preoccupation with death and dying is not just a concomitant of a plot built around a journey into the world of the dead but also an essential trait of his character. His insights into the meaning of death are the fruits of his silences and meditations in which he has pondered, among other things, whether his life and career have moved in the right direction. Early in their relationship Ged remarks to Arren:

Try to choose carefully, Arren, when the great choices must be made. When I was young, I had to choose between the life of being and the life of doing. And I leapt at the latter like a trout to a fly. But each deed you do, each act, binds you to itself and to its consequences, and makes you act again and yet again. Then very seldom do you come upon a space, a time like this, between act and act, when you may stop and simply be. Or wonder who, after all, you are. (*TFS*, pp. 34–35)

Arren is puzzled by Ged's self-doubts, believing that such are proper to adolescents like himself. But Arren is, obviously, in no position to know that what Ged is experiencing is the doubt that often attacks the successful person at the height of his career. To put it another way, what Ged is undergoing is the onset of the process of individuation which, Jung hypothesized, occurs around middle age.

Ravenna Helson, who has utilized Jungian psychology in exploring the relationship between juvenile literary fantasy and self-discovery, describes the process of individuation as follows:

In the second half of life . . . the strong and socially directed ego turns inward to seek a new rapprochement with the unconscious. The middle-aged person begins to feel disenchanted with his social roles. He—or she— feels limited by them and tires of the effort to win admiration of others, to take care of others—always to be doing as others expect him to do. If circumstances and his own standards permit (in many cases one or both do not), he considers himself. With the redistribution of energies that accompanies this shift in attention, there may be a weakening of defenses, perhaps a breakthrough from the unconscious. Anxiety may be so great that the process stops. However, if it continues, an awareness of the "self" begins to develop.[11]

A good part of *TFS* reveals a Ged who has become dissatisfied with his public role. Gnawing away at his self-assurance is the deepening realization that doing, even doing magic, in spite of the good its practice can bring about, is not the entire purpose of living. Perhaps Ged even suspects that his original commitment to a life of action, although readily justified ethically and psychologically, was unduly influenced by youth's conviction that virtually all options and possibilities are available to it. But the imminence of death drastically narrows these and forces a reconsideration of what a person must do. Ged says as much to Arren.

> You are young, you stand on the borders of possibility, on the shadowland, in the realm of dream, and you hear the voice saying *Come.* But I, who am old, who have done what I must do, who stand in the daylight facing my own death, the end of all possibility, I know that there is only one power that is real and worth the having. And that is the power, not to take, but to accept. (*TFS,* pp. 137–38)

The power to accept is attainable not by seizing at it or aggressively pursuing it but by not doing anything except to stand quiet in the presence of life. Thus, as he approaches the shore of Selidor and the confrontation with Cob, Ged looks forward to what he senses may be the final and most important phase of his life: "There is no kingdom like the forests. It is time I went there, went in silence, went alone. And maybe there I would learn at last what no act or art or power can teach me, what I have never learned" (*TFS,* p. 156).

After Ged's quest is completed—paradoxically using every bit of his magic—and he is "done with doing," a new integration of inner resources will take place, and a new "self," a new Ged will develop. Like coming of age, coming of old age marks the end of one period of life and the beginning of another, momentous and challenging. Of this new self, this new Ged, nothing is known except for the provocative remark of King Lebannen: "He rules a greater kingdom than I do" (*TFS,* p. 197).

Old age and death are subjects not often found in children's literature. It is as if many authors of children's books play with their readers a game of "let's pretend" in which the inevitability of growing old and dying are deliberately ignored or, worse yet, denied. The excellence of the Earthsea trilogy as ethical fantasy stems, in large part, from the fact that Le Guin has not been afraid to confront the fact of human mortality. Her lack of fear amounts to more than just the fortitude not to back off from a distasteful subject. Rather, Le Guin is positive, insistent, celebratory: growing old is as natural, necessary, and good as leaving behind youth and becoming adult. Maturation, moreover, implies a constant coming of age; and admitting responsibility for one's actions involves meeting the challenges old age entails.

This does not mean that Le Guin believes that growing old is any easier or less troublesome than maturing and becoming adult. *TFS* testifies to both the inevitability of the aging process and the difficulty of accepting and adjusting oneself to that inevitability. The novel also testifies that old age may be the best portion of life in that it allows an individual, provided he or she sloughs off a frenzy for doing and getting, to contemplate, to open himself or herself to the ultimate potentiality of being human and alive. Unfortunately, this last testimony is—rather, *must be*—more exhortative than definitive, as Le Guin herself intimates.[12] The difference between exhortation and statement, furthermore, affects the narrative quality of the trilogy. The first two novels, compared with the last, are lean and economically written—the result of speculation annealed by experience. The third is lengthy, filled with *sententiae,* and bordering on verbosity—as if its author, trying to convince herself of the validity of what her protagonist says, needs to repeat, coax, and underline. Nonetheless, what seems weakness may be, paradoxically, a source of strength whereby the trilogy becomes outstanding ethical fantasy. For the weakness, as regrettable as it may be, is the unavoidable result of Le Guin's attempt to render more honestly and courageously than any other writer of juvenile fantasy what constitutes the process of coming of age.

PART 4

VOYAGE TO ANARRES

There was a Wall.

The Dispossessed

ELIZABETH CUMMINS COGELL

TAOIST CONFIGURATIONS
"The Dispossessed"

THE ROLE OF TAOISM IN LE GUIN'S WORK

Taoist philosophy is a basic pattern in Ursula K. Le Guin's stories and novels,[1] as verified by both external and internal evidence. Her father, the noted anthropologist Alfred Kroeber, read the Taoist books, particularly Lao Tzu's *Tao te Ching,*[2] and his religion had many Taoist parallels.[3] Her own interest in this philosophy has been openly acknowledged in her use of the writings of Lao Tzu and Chuang Tzu, the two philosophers to whom most of the Taoist writings are attributed.[4] Several characters in her 1966 novel *City of Illusions* cite passages from Lao Tzu, and in 1971 *The Lathe of Heaven* contained quotations at the beginnings of a number of chapters from Lao Tzu and Chuang Tzu. Le Guin again refers to Chuang Tzu in the December, 1974, issue of *Vertex,* commenting, "I've been deeply influenced by his ideas."[5] More recently she uses one section of her 1976 essay in *Science-Fiction Studies* to correct certain scholars' statements about Taoism, asserting that "the central image/idea of Taoism is an important thing to be clear about."[6] In this same article she refers to particular Taoist translations and explications which she has studied, and she has expanded this list in helpful correspondence with the author of this essay.

While a few scholars have noted some Taoist influences in Le Guin's work,[7] most have not. Of the former, Darko Suvin, one of science fiction's leading critics, has expressed the belief that we must go beyond Taoism to understand Le Guin. He has argued that "the attempts to subsume her under Taoism (which has undoubtedly had an influence) are in view of her development after *LOH* not only doomed to failure but also retrospectively revealed as inadequate even for her earlier works."[8] Suvin goes on to assert that Taoism is a confining label because "Leguinian ambiguities are in principle dynamic, and have through her evolution become more clearly and indubitably such."[9]

Suvin's argument is clear and effective, but this essay will argue that an understanding of Le Guin's Taoism is essential for a fuller appreciation of the pattern and order within her works. Admittedly, it does not totally exhaust the sources which have influenced her thought. Le Guin's reading, for example, has ranged from Henry James to the anarchists Paul Goodman and Pëtr Kropotkin and to the existentialists; she states, "It seems to me that when you stop being influenced by other people's ideas, you might as well dig your grave and crawl into it."[10] Significantly, however, these writers are arguing for principles, especially anarchy, which are compatible with Taoism. Moreover, Suvin is somewhat too categorical when he implies that to associate Le Guin's writing with Taoism obscures the dynamism of her ideas. The key to Taoism is that change is eternal, therefore reality is process and truth is relative. So to recognize her Taoism is to be prepared for the concept that "Leguinian ambiguities are in principle dynamic."

In Le Guin's science fiction Taoism affects the form and content in a variety of ways. *City of Illusions,* for example, is a clear metaphor for the search for the Way; "Vaster Than Empires and More Slow," on the other hand, is a complex assimilation of Taoism in setting, characterization, and the value system which resolves the conflict.[11] When her novels are viewed chronologically in terms of composition, a spiral of increasing complexity emerges.[12] The individual's reliance on Tao is well explored in *City of Illusions* (1966); in *The Left Hand of Darkness* (1967–spring 1968) Le Guin adds a preliminary investigation of Tao in political and social theory. "Vaster Than Empires and More Slow" (1970) and *LOH* (1970) return to more extensive investigations of Taoism in the development of the individual. Finally, *The Dispossessed* (1971–74) is a successful synthesis of the theory of personal development with social and political theories.

SCIENCE AND TAOISM IN *THE DISPOSSESSED*

It is the thesis of this essay that Taoist philosophy, especially through three of its major principles (following the model of Nature, the Theory of Letting Alone, and the eternality of change), is more fully integrated into the structure and content of *DIS* than in any other science fiction by Le Guin. The novel's unity is based on the Taoist pattern found in the areas of science, personal development, society, and government as they are presented in the work. A discussion of the first, science, will introduce the reader to the foundations of Taoism; following this, personal development, society, and government will be examined in the light of each of the three major principles of Taoism named above.[13]

Taoism is compatible with science and its literary, philosophical relative, science fiction. As Joseph Needham has thoroughly documented, "It is among the Taoists that we have to look for most of the roots of Chinese scientific thought."[14] Out of the concept of Tao comes the belief in the unity and spontaneity of nature which results in a pantheistic view. The Taoist appreciates the value of scientific knowledge about the universe and believes it increases his understanding of Tao but never completes it. Le Guin, a recognized leader in science fiction, has noted that "the figure of the scientist is a quite common one in my stories, and most often a rather lonely one, isolated, an adventurer, out on the edge of things" (*The Wind's Twelve Quarters*, p. 40). Among her literary creations have been Rocannon in *Rocannon's World* and Lyubov in *The Word for World Is Forest* as ethnologists, Falk-Ramarren, navigator of an FTL ship in *City of Illusions*, the science-trained Jakob Agat of *Planet of Exile* and Genly Ai of *LHD*, and the physicist Shevek of *DIS*.

Like the other protagonists, Shevek's science takes him on a quest. He lives on Anarres in an anarchist society established 170 years earlier by colonists who fled the authoritarian and bureaucratic government of a sister planet, Urras. The novel covers about forty years of Shevek's life, tracing, on the one hand, his burgeoning genius in physics and his increasing commitment to others, especially his partner Takver and their two children and, on the other hand, his developing criticism of Anarres as it moves toward a formalized government which restricts his psychological, intellectual, and social growth. Believing that his society's anarchism (based on the principles of its founder Odo) will survive only if it continues to change, Shevek participates in two revolutionary actions. He joins the Syndicate of the Initiative, a group of individuals who are striving to revitalize the spirit of anarchism, and he travels to the country of A-Io on Urras as a gesture of good will and an opening of communication between the two circling planets. There he completes his unified theory of time and intensifies his belief in and understanding of anarchism.

Unlike many other Le Guin protagonists, Shevek is engaged in theoretical, not applied, science. Further, more explicitly than in any of her other quest novels, science affects the protagonist's personal development and the sociopolitical development of his country. Shevek's unified theory of time reflects the very nature of Tao. This is most clear in his reply to an Ioti on Urras, who has argued that two contradictory statements about the same thing can not be asserted: "Can one dismiss either being, or becoming, as an illusion? Becoming without being is meaningless. Being without becoming is a big bore. . . . If the mind is able to perceive time in both these ways, then a true chronosophy should provide a field in which the relation of the two aspects or processes of time could be understood" (*DIS*, p. 180). Shevek's emphasis on being and becoming is implicit in the sage's concept of Tao.

There was something undifferentiated and yet complete,
Which existed before heaven and earth.
Soundless and formless, it depends on nothing and does not change.
It operates everywhere and is free from danger.
It may be considered the mother of the universe.
I do not know its name; I call it Tao.[15]

Explicators and commentators have defined Tao variously. Joseph Needham describes it as "the way in which the Universe worked; in other words, the *Order of Nature*."[16] Burton Watson states that it is "the underlying unity that embraces man, Nature, and all that is in the universe."[17] Closer to pantheism than to theism, it is an impersonal force working throughout the universe yet not identical with it. It is the natural laws which give harmony and wholeness to the universe and is more than the natural laws. Its definitions are often paradoxes—it is both being and nonbeing, named and nameless, action and no-action, being and becoming. One of the clearest explanations of these paradoxes is given by Holmes Welch.

We can, for instance, imagine a universe packed with primordial substance. Since there is no space—no nothing—to differentiate substance from substance, an observer would not see anything. He would, in effect, see nothing. But now, within this primordial substance, interstices develop. Things take shape. What makes them take shape? The nothing that separates them one from the other. And so out of "nothing," nothing has produced everything.[18]

Immediately following this analogy, Welch comments, "Like many archaic pictures of creation it is vague enough to suggest some of the concepts of contemporary physics." Chan, quoting Homer H. Dubs, is more specific: "Only Einsteinian space-time—which is nothing, yet directs the motion of particles—comes at all close to the *Lao Tzu*'s concept of nonexistence."[19] The Unnamable is, then, both Being (always existing, i.e., simultaneity) and Becoming (always creating, i.e., sequence).

Given this view of the universe, it is not surprising that Le Guin's physicist, Shevek, would have developed a theory of this magnitude. The subject he explores and the attitude of mind he develops reflect Taoist influences.

Shevek's belief in the unity and spontaneity of nature entails two Taoist principles. First, the Taoist recognizes that within one concept or entity is always contained its other, that there are no true opposites but that all possibilities are contained within one. Sequency and simultaneity are opposing concepts, yet Shevek is searching for their unity, as he explains in the following metaphor: "The book is all there, all at once, between its covers. But if you want to read the story, and understand it, you must begin with the first page, and go forward, always in order" (*DIS*, p. 178). The second Taoist principle on which Shevek's search is founded is that change is eternal, reality is process. As Shevek describes it, "Our model of the cosmos must be as inexhaustible as the cosmos. A complexity that includes not only duration but creation, not only being but becoming, not only geometry but ethics" (*DIS*, p. 182). Needham translates this belief as "the doctrine of cyclically recurring differences,"[20] which is akin to Shevek's overall philosophy (rooted in his physics) that "*you can* go home again . . . so long as you understand that home is a place where you have never been" (*DIS*, p. 44). It is also akin to Odo's "causative reversibility" (*DIS*, p. 37).

It should be noted that not only are Shevek's ideas based on Taoism but so is his method of explanation. As did Lao Tzu and Chuang Tzu, Shevek explains abstract theory by using concrete analogies, specifically water. In Taoism water is frequently an analogy for the containment of all things in unity and without differentiation. Early on in his work, for example, Shevek dreams of the simultaneity theory; "He saw time turn back upon itself, a river flowing upward to the spring. He held the contemporaneity of two moments in his left and right hands; as he moved them apart he smiled to see the moments separate like dividing soap bubbles" (*DIS*, p. 91).

In the final analysis, it is not the temporal theory itself which has the greatest significance, but rather the attitude of open-mindedness, the freedom to search for an answer outside the realm of logic. Given the understanding of Tao and of the unity, spontaneity, and eternal change of nature, Shevek approaches nature, as does a Taoist sage, without preconceived theories. As Lao Tzu explained, the sage is imitating nature in this respect.

The supreme Tao, how it floods in every direction!
This way and that, there is no place where it does not go.
All things look to it for life, and it refuses none of them;

Yet when its work is accomplished it possesses nothing.
Clothing and nourishing all things, it does not lord it over them.[21]

Needham explains that "the sage is to imitate the Tao, which works unseen and does not dominate. By yielding, by not imposing his preconceptions on Nature, he will be able to observe and understand, and so to govern and control."[22]

Shevek is open-minded because of his Odonian teaching that the means are the end. His goal is not the unified field theory at all costs; his goal is the means—the open-mindedness and freedom to do physics. In fact, Shevek asserts, "It is not the answer we are after, but only how to ask the question" (DIS, p. 182). This attitude is the same as the Gethenian Foretellers in LHD; Le Guin makes it an integral part of the protagonist and plot development in DIS.

Shevek's attitude also reflects the influence of his culture. Coming out of a cooperative collectivist society, Shevek is better able to accept the unprovable assertion as the basis of his general field theory than are the propertarian Urrasti scientists. There is a parallel here to Needham's historical survey of Taoism. He argues that the Taoist religion which fell into theism, secret rituals, and fortune telling is to be blamed on a "socio-economic system of feudal bureaucratism . . . which sterilized the sprouts of natural science. . . ."[23]

Also, as a member of the Syndicate of the Initiative, the new Anarrasti revolutionary group, Shevek is better able to make the connection than Sabul, his former physics teacher who stifled and censured Shevek's work as he outstripped Sabul. His teacher is similar to the scientists whom Henri Bergson, the French philosopher and scientist, criticizes for using static, separate concepts to explain the dynamic flow of reality. Sabul uses scientific analysis to solve problems, while Shevek uses what Bergson calls intuition, an intellectual sympathy.[24] Interestingly, Needham asserts that the Taoist metaphysicians, in the forefront of their science, were comparable to the mystics of the Renaissance. Shevek is like those mystics; Sabul is like the rational scholastics. Needham asks what social conditions allow mysticism rather than rationalism to become a progressive social force. His answer describes Sabul and the movement toward bureaucracy on Anarres. "When a certain body of rationalist thought has become irrevocably tied to a rigid and outdated system of society, and has become associated with the social controls and sanctions which it imposes, then mysticism may become revolutionary."[25]

Shevek is finally able to complete the unified temporal theory because his attitude allows him to assume the unprovable, an action of one who believes in means, not ends, of one who recognizes the relativity of truth.

The moment of his realization is like a Taoist mystical experience (similar to Falk-Ramarren's in *City of Illusions* the night before his second mind razing, and Genly Ai's with the Foretellers in *LHD*). The Taoist mystical experience involves a unique state of awareness that dissolves the finite point of view holding an individual. It allows the mystic to see behind the flux and finiteness of things around him to the unity of all things rooted in Tao. Lao Tzu describes it as follows:

> Push far enough towards the Void,
> Hold fast enough to Quietness,
> And of the ten thousand things none but can be worked on by you.
> I have beheld them, whither they go back.
> See, all things howsoever they flourish
> Return to the root from which they grew.[26]

Unlike most mystics, the Taoist experiences no explicit visions. There is no ecstasy; there is no allegorical description or emotional experience.[27] There is, Welch explains, a state in which the Taoist reaches new knowledge and understanding of Tao; he attains a "consciousness that all these [finite] distinctions have ceased—consciousness, one might say, of Non-Being."[28] This parallels Le Guin's description of Shevek's experience: "There were no more abysses, no more walls. There was no more exile. He had seen the foundations of the universe, and they were solid" (*DIS*, p. 226). The experience does not lead to the attainment of paranormal powers, but it does lead to a religious dimension beyond an understanding of the physical universe. This relationship between physics and ethics is suggested by Shevek when he tries to explain the Odonian concept of religion to the curious Urrasti doctor on the spaceship taking Shevek to Urras.

In Pravic the word *religion* is seldom. No, what do you say—rare. Not often used. Of course, it is one of the Categories: the Fourth Mode. Few people learn to practice all the Modes. But the Modes are built of the natural capacities of the mind; you could not seriously believe that we had no religious capacity? That we could do physics while we were cut off from the profoundest relationship man has with the cosmos? (*DIS*, p. 12)

Of immediate practical benefit to Shevek and the Taoist sage is the acquisition of *te,* meaning "power" or "virtue." It is that quality which enables the sage "to turn the human forces around him to his own advantage because he understands them."[29] Shevek, after completing his theory on Urras, joins the revolutionary brothers and rejects giving his work to the nonanarchists. He realizes that knowledge of his theory will only give more power to those who have it and use it for oppression.

Clearly, then, Shevek's scientific work to unify sequency and simultaneity into a single theory of time reflects the very nature of Tao. His inquiries reflect the Taoist emphasis on science as a valuable way to knowledge about Tao, the attitude toward nature, and the mindset which results from this attitude and knowledge, including the mystical experience.

FOLLOWING THE MODEL OF NATURE

The preceding examination of science in *DIS* provides the background for understanding the remaining elements in Le Guin's Taoist configuration—personal development, society, and government. In Odonianism, Le Guin's invented anarchistic theory upon which the society of Anarres is built, these elements are so interwoven that they must be discussed together. Generally, they all rest on three Taoist principles: following the model of Nature; the Theory of Letting Alone; and the eternality of change. Each of these will be discussed in the remaining sections of this essay.

Nature, as a manifestation of Tao, serves as a model for the individual seeking the Way. Lao Tzu, arguing with Confucius, is reported to have said:

If you indeed want the men of the world not to lose the qualities that are natural to them, you had best study how it is that Heaven and Earth maintain their eternal course, that the sun and moon maintain their light, the stars their serried ranks, the birds and beasts their flocks, the trees and shrubs their station. Thus you too shall learn to guide your steps by Inward Power, to follow the course that the Way of Nature sets.[30]

The particular pattern nature offers is the undifferentiated society. "Just as there was no real greatness and smallness in Nature," Needham explains, "so there should be none in human society. The accent should be on mutual service,"[31] echoed in Le Guin's "mutual aid." Partaking of the elements of anarchistic theory, the classless society of Anarres reflects this social homogeneity in the four concepts of sharing, cooperative labor, mutual aid, and anarchy. In contrast, the class society of A-Io on Urras in its possessiveness, capitalism, mutual aggression, and government bureaucracy reflects the feudalism the Taoists argued against.

On Anarres people are to be "sharers, not owners" (*DIS*, p. 241). Therefore, there are communal dormitories, not private housing. Meals are prepared at central refectories, and central depositories have the necessities of clothing, shoes, and bedding. Children are educated and cared for in learning centers. Institutions are equally affected as exemplified by Odo's renouncement of both marriage and prostitution because both may lead to possessiveness. Shevek tells the Ioti revolutionaries that if they wish to come to Anarres, they must come "naked, as the child comes into the world, into his future, without any past, without any property, wholly dependent on other people for his life" (*DIS*, pp. 241-42). The naked child, common in Taoist writings, symbolizes the natural self, uncorrupted by civilization, its values and laws. As Odo wrote in *The Social Organism*, "To make a thief, make an owner; to create crime, create laws" (*DIS*, p. 112). This closely parallels a number of passages in *Tao te Ching*, for example:

> The more laws and orders are made prominent,
> The more thieves and robbers there will be.[32]

Although Anarres is falling away from its Odonian ideal, as reflected in the private room and private knowledge that Shevek encounters when he goes to study with Sabul in the major city, Abbenay, Ioti society is still the opposite of Anarres in its excess of material goods, as represented in flamboyant dress and decor and in luxurious bathrooms (to Shevek "a kind of ultimate apotheosis of the excremental" [*DIS*, p. 52]). Lao Tzu also denounced extravagance:

> Elegant cloths are worn,
> Sharp weapons are carried,
> Foods and drinks are enjoyed beyond limit,
> And wealth and treasures are accumulated in excess.
> This is robbery and extravagance.
> This is indeed not Tao (the Way).[33]

Shevek is literally sickened by the "acres of luxuries, acres of excrement" (*DIS*, p. 106) for sale in the shopping area of Nio Esseia on Urras. Further, he sees male-female relationships as being an exchange of possessions. Their materialism overrides any other values, as evidenced by the Ioti physicist Oiie, who adjusts his beliefs about Shevek and war to protect his property.

Following sharing, the second concept in Odonian society with overtones of Taoist social homogeneity is cooperative labor, which defies a class society and includes the equality of men and women. On Anarres work is coordinated through the Division of Labor Central Posting with all individuals willingly rotating through even the menial positions. The

Anarresti are motivated by work for work's sake; in fact, the word for work and play is the same. The reward for work is its own pleasure and the respect of others. Although a few jobs are specialized, many tasks are not. Again, Shevek and the Syndicate of the Initiative become critical of Anarres when they believe the system is acquiring too much power, thus being able to punish individuals by not giving them postings which match their skills. After several years of famine the Syndicate also notes that cooperation with Central Posting has been reduced to obedience.

In contrast, the whole concept of work on Urras is affected first by the principle of possessiveness and second by a central belief in superiority and inferiority. The Ioti are walled in by complex social mannerisms; worse yet, the lower classes, who must perform the least attractive jobs, lead miserable lives.

After sharing and cooperative labor, the third concept in Odonianism which reflects Taoism is voluntary mutual aid. Obviously influenced by her reading of the nineteenth-century Russian anarchist Pëtr Kropotkin (especially *Mutual Aid*), Le Guin must have absorbed these ideas partly because of her already solid Taoist philosophy. The Odonians argue that the only law they follow is that of human evolution, which means that since humans are a "social species," the strongest are the "most social. In human terms, most ethical" (*DIS*, p. 177). Shevek explains the principle of mutual aid to the Ioti revolutionaries. "We know that there is no help for us but from one another, and that no hand will save us if we do not reach out our hand. And the hand that you reach out is empty, as mine is. You have nothing. You possess nothing. . . . You are free" (*DIS*, p. 241). The famine years demonstrate the unity and solidarity of Odonian society. During the long drought and resultant deprivation members are pleased to find their solidarity still strong; "Mutual trust allayed depression or anxiety. 'We'll see each other through,' they said, serenely. And great impulses of vitality ran just under the surface" (*DIS*, p. 199).

Legislated morality, the Taoists felt, was without value; Lao Tzu wrote:

> When the great Tao declined,
> The doctrine of humanity and righteousness arose.
> When knowledge and wisdom appeared,
> There emerged great hypocrisy.[34]

Laws mean the end of an individual's responsibility and freedom; as Shevek expresses it:

It's . . . our common nature to be Odonians, responsible to one another.

And that responsibility is our freedom. To avoid it, would be to lose our freedom. Would you really like to live in a society where you have no responsibility and no freedom, no choice, only the false option of obedience to the law, or disobedience followed by punishment? (*DIS,* p. 36)

Ultimately, the power of moral choice resides in the individual, and it is this characteristic which sets Shevek apart from the majority of his associates; he relies more on inner decision than do most. He is in striking contrast to one of his childhood friends, Tirin, who writes a comic drama which the literalists interpret as anti-Odonian. Their criticism, as well as his subsequent postings to physical labor in outlying communities, drives him insane. Thus, others may be subjected to considerable pressure by those using social responsibility as a form of power.

On the parent planet, however, morality must be legislated because the Urrasti system is based on mutual aggression. The value system becomes clear when Shevek realizes that many of its laws and social customs are designed to protect wealth and power. For example, when Shevek slips away from the University in A-Io and spends the day in the capital city of Nio Esseia with Vea, Oiie's sister, he finds that money seems to buy politeness from the shopkeepers, pictures are painted to be sold, not to express the creative urge, and women use "their sexuality as a weapon in a power struggle with men" (*DIS,* p. 171). Further, in his conversations with Vea, Shevek recognizes that when morality must be legislated, it is already lost, a principle asserted by the Taoist philosophers in criticizing the myriad regulations of Confucian governments.

Thus, anarchy is the fourth concept which, in addition to sharing, cooperative labor, and mutual aid, characterizes Taoist/Odonian collectivism. In *DIS* government is defined as "the legal use of power to maintain and extend power" (*DIS,* p. 134). This is exactly what the Odonians try to avoid. As Le Guin wrote in her introduction to "The Day before the Revolution":

Odonianism is anarchism. Not the bomb-in-the-pocket stuff, which is terrorism, whatever name it tries to dignify itself with; not the social-Darwinist economic "libertarianism" of the far right; but anarchism, as prefigured in early Taoist thought, and expounded by Shelley and Kropotkin, Goldman and Goodman. Anarchism's principal target is the authoritarian State (capitalist or socialist); its principal moral-practical theme is cooperation (solidarity, mutual aid). It is the most idealistic, and to me the most interesting, of all political theories. (*WTQ,* p. 285)

On Anarres the Production and Distribution Coordination (PDC) is a network which coordinates individuals, federatives, and syndicates engaged in communication, travel, shipping, and other productive work. The rotation of administrative posts and the voluntary nature of work groups are designed to prevent power positions from developing. To Shevek, the most obscene thing he ever did was to play the role of a jailer in a prison reenactment during his adolescence. Shevek finally initiates the prisoner's release because he feels disgusted, "vile," and declares, "I want to respect myself" (*DIS*, pp. 31–32). Much of the plot's conflict stems from the Anarresti movement toward a power structure. For example, Sabul and the Physics Federation have acquired power over the community of physicists by determining who will teach and what will be published, children parrot Odo's words so that they become laws, and public disapproval has excommunicated Tirin, virtually reducing him to a criminal. The group of revolutionaries, however, moves closer to the Odonian ideal. One must remember that Odo's ideas were only theories, written into manuscripts. She never lived to come to the Settlement on Anarres and to the practical working out of her idea. The novel derives tension and vitality from this testing of Odo's theories.

In contrast A-Io, like modern Earth, is bureaucratically laden. The powerful governments control their people through funding, spies, bugging, and, when all else fails, violence. When Shevek realizes that his acceptance of Ioti hospitality is tantamount to selling himself to its government, he faces a dilemma. "The individual cannot bargain with the State. The State recognizes no coinage but power: and it issues the coins itself" (*DIS*, p. 219). The symbol of its oppressive power is the prison, whose existence was denied by his Ioti guides. ". . . up on the bluff there was a building, heavy, ruinous, implacable, with broken towers of black stone. Nothing could have been less like the gorgeous lighthearted buildings of the Space Research Foundation, the showy domes, the bright factories, the tidy lawns and paths. Nothing could have made them look so much like bits of colored paper" (*DIS*, p. 70).

The Taoist belief that man should model his social and political behavior after nature also extends to the self. The earliest recorded event in Shevek's life involves learning not to be possessive. At about the age of one year, indignant over another baby having crowded him out of a patch of sunlight in the dormitory playroom, Shevek cries out, "Mine sun!" He is reprimanded by the woman in charge that all things are to be shared, not owned (*DIS*, p. 22). The very next recorded event demonstrates Shevek's recognition, at the age of eight, of the unity in nature, an event which will affect his personality and lifestyle. In the Anarresti education system, one part of the child's day is spent in a Speaking-and-Listening group, directed by a teacher. Here the children learn that "speech is a two-way function" (*DIS*, p. 24); ideas are to be shared, not used to enhance the ego of the speaker. Shevek tries to share his concept of Zeno's paradox, but because his ideas are viewed as disruptive by the teacher, he is reprimanded and expelled from the group.

The pain Shevek feels is assuaged by turning to knowledge of numbers. He does not understand their relationships but senses their pattern, equality, and solidity. Six weeks later, when he has an opportunity to ask his father, he is rewarded with an understanding of numerical relationships. That very night he dreams of discovering the primal number. This discovery, which gives him so much satisfaction that he refers to it as coming home, indicates that his special ability in mathematics reflects his basic nature. The unity and equality he sees, symbolized by the number one, he adopts as his attitude toward life; the plurality, symbolized by the number five, he recognizes as the diversity of nature, that is, that no two things are the same but that the whole is always present.

The juxtaposition of these two experiences is significant for another reason. The former illustrates the society teaching personal attitudes to the individual. But the latter illustrates that the self must develop independently of the society, that the individual can learn from sources other than society—in this case, nature and the pain caused by an unsatisfactory social encounter.

According to Burton Watson, "The central theme of the *Chuang Tzu* may be summed up in a single word: freedom." The basic question of all ancient Chinese philosophers, Watson asserts, was, "How is man to live in a world dominated by chaos, suffering, and absurdity?"[35] This may be viewed as Shevek's problem also. Through the pain of four famine years and his separation from his partner Takver, Shevek learns that his individual responsibility is to develop his own talents. Freedom, says Shevek, is "that recognition of each person's solitude which alone transcends it [solitude] " (*DIS,* p. 86). Even earlier, at the age of nineteen in a discussion with his friends, Shevek understands that pain is man's basic experience. In true Taoist fashion, he sees the opposites which an individual encounters, that is, happiness and pain. "And yet, I wonder if it isn't all a misunderstanding—this grasping after happiness, this fear of pain. . . . If instead of fearing it and running from it, one could . . . get through it, go beyond it. There is something beyond it. It's the self that suffers, and there's a place where the self—ceases" (*DIS,* p. 48). Yet, as will be shown later, while Shevek comes to understand himself, he also recognizes his need for interpersonal relationships. At the conclusion of this same discussion with his friends, he asserts that brotherhood "begins in shared pain" (*DIS,* p. 50).

The pattern of the undifferentiated society which nature offers allows Shevek to develop beyond the social homogeneity of the Odonian society.

New individual meaning and significance is thus given to the principles of sharing, cooperative labor, mutual aid, and anarchy.

THE THEORY OF LETTING ALONE

The second major Taoist principle which affects the three elements of personal development, society, and government in Le Guin's *DIS* is the Theory of Letting Alone *(wu wei)*. Joseph Needham translates *wu wei* as "refraining from activity contrary to Nature," that is,

from insisting on going against the grain of things, from trying to make materials perform functions for which they are unsuitable, from exerting force in human affairs when the man of insight could see that it would be doomed to failure, and that subtler methods of persuasion, or simply letting things alone to take their own course, would bring about the desired result.[36]

Basically a guide for relationships with both the inanimate and animate, it is based on two concepts—passive receptivity and the relativity of truth. The Odonian attitudes toward relationships parallel *wu wei;* the Urrasti attitudes reflect the opposing principle, *wei,* which Needham explains as "'forcing' things, in the interests of private gain, without regard to their intrinsic principles, and relying on the authority of others."[37] The Theory of Letting Alone will be discussed first in sociopolitical terms and then in relation to the development of the self.

The Taoists frequently used the analogies of water and the feminine Valley spirit to explain passive receptivity, as Lao Tzu suggested in the following lines:

The great rivers and seas are kings of all mountain streams
Because they skillfully stay below them.[38]

These models demonstrate the right action in human relations where "force defeats itself. Every action produces a reaction, every challenge a response."[39] When Needham discusses the feminine principle, he contrasts it to the masculine principle dominant in Confucianism. His discussion includes the following contrast. "The Confucian . . . social-ethical thought-complex was masculine, managing, hard, dominating, aggressive, rational and donative—the Taoists broke with it radically and completely by emphasizing all that was feminine, tolerant, yielding, permissive, withdrawing, mystical and receptive."[40]

The feminine model for the Anarresti is Odo, the woman who founded the Anarresti society[41] and emphasized the equality of all individuals. The masculine principle dominates in Ioti society. In fact, Atro calls the Odonians "womanish" because their society "simply doesn't include the virile side of life" (*DIS*, p. 230), i.e., the shaping of masculinity in battle. In striking contrast, Shevek notes the rejection of the natural feminine principle in the Ioti, particularly in the construction of their furniture: "Apparently they [the Ioti], like the tables on the ship, contained a woman, a suppressed, silenced, bestialized woman, a fury in a cage. He had no right to tease them. They knew no relation but possession. They were possessed" (*DIS*, p. 60).

The Odonians are like the Taoist sage and other Le Guin protagonists who recognize that, because every object and arrangement resists a challenge to its existence, they must avoid "all hostile, aggressive action."[42] One immediately thinks of the behavior of Rocannon and Falk in their journeys across rivers and land masses. Each is respectful of the natural environment—these are no stereotyped males who prove their masculinity by hacking their way through trees and prairie grass, whooping after animals for the sport of the hunt. They travel among or over trees, killing only what is necessary for food.

In *DIS* this receptivity to nature is held by the entire society of Anarres, a clear example being their ecological practices. Faced with a desert and a dearth of trees, the Anarresti choose to plant seedlings, not in a new area but in the dust which had once been forest. "Millennia of drought had killed the trees and dried the soil to a fine grey dust that now rose up on every wind, forming hills as pure of line and barren as any sand dune. The Anarresti hoped to restore the fertility of that restless earth by replanting the forest" (*DIS*, p. 37). A second notable example is the behavior of the people during the devastating drought. The society pulls through because the majority accept emergency work postings and reduce their food consumption. They do not riot because there is nothing to riot against—drought is a natural condition and can be survived by hard work and cooperation. The Urrasti, of course, are also ecologically minded, but theirs is an ecological *policy*, existing by means of rules and regulations enforced by the government. Although their resources are thus conserved, there is no equality in who conserves. The wealthy and the powerful have their needs fulfilled; the poor, working class do without.

In offering examples of the violation of *wu wei* in political relationships, the Taoists were particularly critical of capital punishment, believing that it was a sign of governmental failure. If living conditions were so disagreeable that people turned to crime, then punishment by death would be no threat to them.[43] This is reflected in the actions of the new revolutionaries on Urras. Shevek escapes from the Ioti government spies and offers to aid the revolutionaries who are modeling themselves after the Odonians. While speaking at a mass demonstration, Shevek and thousands of working class people are fired on by Ioti government helicopters. The Ioti police then swarm into the district to kill or arrest the revolutionaries. In spite of the government's brutal punishment and the possibility of death, the brotherhood still aids Shevek in escaping to asylum in the Terran embassy. In denying the significance of eternal punishment, they exemplify Odo's words, "No man earns punishment, no man earns reward" (*DIS,* p. 288).

The best society provides the individual the freedom to develop a talent and to share his achievements with others. The Taoists believed that the manifestation of Tao in each individual was *te,* usually translated as "virtue." It was regarded as either being inherent in each individual[44] or developing "from following Tao."[45] In either case, it is that specific ability of each individual. The Odonian society is committed to allowing each individual as much freedom to develop as possible. This is clearly stated by Shevek. After nearly a year on Urras, frustrated over his own naiveté and helplessness in the face of a highly organized bureaucracy, he reassesses his actions and asks, "Well, what had he come here to do?" He answers himself, "to do physics. To assert, by his talent, the rights of any citizen in any society: the right to work, to be maintained while working, and to share the product with all who wanted it. The rights of an Odonian and of a human being" (*DIS,* p. 222).

In contrast, the Ioti government uses its people to further the wealth and power of a few. Lao Tzu denounced a society very similar to Urras for using the individual in two ways; as Holmes Welch explains, the individual "becomes a reservoir of aggression on which society can draw to produce its goods competitively, fight his wars fiercely...."[46] These two factors of materialism and militarism are the same avenues through which Le Guin contrasts Urras and Anarres. The opposing attitudes toward materialism are neatly caught in descriptions of the business districts of the two planets. Shevek's first visit to a street of retail shops in Nio Esseia on Urras exhausts and confuses him, giving him nightmares for many months. Not only is it a show of excessive, useless items, but "all the people in all the shops were either buyers or sellers. They had no relation to the things but that of possession" (*DIS,* p. 107). In contrast, his first visit to the production communities of Abbenay excites him. "There were no disguises and no advertisements. It was all there, all the work, all the life of the city, open to the eye and to the hand" (*DIS,* pp. 80-81). The austere background only emphasizes the holiday atmosphere of people enjoying their work. Odo wrote, "A child free from the guilt of ownership and the burden of economic competition will grow up with the will to do what needs doing and the capacity for joy in doing it. It is useless work that darkens the heart" (*DIS*, p. 199).

The other way, in addition to materialism, in which such a society exploits its people is militarism. Anarres has no war; on Urras it is common. Shevek discusses the concept of the military with Atro, the renowned Ioti physicist, and is horrified by his suggestion that one justification for the common man's existence is to fight wars. As an honest Odonian, Shevek's response reflects the concept of passive receptivity upon which *wu wei* is based.

After passive receptivity, the second concept underlying *wu wei* is the relativity of truth. As Welch explains, "The Sage never tries to do good, because this requires having a concept of good, which leads to having a concept of evil, which leads to combatting evil, which only makes evil stronger."[47] Not only is this approach effective, it is also ethical. First, no action or opinion, in the complex ways of man, is ever entirely good. As Welch comments, "Reward the deserving man with a prize and we plant envy in the hearts of the undeserving."[48] Second, because good and evil are subjective, there must be truth in all opinions. The relativity of truth is a rejection, not of the absolute concepts of good and evil as demonstrated in nature and thus in Tao, but a rejection of the subjective value systems which make these false distinctions. It is now clear why legislated morality, discussed in the previous section as an object lesson learned from nature, is impractical. In fact, Shevek says as much when he arges Vea to "throw out the moralizing, yes—the rules, the laws, the punishments—so that men can see good and evil and choose between them" (*DIS*, p. 176).

The Urrasti motives of fame, money, and power are clearly misdirected. In fact, both Lao Tzu and Chuang Tzu spoke out against them. Lao Tzu was succinct:

When Tao prevails in the world, galloping horses are turned back to fertilize (the fields with their dung).
When Tao does not prevail in the world, war horses thrive in the suburbs.[49]

Chuang Tzu was more explicit when he described those who honored "wealth, eminence, long life, a good name."

People who can't get these things fret a great deal and are afraid—this is a stupid way to treat the body. People who are rich wear themselves out rushing around on business, piling up more wealth than they could ever use—this is a superficial way to treat the body. People who are eminent spend night and day scheming and wondering if they are doing right—this is a shoddy way to treat the body.[50]

Ideally, Odonians are motivated by their own initiative first, balanced with the opinion of others second; public opinion which offers favor or power is rejected. However, as has been mentioned before, much of the tension of the novel results from the movement of Anarres toward a more materialistic, bureaucratic society. This is particularly evident in the Physics Federation, which violates *wu wei* when it becomes motivated by power and ceases to recognize the relativity of scientific truth. Chuang Tzu's description thus applies to Sabul as he struggles to maintain power over Shevek and prevent him from freely developing his *te,* i.e., exploring the simultaneity theory of time, rather than the sequential theory which Sabul prefers. These factors solidify Bedap and Shevek's late night discussion group into the Syndicate of the Initiative. Their open meetings follow the standard of *wu wei,* as all meetings are supposed to. "There were no rules of parliamentary procedure at meetings in PDC. Interruptions were sometimes more frequent than statements. The process, compared to a well-managed executive conference, was a slab of raw beef compared to a wiring diagram. Raw beef, however, functions better than a wiring diagram would in its place—inside a living animal" (*DIS,* p. 283). Any Anarresti may attend the Syndicate's meetings, and the growing conflict among Odonians becomes clear in their discussions. For example, at one meeting during the Syndicate's third year of existence, Bedap initiates discussion of travel between the two planets. Because Anarres has been closed to new colonists since its founding, discussion is vigorous. However, the member who threatens physical violence to anyone who goes to Urras and tries to return has taken up the ways of the Ioti.

Passive receptivity and the relativity of truth merge to support the natural development of *wu wei,* resulting in an anarchistic society. As Odo might have theorized, if an entire group of people have the attitude of *wu wei,* then there is no need for a government which leads from above; "government" will be from within. The Odonians, in fact, look forward to the Promised Man, who like Chuang Tzu's Perfect Man, would exhibit *wu wei:*

His bearing was lofty and did not crumble; he appeared to lack but accepted nothing; he was dignified in his correctness but not insistent; he was vast in his emptiness but not ostentatious. Mild and cheerful, he seemed to be happy; reluctant, he could not help doing certain things; annoyed, he let it show in his face; relaxed, he rested in his virtue. Tolerant, he seemed to be part of the world; towering alone, he could be checked by nothing; withdrawn, he seemed to prefer to cut himself off; bemused, he forgot what he was going to say.[51]

In order to achieve these characteristics, the Taoist believed the individual must develop the self first and then participate in society.

As is clear from the Taoist writings, the emphasis is simply one of degree; an individual cannot grow in a vacuum but is always a member of society. The shifting from self to society is apparent in Shevek's personal development. If the Anarres chapters in *DIS* are read chronologically, they cycle through this shifting emphasis twice. Chapters 2, 4, and 6 trace the development of Shevek's natural self, followed by his recognition of his role in society, followed by specific action in chapter 8 within that society. Chapters 10 and 12 repeat the cycle. Even though the chapters return to the same problems, the problems have altered. Earlier decisions of the problems are relevant, but the new decision required is on a different level. Thus, at the end of chapter 2 Shevek resolves the problem of pain by recognizing it as the beginning of brotherhood between individuals, while at the end of chapter 10 the problem of pain is viewed as necessary in the larger context of interacting groups within the society.

Chapter 12 brings the two emphases into balance because Shevek's decision to go to Urras fulfills both his individual and social functions. When the Urras chapters are read in chronological order, two more cycles emerge. The trip to Urras in chapter 1 is a third cycle of the creative individual developing within a different society; chapter 13 is the fourth cycle—the individual, now changed, returns to his former society, which has also changed in his absence and will continue to change in his presence. Viewed from this perspective, the demonstration of the dynamic relationship between individual and society is perfectly clear.

In order to practice *wu wei*, the individual must have the natural self as a foundation, uncontaminated by society's subjective value systems which emphasize false motivations of wealth, fame, and power. Shevek's early experiences recounted in chapter 2 show both the success and failure the Anarresti have had in teaching the relativity of truth. His freedom to engage in and disengage from the prison experiment demonstrates their success. The episode results in the painful violation of *wu wei* as the boys take on the unnatural roles of the jailer and the jailed. Shevek initiates the prisoner's release, not because of external pressure but because he has lost respect for himself. On the other hand, Shevek's excommunication from the Speaking-and-Listening group demonstrates a flaw in the teaching. The conformity which the teacher insists on must be avoided, as the Taoists argued, if the natural self is to develop.

Shevek's natural self develops through his early schooling, friendships, and work experience. As Chuang Tzu prescribed, Shevek has few desires, is motivated by his own initiative, and exhibits passive receptivity. Further, he has found his special talent in physics which, like Chuang Tzu's parables of the butcher and swimmer, comes so easily to him that he does not have to be conscious of the processes. Bedap, in fact, recognizes

Shevek's natural skill: "You don't have to be able to swim to know a fish . . ." (*DIS*, p. 133). Shevek, like Chuang Tzu's artisans, represents the broader category of the creative individual in society; Le Guin has written that she has used "science as a synonym for art" (*WTQ*, p. 218). Strong as this self is, it is flawed in its hermeticism. Shevek's inwardness is like the Taoist striving to become the Sage, to complete his virtue. It is this quality which allows Shevek time to develop his talent, but it also causes him to overwork and become ill.

Juxtaposed with his illness are two events which seem to remind Shevek of his role in society—his bargain with Sabul and his rejection of his mother. Shevek requests that his paper on Reversibility be sent to Atro for publication on Urras. Sabul, who has been claiming coauthorship on Shevek's previous works in return for assuring publication on Anarres, adamantly refuses. As Shevek bargains with Sabul, he is both violating and demonstrating *wu wei*. Because he has entered into an exploitative relationship, he violates *wu wei;* but Shevek never aggressively confronts Sabul with an accusation about Sabul's striving for power or his inferiority to Shevek. Instead, he uses more subtle means, as Lao Tzu recommended. In this particular disagreement, Le Guin describes Shevek's manner as follows: "His gentleness was uncompromising; because he would not compete for dominance, he was indomitable" (*DIS*, p. 94). Lao Tzu, in like vein, described the sage: "It is precisely because he does not compete that the world cannot compete with him."[52]

Immediately following this confrontation, Shevek is hospitalized with a pneumonic illness. Fevered and drugged for many days, he is cared for by his mother, Rulag, whom he has not seen since he was a toddler. When he recovers, however, he refuses to establish any relationship with her. In her life her work had always come first, so she had taken engineering postings which had kept her separated from Shevek and her partner, Palat. Shevek knew that the separation had pained his father and that "his father's loyalty [was] that clear constant love in which his life had taken root" (*DIS*, p. 100). Shevek's rejection of his mother is a painful reminder of his present isolation in contrast to his former closeness to his father, now deceased.

In chapter 6, then, Shevek consciously begins his socialization process. He initially reaches out for intimate one-to-one personal relationships, first with Bedap, then with Takver. Bedap is a childhood friend whom Shevek accidentally meets in Abbenay. Not only does Shevek live and have sex with Bedap, but he enters fully into running arguments with him over the nature of the Odonian society and the individual's role in it. In his bonding with the woman Takver, however, his *te* is challenged and strengthened by acceptance. The physical setting surrounding their pledge is significant because it merges the two Taoist models for *wu wei,* water and the valley. Takver and Shevek are sitting on a steep slope, looking down at a swift mountain stream in a shadowy ravine. As they talk, the tension of each, hesitant and unsure of revealing their inner feelings, is reflected in the noise of the water rushing down to the lowest level—"a ceaseless harmony composed of disharmonies" (*DIS,* p. 145). When Takver admits she needs the bonding, Shevek's realization is expressed in a simile. "Joy was rising mysteriously in him like the sound and smell of the running water rising through the darkness. He had a feeling of unlimitedness, of clarity, total clarity, as if he had been set free" (*DIS,* p. 146). When the bond of partnership for life is sealed, the symbols echo it: "Life, said the stream of quick water down on the rocks in the cold dark" (*DIS,* p. 147).

From the vantage point of his relationship with Takver, Shevek now sees that he must accept his role in society. Later, during the famine years, he chooses to travel to emergency postings rather than refuse such jobs in order to stay with Takver and their daughter Sadik. It is this commitment which subsequently induces him to go to Urras. The Shevek we meet in chapter 1 on his way to Urras is like the sage described by Lao Tzu who has attained the natural self. It is one of two poetic portraits which Welch quotes in toto.

> Circumspect [he seems], like one who in winter crosses a stream,
> Watchful, as one who must meet danger on every side.
> Ceremonious, as one who pays a visit;
> Yet yielding, as ice when it begins to melt.
> Blank, as a piece of uncarved wood;
> Yet receptive as a hollow in the hills.[53]

Shevek's attitude on Urras seems to be molded on the advice which Chuang Tzu offered an individual being sent on a diplomatic mission. First, the emissary must act from the solidity of his *te,* which includes understanding and accepting that which one can do nothing about, that is, the mode of passive receptivity. So Shevek, horrified or pleasured as he is by the Ioti society, does not preach politics. Second, in warning the emissary there may be communication problems, Chuang Tzu advises, "Transmit the established facts; do no transmit words of exaggeration."[54] Shevek's main approach is to tell the truth "without either forgiveness or anger" (*DIS,* p. 65). He is particularly careful to follow this aspect of *wu wei* with Oiie's children when they question him about Anarres. "Shevek kept out of the ethical mode with some scrupulousness; he was not there to propagandize his host's children" (*DIS*, p. 120). Finally, Chuang Tzu urges the emissary to avoid "parading your store of talents."[55] On Urras, where he is considered a great man, Shevek's modesty is continually emphasized in his rejection of the honorary title of "doctor," his request to be treated as an equal, and his gentle explanations of Odonian morality and government.

At the end of chapter 4 Chuang Tzu warns his readers to beware of being usable; he suggests that long life depends on being useless, and he cites the example of the enormous oak tree which has never been cut because it is so gnarled. Shevek errs in this respect; after several months on Urras, he discovers that the physicists believe their Ioti government has bought him; that is, by bringing him to the planet and supporting him all these months, they expect to be repaid with Shevek's unified theory of time. The mode of *wu wei,* however, also allows for exceptions; like a true Taoist, when backed into a corner, Shevek rebels. He flees his jailers, offers help to the revolutionaries, and refuses to give his theory to the Ioti or any Urrasti government to further their political power. Like the sage, he does not enjoy his deviousness; it is simply an unpleasant necessity.

The reflection of the Taoist principle of *wu wei* in Le Guin's *DIS* gives the novel much of its unity. Passive receptivity and relativity of truth guide the development of anarchy in Odonian social and political relationships, as well as in Shevek's natural self and *te.* Shevek's commitment to himself, his family, and his society is a crucial configuration in the novel. As Shevek recognizes, "It is not until an act occurs within the landscape of the past and the future that it is a human act. Loyalty, which asserts the continuity of past and future, binding time into a whole, is the root of human strength; there is no good to be done without it" (*DIS,* pp. 268–69). The interactions between the individual and society are reciprocal and dynamic.

THE ETERNALITY OF CHANGE

The third and final principle of Taoism, which lies behind Le Guin's development of Shevek and the sociopolitical conflicts of Anarres and Urras in *DIS,* is that change is eternal and reality is process. What is immediately clear is that the structure of *DIS* is cyclical. Changes often occur in cycles, the Taoists observed, thus resulting in tension between the old and the new. Nearly two hundred years ago the Odonian revolution began, culminating in the founding of Anarres by the Settlers, but the barrenness of the planet caused them to revise some of Odo's principles. This modification begins a spiraling process which includes Shevek's new revolutionary group (the Syndicate of the Initiative) and the Urrasti brotherhood. Even the original Settler cycle is not a closed circle. In the last chapter, as the Hainish spaceship which has brought Shevek back from Urras to Anarres is preparing to land, one of the Hainishmen requests permission to debark with Shevek. Shevek's agreement includes the admonition that "once you walk through the wall with me, then you are one of us. We are responsible to you and you to us" (*DIS*, pp. 309–10). Because each of these cycles is slightly different from the previous ones, they exemplify Taoism's "cyclically recurring differences."[56] Odo's epitaph is a cryptic statement of this principle, "True voyage is return" (*DIS*, p. 68). Significantly, Joseph Needham translates chapter 40 of *Tao te Ching* as "Returning is the (characteristic) movement of the Tao."[57]

The Taoists recognized the difficulty of denoting the point when "the limits of one category have been overpassed and the next category entered."[58] This was the major subject of Chuang Tzu's second chapter, which included the famous parable of "Three in the Morning":

But to wear out your brain trying to make things into one without realizing that they are all the same—this is called "three in the morning." What do I mean by "three in the morning"? When the monkey trainer was handing out acorns, he said, "You get three in the morning and four at night." This made all the monkeys furious. "Well, then," he said, "you get four in the morning and three at night." The monkeys were all delighted. There was no change in the reality behind the words, and yet the monkeys responded with joy and anger. Let them, if they want to. So the sage harmonizes with both right and wrong and rests in Heaven the Equalizer. This is called walking two roads.[59]

Shevek's discussions with Bedap in chapter 6 demonstrate that he shares this dilemma with the Taoists; it is difficult for him to recognize that Anarres is in a cycle leading away from anarchy. Bedap argues, "The circle has come right back around to the most vile kind of profiteering utilitarianism" (*DIS*, p. 142). Shevek, as has already been shown, eventually agrees with Bedap, thus demonstrating the maturation of the Taoist sage.

The assumption that change is inevitable and invaluable characterizes the Anarresti society. The Settlers established the communication network first, as Odo had planned, so that "no community should be cut off from change and interchange" (*DIS*, p. 77). Bedap emphasizes the necessity of change in his early discussions with Shevek over the nature of society. He asserts that the basis of Odonianism is, "Change is freedom, change is life" (*DIS*, p. 135). Several years later, when arguing for the freedom of an Anarresti to visit Urras, Shevek restates Bedap's assertion:

"If it [the revolution] is seen as having any end, it will never truly begin" (*DIS*, p. 289).

The Taoist/Odonian society, having accepted change as the natural characteristic of life, accepts two other concepts. First, if reality is process, then means are the ends; second, if change is eternal, then truth is relative. The first embraces the recognition that accomplished ends in a reality of process are lost the moment after they come into being. The characteristics of the self, then, are determined by the individual's actions in the process of living, not by his completed goals. For Shevek this means that the goal is doing physics, not publishing his results nor seeing them used by one individual or government to gain an advantage over another. The second embraces the recognition that change gives openness to reality. New realities can come into being and old truths do not necessarily apply to them. Both these concepts are organic in Taoism.

In A-Io, where society is based on profit and power, those with the most power and profit work hard to prevent change. For example, when revolutionary forces in Benbili, a large nation in the Urrasti western hemisphere, overthrow the military dictator, A-Io sends in forces to aid the deposed government. The war is a power struggle, and the superiority of Ioti forces will help restore the status quo in Benbili. Shevek, sickened by the war, finds he has no one to talk to, not even Oiie, the Ioti physicist who frequently invites Shevek into his home. "Oiie was an ethical man, but his private insecurities, his anxieties as a property owner, made him cling to rigid notions of law and order. He could cope with his personal liking for Shevek only by refusing to admit that Shevek was an anarchist" (*DIS*, p. 163). Shevek strongly condemns the Urrasti in his recurrent image of resistance to change—the wrapped package. "Urras is a box, a package, with all the beautiful wrapping of blue sky and meadows and forests and great cities. And you open the box, and what is inside it? A black cellar full of dust, and a dead man" (*DIS*, p. 278). Ironically, it is the enemy (Pai, the Ioti government's spying physicist) who gives him the truth (Ainsetain's theories) he needs to complete his temporal theory. This is more than literary irony of situation; it is a demonstration of the relativity of truth and has occurred consistently in Le Guin's novels. In *Rocannon's World* Rocannon learned what he valued most when the enemy killed his alien friend Mogien; Rolery, daughter of the old leader of the native race, learned love and biological truth in the enemy's city in *Planet of Exile;* Falk-Ramarren in *City of Illusions* learned his identity in the enemy's city;[60] Ai learned of Estraven's loyalty in enemy territory in *LHD;* Orr of *LOH* learned truth about reality in the enemy-doctor's office. So knowledge is to be gained everywhere, even from the enemy.

After aiding the revolutionaries of A-Io, Shevek finds asylum in the Terran embassy on Urras. There, in conversations with the ambassador Keng, he learns that Earth also resists change. Lamenting that men on Earth failed, she asserts, "We forfeited our chance for Anarres centuries ago, before it ever came into being" (*DIS*, p. 280). Shevek sees this as a denial of change; he argues that time cannot be sectioned into past, present, and future. "Things change, change. You cannot have anything. . . . And least of all can you have the present, unless you accept with it the past and the future" (*DIS*, p. 280). This failure to understand the nature of reality convinces Shevek that the world is not ready for the reality of an Odonian society.

Just as Odonian social and political action is based on the permanence of change, so are the individual Odonian's actions. Shevek, convinced by Bedap's evidence, chooses to work for change:

Bedap had forced him to realize that he was, in fact, a revolutionary; but he felt profoundly that he was such *by virtue of* his upbringing and education as an Odonian and an Anarresti. He could not rebel against his society, because his society, properly conceived, was a resolution, a permanent one, an ongoing process. To reassert its validity and strength, he thought, one need only act, without fear of punishment and without hope of reward: act from the center of one's soul. (*DIS*, pp. 142–43)

In the novel Le Guin has carefully prepared us for accepting Shevek's decision. His early interest in mathematics, which has already been noted, is also a recognition of change. "Everything could change, yet nothing would be lost. If you saw the numbers you could see the balance, the pattern. You saw the foundations of the world. And they were solid" (*DIS*, p. 25). Because of his interest in theoretical physics and his hermetical nature, Shevek, more than most members of his society, relies on his own opinions to make decisions. His morality is rigid, a result of teaching by mediocre adults, so there is a need for change within himself which he must accept.

In a sense, Shevek's quest is also maturation. It is the actualization of Odonianism; he shifts from acting as a result of past teaching to acting as a result of his thoughts about past teaching and the present situation. This is the shift which takes place in his first discussion of revolution with Bedap. Only his belief that his past teachers were right would lead him to consider suicide. While he argues, the "walls of his hard puritanical conscience were widening out immensely" (*DIS*, p. 140). His bonding with Takver further convinces him that the process of change is the essence of life. He recognizes that "everything that had happened to him was part of what was happening to him now" (*DIS*, p. 148). Or, as he explains to Takver, "unless the past and the future were made part of the present by memory and intention, there was, in human terms, no road, nowhere to go." (*DIS*, pp. 148–49). It was this same attitude that furthered his work on the general temporal theory. Further, his decision to go to Urras is based on the belief that because of the cycle of change and of time he cannot deny his past, because that would be to deny his future; "To deny is not to achieve" (*DIS*, p. 72). His life's work illustrates unity in change, so prominent in Taoism and in Le Guin's opus.

In light of the principle of change, then, the relationship between the individual and society must be dynamic. In fact, Shevek's search for the unity between sequency and simultaneity in the temporal theory parallels his increasing understanding of the complex relationship between the individual and society. Odonians believe, as did the Taoists, that the individual must be sound in the Way before he can be of much value to the society. As Shevek points out, "The duty of the individual is to accept *no* rule, to be the initiator of his own acts, to be responsible. Only if he does so will the society live, and change, and adapt, and survive" (*DIS*, p. 288). If an individual mistakenly views the society as more basic, then it becomes the State; and, as Shevek saw demonstrated on Urras, "The individual cannot bargain with the State" (*DIS*, p. 219).

When Shevek sees the rudiments of a bureaucratic government developing on Anarres, he rebels for the sake of the anarchistic society. "Sacrifice might be demanded of the individual, but never compromise: for though only the society could give security and stability, only the individual, the person, had the power of moral choice—the power of change, the essential function of life. The Odonian society was conceived as a permanent revolution, and revolution begins in the thinking mind" (*DIS*, p. 267). He realizes that his error in the mission to Urras was believing that he could bring them the model of his anarchist society. Instead, Shevek recognizes that the people themselves must change. When their values are more like the Odonians', then they will naturally select anarchy. Thus, Shevek says to the Terran ambassador, "We can only wait for you to come to us" (*DIS*, p. 281). Both Odonians and Taoists recognize that individual development is certainly aided by a society which gives one the freedom to make choices. The subtly shifting relationships between the two are similar to the paradoxical union of sequency and simultaneity in Shevek's unified temporal theory. The Taoist recognition of the eternality of change, then, affects the movement of *DIS* in a variety of ways. Chronologically, there is the revolutionary cycle which begins and ends the contrasts between Anarres and Urras, and there is the scientific quest of Shevek. Structurally, there are the alternating chapters which reflect the juxtaposition of the present with the past and future.

DIS is clearly the culmination of Taoist philosophy in Le Guin's writing. The Taoist configuration includes the model of nature which offers the anarchist and revolutionary pattern for society, the attitude of *wu wei* in human relationships which unifies the novel, and the acceptance of the eternality of change which structures the novel. To argue that Le Guin has been influenced by Taoism is not to rule out additional influences nor to say that Taoism totally explains her writing. It is to say, however, that Taoism is the basic substance out of which the other threads are made. A study of Le Guin's writing reveals the pattern and configuration which are at the heart of her work.[61] That heart is Taoism. Living in a period of rapid change and search for meaning, she has rediscovered, updated, and brought to our attention the philosophical responses of ancient China to similar challenges.[62]

LARRY L. TIFFT AND
DENNIS C. SULLIVAN

POSSESSED SOCIOLOGY AND LE GUIN'S DISPOSSESSED
From Exile to Anarchism

If any single judgment can be rendered against Western sociology, it is that it has traded the totality of human experience for its own possessive, self-righteous exile. With but few historical exceptions, Western sociology has preferred to remain isolated from human community, maintaining the observed detachment and singular smugness of a diplomat. If Western sociology has become dogmatic, as Bakunin predicted it would, it is because it conceives of itself more as the parent and healer of human experience, than as one ideological derivative of it.

Some sociologists now recognize the seriousness of this isolation and speak of an impending crisis in Western sociology. Yet if we are honest about our heritage, we must admit that Western sociology has been in crisis since its inception. Sociology has rarely been grounded in, and is now far removed from, human experience and community.

POSSESSED SOCIOLOGY AND LE GUIN'S DISPOSSESSED

Fearful of the changes, the pain, and the suffering they might have to undergo once grounded in human relationship, sociologists have become increasingly possessive of their own "status" and "professional" boundaries, manufacturing conceptual languages and methodological technologies which mystify and conceal but never allow for experience. The sociologist who experiences is labeled the "corrupted" sociologist. The sociologist who struggles to find life's meaning is accused of producing "meaningless" sociology.

As ethical decisions are life decisions, sociology has become nonethical, value-free, neutral, removed from personal and life experience. Sociological endeavor, therefore, has become increasingly private, as private as the properties, ideological as well as material, it has come to protect. But since sociologists have remained above the experiences of community, they have rarely recognized the effects of their privatization; have rarely recognized the ways in which they have facilitated possessive and oppressive relationships designed to prevent and/or destroy organic human community. Self-rendered beyond human experience, sociology has not been capable of recognizing its own part in the conceptualization and concretization of sexism—differentiating male from female; or ageism— separating the young and the old; of racism—the dark from the light; of classism—the unpossessing from the possessing; of militarism—the weapon from the olive branch. As a sociology of possession and exile, Western sociology has sadly come to be a sociology of emptiness and abstraction, not of pain or suffering or joy or human experience. These it has forfeited for method, neutrality, and isolation, for service to power.

By dividing the world into parts, sociologists have continued to think in parts. Because sociologists have created a fragmented world of sociological thinking, mirroring the possessed social orders in which they live, there has been little connectedness between theory and practice, between words and deeds, between feelings and rationality.

Even in its more militant Marxist versions, sociology has been reform sociology, possessed sociology, or a sociology of exile because it has been concerned solely with boundaries and partitioning, not with journey and connectedness. If revolutionary thinking has been absent from the sociological landscape, it is because sociologists have been unwilling to risk the journey from the safety of their isolation. A sociology that engages revolution is a sociology of risking one's possessions for wholeness and connectedness; is a sociology of the linked present, for only in the linked present do connectedness and wholeness have meaning.

If anarchism as a sociology has been *lost* or absent, it is because sociologists have preferred the safety of possession to the suffering and joy of human experience. It is because sociologists themselves have been lost in time, in exile, divided between the past and the future, without any grounding in the present. It is because they have abstracted themselves from the sociological enterprise, acting more like pompous bishops preaching thoughts of healing from their sacred pulpits than physicians immersed in and aware of the pain of healing the sores of persons who are themselves.

We are not surprised that sociologists find the risk of journey overwhelming, for they have no particular place, relationship, to which to return. Nor is it surprising to find anarchism as a sociology being *found,* for it is a sociology of connectedness, a sociology that allows the exile to return, that provides the opportunity for grounding and for seeing human experience in terms of "a coherent process in which the bifurcations of thought and activity, mind and sensuousness, discipline and spontaneity, individuality and community, man and nature, town and country, education and life, work and play are all resolved, harmonized, and organically wedded in a qualitatively new realm of freedom."[1]

As sociologists, we are aware of the pitfalls of possessive sociology, for we are its children. We are critically aware that the risk we take in an analysis or critique of a work of art, another person, or life itself is that in dividing the whole into distinct parts, in constructing boundaries for the purpose of understanding unity and elucidating meaning, we quite possibly destroy or conceal meaning, leaving ourselves with a juxtaposition of fragments and as isolated from meaning as ever. By constructing boundaries and dividing the whole of Le Guin's novel *The Dispossessed*,[2] we risk separating her ideas from her feelings, her characters from her landscapes, her history from her presence, her fears of isolation from her total engagement in life which she so sensitively projects. We take the risk of making of her an exile in her own world of meaning. But to do otherwise is to remain in isolation, to be the sociological exiles on whom Western sociology has survived. If we are to discover meaning, we must risk forfeiting the safety of exile status. The alternative is possessed sociology, to preserve our own isolation from Le Guin's gift, to abstract ourselves from her consciousness and poetry, and face the reality of never being grounded. From this paradox no exit exists.

This paradox is a major theme of Le Guin's novels and one which she faces in responding to others' commentaries. Contradictory needs and possibilities lie in reaching out to others while realizing that "it's so hard to talk about the *ideas* in a quartet or a watercolor...."[3] Or a novel? Le Guin is aware that what she knew when she wrote *DIS* she now knows differently. For her to express what she meant then is to recreate the past through the present and, also, to place boundaries on, constrain, and restrict the novel's meaning. It is to require of her another mode of expression. It is possibly to deny to us, the present participants in the novel, our own creativity, our own journey. It is possibly to deny to us the construction of meaning the novel has for our lives and future. But if we are denied these possibilities we may not discover the meaning in the gift she has given. We may not understand that, through shared speech about shared journeys, collective understanding emerges and barriers fall.

While it might be desirable to explore totally a novel or a life for meaning, we cannot, for it is an unresolved, ever-changing journey. The sharing of meaning comes through traversing the boundary of self and negating the isolation of existential and physical separateness, by becoming connected, by becoming more whole, by initiating collective understanding. Sharing is to continue one's own journey while extending its meaning to others. It is to open oneself up for introspection and exploration by others, to become vulnerable. And by becoming vulnerable while in the midst of our journey, we risk not being able to continue, risk forfeiting future meaning. Without vulnerability, however, there is no journey, at least no journey that fords the isolation of our exiled self. For to be vulnerable is to bring death to the exile.

Though the risks of introspection and exploration are uncertainty and pain, they are as well joyous, for we share ourselves. To risk, to share her gifts, to be vulnerable, as was Shevek in *DIS* in his sharing, is Le Guin's chosen valued journey. To withhold sharing is to journey only within self-boundaries, to close oneself off *from* others and *to* others. It is a mockery of revolution.

To make a choice to adhere to any boundaries, those of self, gender, age, race, culture, or ideology, is to choose not to explore, not to recognize and journey with different others. It is thereby to activate the values generated by an inward journey. We do not deny the reality of a journey within the boundaries or barriers of self, gender, culture, or ideology. We do recognize, however, that this is a journey of isolation, segregation, and an inner dynamics that yields entropic processes. It is a journey that dwarfs, that structures a life of false proportions, that protests against the pain of the reality of facing the whole, of struggling to discover unity. It is a journey that is situated in the past or future, that permits no existential present. There may *be* a journey, but it is neither human nor personal.

As one introspectively journeys and creates realities from within, one removes and is removed from others with whom this reality is not shared. The personally or socially disconnected reality created is either destructive or socially meaningless and unvalued. Shevek's initial introspective journey into (the world of) physics is disconnected from the needs of, and from any commitment to, others. Others merely intrude upon his physically and mentally self-destroying search. His physics and social relations are catatonic, locked in mental solitary, severed from the nurturance of spiritual, moral, social, whole human-self. We see a journey of disconnected parts coming unglued as a result of unidimensional blindness rather than being connected by hope or love.

Shevek's physics begins to develop and becomes meaningful only when he realizes he must release himself from his confinement. It is as William Butler Yeats said:

Nothing can be sole or whole
That has not been rent.

Through becoming more whole and connected to Takver, his beloved female partner, his rent physics and life gather meaning, for both are now grounded in the poetry of human relationship. Through this grounding he begins to acquire a language for the expression of his physics as it relates to the universe, for he is already grounded in that universe. He realizes, as a courier true to his talents, that he must take his physics and connect himself with persons and realities who pose a threat to the persons of anarchistic Anarres. The irony is, however, that the more he becomes grounded in personal realities and in the particularities of place (the blade of grass), the farther he can journey, the greater the risks he takes, the more meaning his physics has for the universe. His physics of life, once grounded, allows him a metaphysics of possibility.

To most of those living on Anarres, Shevek's physics is unvalued because its meaning threatens their isolationist values, as the promise of any grounding in reality always threatens the isolated. In order to understand him, his physics, his journey, they too must ground themselves in connectedness, which means they too must traverse the sacred boundaries of the reality they hold. Separation in time and space from the possessed world of Urras is for those on Anarres a believed barrier *for* survival. Yet to Shevek, this separation is a barrier *to* survival, reeking of a despair as desolate as the Anarres landscape.

To Shevek and Le Guin the hope *for* survival is the ever continuous breaking down of barriers, never pausing, but never pressing revolution. It entails continuous change, a never-wavering commitment to risk, to the negation of certainty, for to be certain is to be an exile. The journey out of boundaries negates the journey within and lays open the possibility of being whole. The within journey, the creation and maintenance of barriers, propels the degenerating processes of separateness and alienation, power and hierarchy, superiority and possession. The journey within fosters the isolation of self from self, from others, and from meaning. The challenge to connect worlds of ideology, the challenge to connect our own worlds of mind and body, is voided.

LANDSCAPES FOR HUMAN SURVIVAL

Through the juxtaposition of two worlds we trek across the possessed political economics of current capitalist and socialist states (A-Io and Thu on Urras) and journey into the possible, the known and familiar world of anarchism which lies "like a seed beneath the snow, buried under the weight of the state...."[4] The possessed life of the United States is our past, the dispossessed life of anarchism our future; in the creative joining of the two is our present, is our journey, is the invitation for us to be whole.

The dispossessed persons of Anarres have no possessions, are no longer possessed or obsessed by the principle of *having* in contrast to that of *being.* They no longer possess things, knowledge, self-attributes, nature, or other persons. They no longer construct barriers between self and others, self and nature, for all is part of the natural and the organic. They no longer package, market, sell, or consume one another, for to consume one another is to consume oneself. Nor are they obsessed, as are the possessed, with being or becoming *free from* everything and everyone.[5] Rather, they are *free to* demonstrate their vulnerability and extend themselves to others in human relationships, to be, in a world without the icons of domination-subordination and the leg irons of superiority-inferiority. They live in the present because they experience the presence of someone who cares, because they live in a society in which caring relationships are supported by freedom of choice.

Hierarchy, possession, superiority, and alienation are the cages of an inward journey, artifacts of the walls we build around ourselves, invisible to us, but elements of our thought. In a healthy society an individual recognizes the real mutuality and reciprocity of society and individual, the interdependence between person and environment, both social and physical. "Sacrifice might be demanded of the individual, but never compromise: for though only the society could give security and stability, only the individual, the person, had the power of moral choice . . ." (*DIS,* p. 267). For only the individual can create, and only through moral choice does creation become possible. As Shevek proclaims:

The duty of the individual is to accept *no* rule, to be the initiator of his own acts, to be responsible. Only if he does so will the society live, and change, and adapt, and survive. We are not subjects of a State founded upon law, but members of a society founded upon revolution. Revolution is our obligation: our hope of evolution. "The Revolution is in the individual spirit, or it is nowhere. It is for all, or it is nothing. If it is seen as having any end, it will never truly begin." We can't stop here. We must go on. We must take the risks. (*DIS,* pp. 288–89)

Yet even among the dispossessed of Anarres, convention, moralism, fear of social ostracism, fear of being different, and fear of being free had eroded their consciousness and created barriers to freedom, moral choice, and risk. Their collective journey had become the journey of isolates, an interior journey that preferred the destructive safety of boundaries and separation to the life-giving risk of an exterior journey beyond self, of establishing a present so as to connect with their past and future. This became nearly impossible, for they were becoming slaves to a past dream and a future hope, forfeiting the possibility of a present. Shevek elucidates:

We always think it [I'm a free man], and say it, but we don't do it. We keep our initiative tucked away safe in our mind, like a room where one can come and say, "I don't have to do anything, I make my own choices, I'm free." And then we leave the little room in our mind, and go where PDC posts us, and stay till we're reposted. . . . We're ashamed to say we've refused a posting. That the social conscience completely dominates the individual conscience, instead of striking a balance with it. We don't cooperate—we *obey*. We fear . . . egoizing. We fear our neighbor's opinion more than we respect our own freedom of choice . . . just try stepping over the line, just in imagination, and see how you feel. . . . We have created crime, just as the propertarians did. We force a man outside the sphere of our approval, and then condemn him for it. We've made laws, laws of conventional behavior, built walls all around ourselves, and we can't see them, because they're part of our thinking. (*DIS*, pp. 264-65)

Among the possessed on Urras these same walls were so concretely fortified as to allow only a sliver of hope, of consciousness to enter, but that hope and consciousness are always emerging in the form of persons of moral choice, persons of journey, persons of the present who struggle to connect. On Urras:

. . . there is nothing . . . but States and their weapons, the rich and their lies, and the poor and their misery. There is no way to act rightly, with a clear heart, on Urras. There is nothing you can do that profit does not enter into, and fear of loss, and the wish for power. You cannot say good morning without knowing which of you is "superior" to the other, or trying to prove it. You cannot act like a brother to other people, you must manipulate them, or command them, or obey them, or trick them. You cannot touch another person, yet they will not leave you alone. There is no freedom. It is a box—Urras is a box, a package, with all the beautiful wrapping of blue sky and meadows and forests and great cities. And you open the box, and what is inside it? A black cellar full of dust, and a dead man. A man whose hand was shot off because he held it out to others. (*DIS*, p. 278)

The land (Urras) of possessed abundance, of natural beauty, where people have so much, is the land of surface pleasure and spiritual death. The land (Anarres) of surface dust, darkness, and scarcity is the land of spiritual life and fulfillment. It is not that anarchism is possible only under conditions of scarcity, but that fulfillment has meaning through mutual commitment: "It is not until an act occurs within the landscape of the past and the future that it is a human act. Loyalty [commitment and connectedness], which asserts the continuity of past and future, binding time into a whole, is the root of human strength; there is no good to be done without it" (*DIS*, pp. 268-69). It also has meaning through suffering, which is everywhere. "If you evade suffering you also evade the chance of joy. Pleasure you may get . . . but you will not be fulfilled. You will not know what it is to come home" (*DIS*, p. 268). While individuals suffer their individual pain sequences, pain is universal. Suffering is common to the species because each member of the species is mortal and at the same time struggling to understand and grasp the possibility of this absolute. Through connectedness and mutual aid, meaning is given that defies mortality. Absolutes are seen for what they are, as the presence of the human struggle pervades each act to overcome isolation.

The people of Anarres share a constant threat—extinction in their barren landscape. The scarcity of Anarres is not a statement that whole, connected, changing, moral life can exist only in such a landscape, but rather that barriers are overcome when people recognize and share a constant threat and commitment. In the process of the struggle, understanding, solidarity, cooperation, mutual aid, equality, and appreciation emerge—barriers are broken and new life, new consciousness are born.

The scarcity landscape of Anarres is thus a strength, for it energizes the solidarity, understanding, and processes of constant change. But this scarcity landscape is also Anarres's weakness, making it vulnerable as an economically exploitable colony. Anarres's ideological landscape valuing revolutionary process is a strength, but, as a ground for segregation to insure ideological purity, it is a weakness as well, for it makes itself vulnerable to the stagnation of ideas, to the end of change, process, and revolution. As was the case with Shevek personally, such a ground turns in upon the self, and proclaims an inward journey that defies the possibility of change and meaning.

And yet, while the people of Anarres are struggling with the real human threat, that of *species survival*, for which barriers must crumble, most persons, having lost sight of the connectedness of human life because they live in isolation, perceive the real human threat to be other persons separate from them, on the other side. Ironically, these threats and conquest struggles between persons, sexes, races, cultures, ages, nations, and ideologies generate processes of struggle and solidarity by which barriers are transcended and some sense of the true human condition is learned (freedom, fulfillment, change). But as these struggles are discontinued or successfully removed from consciousness, walls of old stone or new plastic are reconstructed. The temporally known processes of understanding, solidarity, mutual aid, and appreciation are turned under, new and different human victims are sought, the ante of conflict is raised.

Among the possessed of Urras, Shevek experiences episodic mutual trust and understanding only with those persons who are engaged in change, who have a real sense of human struggle: children and revolutionizing workers. Young children are in the process of growing up, temporarily isolated from the absurd exploitative culture. They are novices in the creation of barriers. The unpossessing workers are struggling against the barricades which segregate them from Urras's landscape of material abundance and spiritual scarcity, from useful work, dignity, and honor. In either case, Shevek develops solidarity with the isolated, in order to connect the feelings that lock them out and miniaturize their lives and growth:

Oiie had invited him to dinner several times since his first visit, always rather stiffly, as if he were carrying out a duty of hospitality, or perhaps a governmental order. In his own house, however, though never wholly off his guard with Shevek, he was genuinely friendly. By the second visit his two sons had decided that Shevek was an old friend, and their confidence in Shevek's response obviously puzzled their father. It made him uneasy; he could not really approve of it; but he could not say it was unjustified. Shevek behaved to them like an old friend, like an elder brother. They admired him, and the younger, Ini, came to love him passionately. Shevek was kind, serious, honest, and told very good stories about the Moon; but there was more to it than that. He represented something to the child that Ini could not describe. Even much later in his life, which was profoundly and obscurely influenced by that childhood fsscination, Ini found no words for it, only words that held an echo of it: the word *voyager*, the word *exile*. (*DIS*, p. 157)

PHENOMENOLOGY, CULTURAL RELATIVITY, AND HUMAN VALUES

The protagonists in Le Guin's novels develop an appreciation for the differentness, the uniqueness of others. It is because they too are grappling with an awareness of the pain of their own uniqueness, their own struggle to overcome isolation. Through an awareness of these "same" others, they come to discover and appreciate human similarity, likeness, and commonality, and the bonds for mutual aid. They recognize that the social base of human life beneath the weight of any and all walls is the same. They recognize the necessity of digging beneath these walls to discover one's uniqueness and begin one's journey as a free person in search of connectedness and meaning.

Through struggle and change Le Guin's protagonists learn to appreciate and understand culturally alien others, in the particularity of their own personal struggle as well as in the universality of life struggle.[6] Through the paces of their own journey, they come to appreciate themselves and take the risks of the vulnerable, come to greet the vulnerable, understanding that love can emerge only when people come to meet each other in their individuality. Le Guin has worked through her cultural relativity and authenticating (phenomenological) phase, evident in her previous novels. In the process of working through these ideas, she has changed. Through her struggle to understand, to find meaning in the basic premises, assumptions, and values of current statist political economies, she discovers that cultural, technological, and value exchange is at once productive of change and destructive of values. On her own journey, she inserts herself into her varied landscapes to portray at what points these exchanges enliven or deaden the person, how the human person in the process of change and exchange withdraws at times into isolation, only to return to an understanding that primal experience (change) lies in human connectedness.

She finds that perhaps basic values are not subject to cultural relativism and appreciation after all. One set of values is *not* equally acceptable, *not* as authentic as another. Values, technologies, and consequent social arrangements which segregate and separate humans from each other and from self, which divide the whole, which upset the ecology, the beauty of the diversity of the universe, and which violate the sanctity or sacredness of life, may be understood on their own terms, but they are *not* acceptable.

In this sense, Shevek's journey home is a demonstration of the power of commitment to and the meaning of human values. His trip to Urras and return reaffirms the basic values he has learned in his society on Anarres. His exploration reaffirms their justness and correctness (perhaps their ethnocentricity, but we do not believe so). They are values that assert the necessity of journey, the necessity of grounding, the necessity of return to oneself and one's commitments.

There are basic human values, basic human dilemmas, and emotions which are universal. Shevek's pain is our pain; so also are his isolation, his fears and uncertainties. His pain and fears are those of each person on Anarres and Urras. They are the pain and fears of our parents and our children. They are the core of human life and are forever seeping through the most rigorous walls of our current social orders. They are the backdrop of history, the base of social life, not because they are dictated to us by some authority, but because they boil up everywhere in our facing of questions of authority. Shevek has learned from his journey that within the contrasts and diversity of life is to be found the meaning we search for. The drama of his journey illustrates that connectedness and fulfillment are not found through "variety or experiencing seeking," for the variety-seeking spectator never reaches the insights of fundamental human values, never experiences the pain in journey, the fears and uncertainty in attempting to ground oneself.

The variety seeker never experiences in a human way the dilemmas and emotions that are universal. Variety seeking, as opposed to journey, always comes to an end. One must always "start over," begin a new seeking each time. Without a grounding in the particular there is never a chance for an appreciation of the universal. One never encounters one's person or one's humanity. Life is not, therefore, "...a journey and return, but a closed cycle, a locked room, a cell" (*DIS*, p. 268).

From the spiritual death of the possessed, from the spiritual life of the dispossessed, we see how in *being* rather than in *having* we can free ourselves for life in the present, the opposite of death. Life, quality of life, is seen as possible and provides motivation and encouragement for the risk to free ourselves.

Shevek learned from his journey that there is hope, that he and his values are the hope, that the rejuvenated individual spirit is the hope for humankind, that to return home is a denial of death and isolation. It is the reaffirmation of oneself, not in isolation but as an individual who is alone but also collective. Shevek renews this hope with Ketho, who is to accompany him in Anarres. But for those on Urras, for the possessed, they are his past, our present.

THE JOURNEY OF ANARCHIST SOCIOLOGY

Le Guin thus removes anarchism to our future; while those on Anarres may provide a personal link to the past, they can no longer come to live in Urras (the past). We, you and I, each of us, the nonpossessed, must come to anarchism for the hope and future of humankind, which is to say we must come to recognize and accept our own personal journeys. There is hope; but we, in failing to adapt to the present, in failing to revere human possibility (the future), are forfeiting the opportunity for those who follow us.

There is despair in Shevek's return, for despite the struggle to connect, connectedness may have to be forfeited. But there is also hope in his return, his risk, his spirit. His planetary return signifies his return to his basic human self, which allows him an understanding of the universality, the uniqueness of the human self. It signifies his move to connectedness, not isolation. His return signifies the death of the self-exile he was. His hope is our hope, for it says that, though in grave exile, we can overcome isolation, whether we are possessed or dispossessed; that meaning is not simply possible but close at hand, if only at a risk's distance—the risk to live in the present:

Shevek stood below the window gazing out, the light filling his eyes. "You don't understnad what time is," he said. "You say the past is gone, the future is not real, there is no change, no hope. You think Anarres is a future that cannot be reached, as your past cannot be changed. So there is nothing but the present, this Urras, the rich, real, stable present, the moment now. And you think that is something which can be possessed! You envy it a little. You think it's something you would like to have. But it is not real, you know. It is not stable, not solid—nothing is. Things change, change. You cannot have anything. . . . And least of all can you have the present, unless you accept with it the past and the future. Not only the past but also the future, not only the future but also the past! Because they are real: only their reality makes the present real. You will not achieve or even understand Urras unless you accept the reality, the enduring reality, of Anarres. You are right, we are the key. But when you said that, you did not really believe it. You don't believe in Anarres. You don't believe in me, though I stand with you, in this room, in this moment. . . . My people were right, and I was wrong, in this: We cannot come to you. You will not let us. You do not believe in change, in chance, in evolution. You would destroy us rather than admit our reality, rather than admit that there is hope! We cannot come to you. We can only wait for you to come to us." (*DIS*, pp. 280–81)

Does Le Guin mean that anarchism must be embraced through individual spiritual rejuvenation, that change must come from within? Does she mean that revolution cannot be imposed, else it will stagnate from lack of commitment to revolution as a process? Does she mean that social structures or arrangements are barriers if they are taken as "the way" and not created by those within these arrangements? Yes. And thus she begins to explore the dynamics and dialectics of the relationship between person and social structure. This is the heart of all cogent sociologies (Durkheim, Marx, Kropotkin), and at the heart of anarchist sociology.

But what does Le Guin mean by "the never pressing revolution"? Does she mean that we who are committed to anarchism can only or should only wait for others to journey to our present? Does she mean that we anarchists should wall ourselves off until you come to us, to anarchism, to human values? Perhaps. The original settling of Anarres was a sell-out of revolution, a denial of their past, and our present. The anarchists were given Anarres, the arid moon of Urras, in return for ending their revolution on the home world and for mining raw materials on Anarres needed by Urras. In accepting the agreement, in being bought off and becoming isolated, the settlers relieved the hierarchical elite, the possessed of Urras, of revolutionary change. The promise for the present and future according to Le Guin is to take risks, but what of the revolution during Shevek's journey? What is the moral of Shevek's leaving, the ethics of his leaving? Was he motivated dominantly by his personal interest in getting home, his journey? Was his choice singly to leave-return or be martyred? What if all leave the revolution on earth now, and place it in the future, as Shevek left it in space? Would there be then little hope for present revolution? Are we to remove ourselves and wait for a future revolution, one which shall never occur because of our passivity, our getting home, our wall? No! We cannot merely wait for you to come to us. We must risk, knowing, perhaps lamenting, that such commitment to human values will cut us off from other aspects of life, from others. But Le Guin's characters, too, have such laments. Bedap's lament (*DIS*, p. 297) is that he "never took the time" to relate and, thus, in his "perfect" independence, he could not share the intimacy of human pain. Odo laments her separation from nature: "On ahead, on there, the dry white flowers nodded and whispered in the open fields of evening. Seventy-two years and she had never had time to learn what they were called" (*DBR*, p. 246). But as one can never be whole, only being-becoming more whole, the choice must be made. We must come to you through our journeys, through your own. We must come, we do come, even if you do not want us. We do not come, however, as an elite, as leaders, as those who know best how or through which means to struggle. We come to share our journey, to bare our strengths and vulnerabilities, knowing that there are only means. All are capable of struggle; all do break barriers, albeit different ones. Perhaps, however, Le Guin's selected barrier breakers—Shevek, the scientist; Tirin, the artist; and Odo, the revolutionary philosopher—contradict this truth, for as examples they reinforce the beliefs that science is beneficent, and that intellectual elites alone are capable of, are critically catalytic for, social change and revolution. And yet, her portrayal of them beneath these surface talents or "positions," convincingly, emotionally, tells us they are each of us.

If we, as persons, are outsiders to your presence, your gates, our ideas and our truths lie at the walls of your experience here and now. Hope lies in breaking through hierarchies of consciousness, culture, and social organization, in making ethical choices, in being committed to humanity through experiencing mutual aid, solidarity, understanding, and in personal fulfillment by being connected to others now.

Anarchist sociology assumes that there is a basic unity of all social life which is now walled over from above by archies, power, and possession. Anarchist sociology means struggle between unity and separation. It differs from undialectical sociology, which posits a consensual order, and from marxist sociology which dwells on separation, the struggle, assuming unity after the struggle ends.[7] Thus, for Le Guin there are no resolutions in social life, in *DIS.* There are only choices and risks, in all social landscapes, between the possessing (capital) and the unpossessing (labor); between power, authority, and those repressed; between each and every person and their relations with others (social relations). Yet, these landscapes are as unified as they are separate.

On the personal level, the contradictions of social life are accompanied by the contradictions of consciousness. To journey outward to break down walls, each must assume and create foundations, walls. Only an inward entropic journey results from questioning and breaking through everything, for then there is no base left on which to search, everything becomes meaningless, including life itself. Temporary walls generate further change, new foundations. Wholeness is gained through the consciousness that one is unwhole.[8] The unity of humankind lies in the basic duality of self and other, unique and separate—unified. Wholeness of self is germinated by the distinctiveness of others, from the process of sharing and learning from one another. Each of us is unique, diverse, attracting and interesting to the other. Through these interactions mutual human bonds develop, initiating greater wholeness in each. Wholeness is also generated by the similarity of others, from each one's need to search for understanding, attachment, and support. Awareness has its meaning from connectedness, connectedness from separation. Shevek experienced this in his separation from Takver:

The air is dry and the wind always blowing. There are brief rains, but within an hour after rain the ground loosens and the dusts begins to rise. It has rained less than half the annual average this season here. Everyone on the Project gets cracked lips, nosebleed, eye irritations, and coughs. Among the people who live in Red Springs there is a lot of the dust cough. Babies have a specially hard time, you see many with skin and eyes inflamed. I wonder if I would have noticed that half a year ago. One becomes keener with parenthood. The work is just work and everyone is comradely, but the dry wind wears. Last night I thought of the Ne Theras and in the night the sound of the wind was like the sound of the stream. I will not regret this separation. It has allowed me to see that I had begun to give less, as if I possessed you and you me and there was nothing more to be done. (*DIS,* p. 203)

. . . .

[Shevek's] mutual commitment with Takver, their relationship, had remained thoroughly alive during their four years' separation. They had both suffered from it, and suffered a good deal, but it had not occurred to either of them to escape the suffering by denying the commitment. (*DIS,* p. 268)

. . . .

. . . binding time into a whole, is the root of human strength. . . . So, looking back on the last four years, Shevek saw them not as wasted, but as part of the edifice that he and Takver were building with their lives. The thing about working with time, instead of against it, he thought, is that it is not wasted. Even pain counts. (*DIS*, p. 269)

Bedap's introspective breakthrough was also uncovered by feeling separation:

> Bedap stayed on with them for an hour after dinner in the pleasant, spacious common rooms of the domicile, and when he got up to go offered to accompany Sadik to her school dormitory, which was on his way. At this something happened, one of those events or signals obscure to those outside a family; all he knew was that Shevek, with no fuss or discussion, was coming along. Takver had to go feed Pilum, who was getting louder and louder. She kissed Bedap, and he and Shevek set off with Sadik, talking. They talked hard, and walked right past the learning center. They turned back. Sadik had stopped before the dormitory entrance. She stood motionless, erect and slight, her face still, in the weak light of the street lamp. Shevek stood equally still for a moment, then went to her.
>
> "What is wrong, Sadik?"
>
> The child said, "Shevek, may I stay in the room tonight?"
>
> "Of course. But what's wrong?"
>
> Sadik's delicate, long face quivered and seemed to fragment. "They don't like me, in the dormitory," she said, her voice becoming shrill with tension, but even softer than before.
>
> "They don't like you? What do you mean?"
>
> They did not touch each other yet. She answered him with desperate courage. "Because they don't like—they don't like the Syndicate, and Bedap, and—and you. They call—The big sister in the dorm room, she said you—we were all tr—She said we were traitors," and saying the word the child jerked as if she had been shot, and Shevek caught her and held her. She held to him with all her strength, weeping in great gasping sobs. She was too old, too tall for him to pick up. He stood holding her, stroking her hair. He looked over her head at Bedap. His own eyes were full of tears. He said, "It's all right, Dap. Go on."
>
> There was nothing for Bedap to do but leave them there, the man and the child, in that one intimacy which he could not share, the hardest and deepest, the intimacy of pain. It gave him no sense of relief or escape to go; rather he felt useless, diminished. "I am thirty-nine years old," he thought as he walked on towards his domicile, the five-man room where he lived in perfect independence. "Forty in a few decads. What have I done? What have I been doing? Nothing. Meddling. Meddling in other people's lives because I don't have one. I never took the time." (*DIS*, pp. 296–97)

Our social arrangements develop from these life contrasts and contradictions, from the dualities of self and others. Identity-differentness, loneliness-togetherness, we-they, hope-despair, change-stability are unities of differentnesses. How each person walls in or is walled out creates our social relations and structures, our quality of life, how we possess ourselves or are dispossessing.

A RETURN FROM HUMAN EXILE

The many social contradictions and conflicts we now face abstractly as atomized and isolated individuals can be met directly through mutual support and freedom. In the realization that each of us is unique and of equal humanness, the realization that self is separate and socially constructed, the dilemmas of rationality and freedom, of power and principle, can be met directly and collectively. But there is no social order which we can conceive or bring about which will resolve genuine contradictions, basic dualities, social change, or human suffering. If we wish to live without authority and without being possessed—in the landscape of Anarres—now—to change social arrangements, we must not perpetuate humankind's current inhumanity.[9]

To perpetuate humankind's current suffering, to assume that humans are naturally evil, is to fail to recognize that the extent and frequency of suffering have historic variation. It means to give up the search for an explanation of these variations, both in consciousness and in social structure. It is to reconcile oneself to the current frequency and extent of misery and suffering, to interpret history (the past) and the future as lacking in substantive change, incapable of change. It is to remain possessed, convinced that you cannot change anything. And faced with the fact of doing nothing, one is faced with the reflection that one is nothing.[10]

To counteract this cycle, to journey out of Urras, a spiritual awakening is necessary.

... a devout understanding of life, according to which man regards his earthly existence as only a fragmentary manifestation of the complete life, connecting his own life with infinite life, and, recognizing his highest welfare in the fulfillment of the laws of this infinite life. . . .

Only such a life-conception will give men the possibility . . . of combining into rational and just forms of life.

. . . .

If this be so, then it is evident that it is not to the establishment of new forms that the activity of men desirous of serving their neighbor should be directed, but to the alteration and perfecting of their own characters and those of other people.

Those who act in the other way generally think that the forms of life and the character of life-conception of men may simultaneously improve. But thinking thus, they make the usual mistake of taking the result for the cause and the cause for the result or for an accompanying condition.

The alteration of the character and life-conception of men inevitably brings with it the alteration of those forms in which men had lived, whereas the alteration of the forms of life not only does not contribute to the alteration of the character and life-conception of men, but, more than anything else, obstructs this alteration by directing the attention and activity of men into a false channel. To alter the forms of life, hoping thereby to alter the character and life-conception of men, is like altering in various ways the position of wet wood in a stove, believing that there can be such a position of wet fuel as will cause it to catch fire. Only dry wood will take fire independently of the position in which it is placed.

This error is so obvious that people could not submit to it if there were not a reason which rendered them liable to it. This reason consists in this: that the alteration of the character of men must begin in themselves, and demands much struggle and labor; whereas the alteration of the forms of the life of others is attained easily without inner effort over oneself, and has the appearance of a very important and far-reaching activity.[11]

In essence, the social revolution must come from within and one must attempt to perfect self and construct with others the social institutions of this rejuvenation.[12] Tolstoi's and Le Guin's critique is not so much that of constructing social forms or recounting them historically, but of adopting these forms without spiritual revolution; of presenting these forms as set blueprints for the new order, into which persons must fit and be transformed rather than having themselves been the social creators.

For Tolstoi, as for Le Guin, the struggle to be human requires more than exercising the principle of equity as a base for justice. It requires more than treating others as you would like them to treat you under similar circumstances.[13] It requires more than not wanting to be ruled, and therefore not ruling others. It requires more than feeding the hungry, as one knows hunger's ache. It requires a journey; it requires being present to one's self, to one's life work, and to others in caring relationships. It requires personal commitment to something, to someone, so that a journey (and return home) is possible. It requires us to demonstrate our struggling new consciousness, to energize others with our exuberance and pain, to develop new relationships, and to attempt to be pure and strong while always aware of our mortality and limitations. It is to feel comfortable with ourselves and the organic anarchy of the bounded universe, which is to say with the risk of the dispossessed.

Le Guin demonstrates that it is possible to design and institute constructive programs, to project communes and develop self-rule in agriculture, industry, community, and federation.[14] Yet she warns that institutional means cannot generate a transformation of human heart but only foster possession and isolation. Transformation of heart can occur only through one's personal journey, and only through its sharing can the "new" society emerge. Only then will the journey have meaning, for the exiles will have a home for their return. As Shevek returned to Anarres, the sun rose on the black anarchic land. His hands were empty, as they had always been. And though he had not brought anything, he carried with him all.

NOTES

JOE DE BOLT: A LE GUIN BIOGRAPHY

1. Paul Walker, "Ursula K. Le Guin: An Interview," *Luna Monthly*, March, 1976, p. 1. The present biography largely derives from such previously published material by or about Le Guin and her family; however, Ursula Le Guin has read this biography to check its factual accuracy. A special debt of thanks is owed James Bittner for his useful comments and for his generous sharing of materials on Le Guin.

2. Paula Brookmire, "She Writes about Aliens—Men Included," *Milwaukee Journal*, July 21, 1974; reprinted in *Biography News* (Detroit: Gale Research, 1974), p. 1155.

3. Clifford E. Landers, "Meet Ursula: She Can Shape You a Universe," *Northwest Magazine*, July 26, 1970, p. 9; Anthony Wolk and Susan Stanley Wolk, "Galaxy of Awards for Ursula Le Guin," *Willamette Week*, June 30, 1975, p. 11.

4. Harlan Ellison, ed., *Again, Dangerous Visions* (Garden City, N.Y.: Doubleday, 1972), p. 28.

5. Le Guin, *Dreams Must Explain Themselves* (New York: Algol Press, 1975), p. 36.

6. Barry Barth, "Ursula Le Guin Interview: Tricks, Anthropology Create New Worlds," *Portland Scribe* 4 (May 17-25, 1975), 9.

7. Le Guin, p. 12.

8. This material on Ursula Le Guin's parents and their family life is drawn from a fascinating biography of Alfred Kroeber written by his wife: Theodora Kroeber, *Alfred Kroeber: A Personal Configuration* (Berkeley: University of California Press, 1970).

9. See Theodora Kroeber's entry in *Contemporary Authors*.

10. Kroeber, p. 141.

11. Barth, p. 8.

12. Charles Bigelow and J. McMahon, "Conversations with Ursula K. Le Guin: Science Fiction and the Future of Anarchy" (Portland) *Oregon Times*, December, 1974, pp. 28-29.

13. Brookmire.

14. Win McCormack and Anne Mendel, "Creating Realistic Utopias: 'The Obvious Trouble with Anarchism Is Neighbors,'" *Seven Days*, April 11, 1977, p. 39.

15. Barth, p. 8.

16. Walker, p. 3.

17. Le Guin, "A Citizen of Mondath," *Foundation* 4 (July, 1973): 22.

18. Ibid., pp. 20-21.

19. Walker, p. 7.

20. Le Guin, "A Citizen of Mondath," p. 21.

21. Wolk and Wolk, p. 11.

22. Brookmire. Also see Damon Knight, ed., *Orbit 12* (New York: Putnam's Sons, 1973), pp. 248-49.

23. Le Guin, "A Citizen of Mondath," pp. 22-23.

24. Kroeber, pp. 285-86.

25. Ibid., p. 217.

26. Ibid., p. 216. This is a portion of a longer poem, "Coming of Age," which appears in Le Guin's poetry collection *Wild Angels* (Santa Barbara, Cal.: Capra Press, 1975), pp. 8-16.

27. Le Guin, "A Citizen of Mondath," p. 22.

28. Ibid., p. 23.

29. Le Guin, *The Wind's Twelve Quarters* (New York: Harper & Row, 1975), p. 20.

30. Ibid., p. 33.

31. Le Guin, "The Stone Ax and the Muskoxen," *SunCon Convention Journal* 1 ([no month], 1976): 8.

32. Le Guin, *Dreams Must Explain Themselves*, pp. 7-8.

33. Ibid.

34. Le Guin, *The Wind's Twelve Quarters*, p. 75.

35. Le Guin, "The Stone Ax and the Muskoxen," p. 8.

36. "Le Guin (II)," *Entropy Negative*, no. 3 (1971), p. 23.

37. "Le Guin (I)," *Entropy Negative*, no. 3 (1971), p. 19.

38. Le Guin, *Dreams Must Explain Themselves*, p. 13.

39. McCormack and Mendel, p. 40.

40. Le Guin, *The Wind's Twelve Quarters*, pp. 224-25.

41. Daniel Yost, "Ursula Le Guin: What's Wrong with Our New Left Is We're Trying to Work through the Existing Power Structure," *Northwest Magazine*, February 13, 1972, p. 8.

42. Le Guin, "Open Letter to the *SFWA Bulletin* and/or *Forum* and to *Locus*," *Locus*, March, 1977, pp. 5, 12.

43. Le Guin, "Concerning the 'Lem Affair,'" *Science-Fiction Studies*, March, 1977, p. 100.

44. Bigelow and McMahon, p. 29.

45. Le Guin, *The Wind's Twelve Quarters*, p. 232.

46. Landers, p. 9; Wolk and Wolk, p. 11.

47. Brookmire.

48. Landers, p. 9.

49. Landers, p. 10; Wolk and Wolk, p. 11.

50. McCormack and Mendel, p. 40.

51. Wolk and Wolk, p. 11.

52. McCormack and Mendel, p. 40.

53. Landers, p. 10.

54. "Le Guin (II)," p. 24.

55. Brookmire.

56. Roger Scafford, "Ursula Le Guin," *Prism* (Oregon State University), Fall, 1974, p. 12.

57. Le Guin, "The Stone Ax and the Muskoxen," p. 10.

58. McCormack and Mendel, p. 40.

59. Landers, pp. 9-10.

60. Ibid., p. 10.

61. Le Guin, *Dreams Must Explain Themselves*, pp. 6–7.
62. Walker, p. 2.
63. Landers, p. 10.
64. Le Guin, *Dreams Must Explain Themselves*, p. 6.
65. Landers, p. 10.
66. Le Guin, "A Citizen of Mondath," p. 24.
67. Barth, p. 8.
68. "Le Guin (II)," p. 26.
69. Walker, p. 2.
70. *Colloquy* (May, 1971), p. 7.
71. Le Guin, "The Stone Ax and the Muskoxen," p. 8.
72. Le Guin, "Escape Routes," *Galaxy*, December, 1974, p. 44.
73. Walker, p. 3.
74. Le Guin, "The Crab Nebula, the Paramecium, and Tolstoy," *Riverside Quarterly*, February, 1972, p. 95.
75. McCormack and Mendel, p. 39.

JAMES W. BITTNER: A SURVEY OF LE GUIN CRITICISM

Materials and information for this essay were collected with more than a little help from my friends, some close, some casual: Douglas Barbour, Joe De Bolt, Thomas Clareson, Robert Elliott, Jeff Levin, Naomi Lewis, Lesleigh Luttrell, Ugo Malaguti, Michael McClintock, Terri Paul, Henry-Luc Planchat, Catherine Rasmussen, Thomas Remington, Joanna Russ, Robert Scholes, Charlotte Spivak, Darko Suvin, and Susan Wood. My special thanks go to Ms. Le Guin for answering my queries.

1. Le Guin, "A Citizen of Mondath," *Foundation* 4 (July, 1973): 24.
2. Le Guin, personal correspondence, March 7, 1977.
3. Both Le Guin and her brother Karl Kroeber cite Moore's "Poetry" when discussing imaginary worlds, whether science fiction, fantasy, or other. See "Vertex Interviews Ursula K. Le Guin," *Vertex* 2 (December, 1974): 96; and Kroeber, "Sisters and Science Fiction," *The Little Magazine* 10 (Spring–Summer, 1976): 90. Robert Nye remarks that *WOE* is "an imaginary garden absolutely hopping with real toads" ("Doings in Earthsea," *New York Times Book Review*, February 18, 1973, p. 8).
4. Harper & Row issued *Rocannon's World* in May, 1977. *Planet of Exile* in March, 1978; and *City of Illusions* in June, 1978. All three novels were issued in an omnibus volume by the Science Fiction Book Club in 1978.
5. Eleanor Cameron, "High Fantasy: *A Wizard of Earthsea*," *Horn Book* 47 (April, 1971): 129–38. An early discussion in a fanzine is Banks Mebane, "The Novels of Ursula K. Le Guin," *Double: Bill* 21 (Fall, 1969): 24–26.
6. Nye. Le Guin herself has spoken at length on Americans' low opinion of fantasy, calling it fear in one instance, and "adult chauvinist piggery" in another. See "Why Are Americans Afraid of Dragons?" *PNLA Quarterly* 38 (Winter, 1974): 14–18; rpt. as "This Fear of Dragons" in *The Thorny Paradise: Writers on Writing for Children*, ed. Edward Blishen (Harmondsworth: Kestrel Books, 1975), pp. 87–[92]; and "Dreams Must Explain Themselves," *ALGOL* 21 (November, 1973): 12; rpt. in *Dreams Must Explain Themselves* (New York: Algol Press, 1975), p. 11.
7. For review of *LHD* see *TLS*, January 8, 1970, p. 39; for *LOH*, see *TLS*, June 23, 1972, p. 705; and for *DIS*, see *TLS*, June 20, 1975, p. 704.
8. For Lewis's reviews of the trilogy, see "The Making of a Mage," *TLS*, April 2, 1971, p. 383; "Earthsea Revisited," *TLS*, April 28, 1972, p. 484; and "A

Hole in the World," *TLS,* April 6, 1973, p. 379. In a letter dated March 16, 1977, Ms. Lewis confirmed that she is the author of these reviews, which were originally published anonymously.

9.   For Lewis's reviews of the trilogy in the *Observer,* see May 4, 1971, p. 36; July 30, 1972, p. 32; and May 15, 1973, p. 39.

10.   Anon., "Quests and Tranquillities," *The Economist* 251 (April 13, 1974): 70. This essay discusses the Earthsea trilogy along with Adams's *Watership Down,* Tolkien's *The Hobbit* and *The Lord of the Rings,* and Lewis's Narnia chronicles.

11.   Wendy Jago, "*A Wizard of Earthsea* and the Charge of Escapism," *Children's Literature in Education* 8 (July, 1972): [21]-29.

12.   Le Guin, "The Child and the Shadow," *Quarterly Journal of the Library of Congress* 32 (April, 1975): [139]-48.

13.   Geoff Fox, ed., "Notes on 'Teaching' *A Wizard of Earthsea,*" *Children's Literature in Education* 11 (May, 1973): [58]-67.

14.   Peter Nicholls, "showing children the value of death," *Foundation* 5 (January, 1974): 71-80; rpt. *SF Commentary* 41/42 (February, 1975): 75-79. *SF Commentary,* edited and published by Bruce Gillespie in Melbourne, Australia, is a fanzine equal in quality to many academic journals.

15.   Le Guin, "A Citizen of Mondath," p. 24.

16.   Stanislaw Lem, "Lost Opportunities," *SF Commentary* 24 (November, 1971): 22-24; substantial excerpts, with Le Guin's reply, rpt. in *Women of Wonder,* ed. Pamela Sargent (New York: Vintage, 1975), pp. xxxii-xxxvi. Lem was not alone in his harsh judgment of the novel. In his review of *LHD* Alexei Panshin writes, "Ultimately as a story it is a flat failure" ("Books," *Magazine of Fantasy and Science Fiction* 37 [November, 1969]: 50). But compare Ted White's laudatory review, "The Future in Books," *Amazing* 43 (July, 1969): 124, 128.

17.   Joanna Russ, "The Image of Women in Science Fiction," *Red Clay Reader* 7 (Charlotte, N. C., 1970): 35-40; rpt. without bibliography in *Images of Women in Fiction,* ed. Susan Koppelman Cornillon (Bowling Green, Ohio: Bowling Green University Popular Press, 1973), pp. 79-94; rpt. without either notes or bibliography in *Vertex* 1 (Februray, 1974): 53-57. Russ was the first American academic to comment on Le Guin, but it would be hard to say whether she was doing so in her capacity as an academic or as a writer and critic of science fiction.

18.   George Turner, letter in *SF Commentary* 25 (December, 1971): 8-10, 43. See also Turner's enthusiastic review of *LHD* in "Back to the Cactus," *SF Commentary* 17 (November, 1970): 37-38.

19.   Le Guin, letter in *SF Commentary* 26 (April, 1972): 90-93; rpt. in *Women of Wonder* (see note 16, above).

20.   Brian Aldiss, letter in *SF Commentary* 33 (March, 1973): 22.

21.   David Ketterer, "*The Left Hand of Darkness:* Ursula K. Le Guin's Archetypal 'Winter-Journey,'" *Riverside Quarterly* 5 (April, 1973): 288-97. See also letters of comment from Sheryl Smith and Douglas Barbour in *Riverside Quarterly* 6 (August, 1973): 90-91 and 93-94. Ketterer's essay became chapter 4 of his *New Worlds for Old: The Apocalyptic Imagination, Science Fiction, and American Literature* (Garden City: Doubleday Anchor, and Bloomington: Indiana University Press, 1974), pp. 76-90.

22.   Ketterer, *New Worlds for Old,* p. 194.

23.   Le Guin, "Ketterer on *The Left Hand of Darkness,*" *Science-Fiction Studies* 2 (July, 1975): 137-39. See also the critiques of Ketterer's book by Canary and Fredericks, and Ketterer's response, all in the same issue.

24.   Le Guin, "Is Gender Necessary?" in *Aurora: Beyond Equality,* ed. Vonda N. McIntyre and Susan Janice Anderson (Greenwich, Conn.: Fawcett, 1976), pp. 130-39; and her introduction to a new edition of *LHD* (New York: Ace Books, 1976), pp. [xi]-[xvi]. When Le Guin reprinted "Winter's King," the germ of *LHD,* in

The Wind's Twelve Quarters (New York: Harper & Row, 1975), she changed all the masculine pronouns to "she" to redress the injustice in the English language which denotes the generic third person with "he."

25.   Douglas Barbour, "Patterns and Meaning in the SF Novels of Ursula K. Le Guin, Joanna Russ and Samuel R. Delany, 1962-1972," dissertation, Queen's University (Kingston, Ont.), 1976, pp. 75-177. Two other dissertations include chapters on Le Guin: Sam J. Siciliano, "The Fictional Universe in Four Science Fiction Novels: Anthony Burgess's *A Clockwork Orange*, Ursula Le Guin's *The Word for World Is Forest*, Walter Miller's *A Canticle for Leibowitz*, and Roger Zelazny's *Creatures of Light and Darkness*," dissertation, University of Iowa, 1975; and Joan Perry, "Visions of Reality: Values and Perspectives in the Prose of Carlos Castaneda, Robert M. Pirsig, Ursula K. Le Guin, James Purdy, Cyrus Colter, and Sylvia Plath," dissertation, University of Wisconsin, 1976. Nearing completion is James W. Bittner, "The Fiction of Ursula K. Le Guin," dissertation, University of Wisconsin, 1979.

26.   Barbour, "*The Lathe of Heaven:* Taoist Dream," *ALGOL* 21 (November, 1973): pp. 22-24. A similar study of Taoism in *LOH* appeared in a fanzine: Jerry Kaufman, "Haber Is Destroyed on the Lathe of Heaven," *Starling* no. 27 (January, 1974), pp. 35-40. *Starling* is edited by Hank and Lesleigh Luttrell in Madison, Wisconsin.

27.   Barbour, "On Ursula Le Guin's *A Wizard of Earthsea*," *Riverside Quarterly* 6 (April, 1974): 119-23.

28.   Barbour, "Wholeness and Balance in the Hainish Novels of Ursula K. Le Guin," *Science-Fiction Studies* 1 (Spring, 1974): 164-73; and "Wholeness and Balance: An Addendum," *Science-Fiction Studies* 2 (November, 1975): 248-49.

29.   Darko Suvin, "The SF Novel in 1969," in *Nebula Award Stories 5*, ed. James Blish (Garden City: Doubleday, 1970), pp. 193-205.

30.   Suvin, "SF and *The Left Hand of Darkness*," *seldon's plan* 7 (February-March, 1975): 6-17. *seldon's plan* is edited by Cy Chauvin in Detroit.

31.   Robert Scholes, "The Good Witch of the West," *Hollins Critic* 11 (April, 1974): 2-12; rpt. in his *Structural Fabulation: An Essay on Fiction of the Future* (Notre Dame: Notre Dame University Press, 1975), pp. 77-99. Scott Sanders reviewed *Structural Fabulation* in *Novel* 9 (Winter, 1976): pp. 185-89, disapproving of Scholes's divorcing "fabulation" from "realism," but approving of his moral argument for "fabulation." Thomas J. Remington, in "Three Reservations on the Structural Road," *Science-Fiction Studies* 4 (March, 1977): 48-54, argues that *Structural Fabulation* "condescends to science fiction, oversells it, and badly misrepresents it."

32.   "Ursula K. Le Guin: An Interview," conducted by Paul Walker, *Luna Monthly*, no. 63 (March, 1976), pp. 1-7.

33.   Scholes, "Science Fiction as Conscience: John Brunner and Ursula K. Le Guin," *New Republic* 175 (October 30, 1976): 38-40. The sections on Le Guin in Robert Scholes and Eric Rabkin, *Science Fiction: History–Science–Vision* (New York: Oxford University Press, 1977) add little to Scholes's previous statements.

34.   George Turner, "Paradigm and Pattern: Form and Meaning in *The Dispossessed*," *SF Commentary* 41/42 (February, 1975): 65-74, 64. See also letters of comment from Thomas Disch, Angus Taylor, and Douglas Barbour in *SF Commentary* 44/45 (December, 1975): 89-92.

35.   Joanna Russ, "Books," *Magazine of Fantasy and Science Fiction* 48 (March, 1975): 41-44.

36.   James Tiptree, Jr., "The Time Machine," *Universe SF Review* no. 5 (Sept./ Oct., 1975), p. 2. "James Tiptree, Jr.," is the pseudonym of Alice Sheldon.

37.   Ian Watson, "Le Guin's *The Lathe of Heaven* and the Role of Dick: The False Reality as Mediator," *Science-Fiction Studies* 2 (March, 1975): 67-75.

38.   Gérard Klein, "Malaise dans la science-fiction," *Cahiers du Laboratoire de Perspective Appliquée*, no. 4 (Septembre, 1975); 2nd rev. ed. published separately, Metz, France: L'Aube Enclavée, 1977. English translation by Darko Suvin and Leila Lecorps, "Discontent in American Science Fiction," *Science-Fiction Studies* 4 (March, 1977): 3-13, and "Ursula Le Guin's 'Aberrant' Opus: Escaping the Trap of Discontent," *Science-Fiction Studies* 4 (November, 1977). Other essays by European critics are Anthelme Donoghue, "ursula le guin: une morale pour le futur," *Univers/04* (Paris: Editions J'ai lu, Mars, 1976), pp. 148-[57]; Ugo Malaguti, "Introduzione alla Prima Edizione," and "Commento alla Seconda Edizione" in his translation of *The Left Hand of Darkness, La mano sinistra delle tenebre* (Bologna: Libra Editrice, 1976), pp. 7-19, 313-18; and Carlo Pagetti, "Anarres dopo Anarres," *I reietti dell'altro pianeta (The Dispossessed)* (Milano: Editrice Nord, 1976), pp. i-viii.

39.   Klein's sense of crisis is as strong as Arnold's and Mannheim's were; referring to his essay "L'Avenir d'une crise," *Analyse financiére*, 4e trimestre (1974), Klein says, "We are living the first episodes [of] . . . a grandiose and probably long-lasting planetary crisis."

40.   This summary of the second part of Klein's essay is from my reading of his typed manuscript, kindly supplied to me by Henry-Luc Planchat. The English translation was not available when this book went to press.

41.   "The Science Fiction of Ursula K. Le Guin," *Science-Fiction Studies* 2 (November, 1975): 203-74. Most of the essays were reprinted in *Science-Fiction Studies: Selected Articles*, ed. R. D. Mullen and Darko Suvin (Boston: Gregg Press, 1976). Barbour's "Wholeness and Balance" is included from an earlier issue, and Plank's essay on Le Guin from a later issue was not reprinted.

42.   Le Guin's polemic drew a response from Alex Eisenstein, "On Le Guin's 'American SF and the Other,'" *Science-Fiction Studies* 3 (March, 1976): 97; he charges Le Guin with ignorance, sarcastic misreading, and "offhand slander." On the next page Le Guin explains that her polemic was intentionally irritating and overstated because it was prepared as a talk before a panel on women in science fiction and she wanted to generate a heated discussion.

43.   Le Guin, personal correspondence, March 21, 1977.

44.   Robert Plank, "Ursula K. Le Guin and the Decline of Romantic Love," *Science-Fiction Studies* 3 (March, 1976): 36-43.

45.   Le Guin, "A Response to the Le Guin Issue (*SFS* 7)," *Science-Fiction Studies* 3 (March, 1976): 43-46.

46.   Anthony Wolk, "On the Le Guin Issue," *Science-Fiction Studies* 3 (March, 1976): 95-96. See Suvin's answer, "On Wolk, Eisenstein, and Christianson in SFS # 8," *Science-Fiction Studies* 3 (July, 1976): 211-12.

47.   Ian Watson, "what do you want—the moon?" *Foundation* 9 (November, 1975): 75-83.

48.   Robert C. Elliott, "A New Utopian Novel," *Yale Review* 65 (Winter, 1976): 256-61.

49.   Angus Taylor, "The Politics of Space, Time, and Entropy," *SF Commentary* 44/45 (December, 1975): 24-28; rpt. slightly revised, *Foundation* 10 (June, 1976): 34-44.

50.   Donna Gerstenberger, "Conceptions Literary and Otherwise: Women Writers and the Modern Imagination," *Novel* 9 (Winter, 1976): [141]-50.

51.   Thomas J. Remington, "A Touch of Difference, A Touch of Love: Theme in Three Stories by Ursula K. Le Guin," *Extrapolation* 18 (December, 1976): 28-41.

52.   See R. H. W. Dillard, "Speculative Fantasy and the New Reality," *Chronicle of Higher Education*, February 23, 1976, p. 12; George Turner, "From Paris to Anarres: The Le Guin retrospective," *SF Commentary* 44/45 (December, 1975): 20-23, 28; Gerald Jonas, review of *Orsinian Tales, New York Times Book Review,*

November 28, 1976, pp. 8, 44; and Darrell Schweitzer, "The Vivisector," *Science Fiction Review* 6 (February, 1977): 36–38.
53. Martin Bickman, "Le Guin's *The Left Hand of Darkness:* Form and Content," *Science-Fiction Studies* 4 (March, 1977): 42–47. The other two papers were Wayne Cogell, "Le Guin's Concept of Freedom in *The Dispossessed"* and Terri Paul, "I and Thou: Basic Dualities Underlying Le Guin's *The Left Hand of Darkness.*" One paper, Charlotte Spivak's Jungian analysis of the Earthsea trilogy, "The 'I' in the Islands of Earthsea," was presented at the 1976 Modern Language Association Convention. Seven papers on Le Guin were read and discussed at the 1977 Popular Culture Association Convention, three of them in a symposium on "Defining the Human" in Le Guin's fiction, organized by Thomas Remington. At the 1977 Science Fiction Research Association Meeting, a session was devoted to Le Guin.
54. George Woodcock, "Equilibrations of Freedom: Notes on the Novels of Ursula K. Le Guin," *Georgia Straight* (Vancouver, B.C., Canada), October 21–28, 1976, pp. 4–5, 9; and October 28–November 4, pp. 6–7.
55. George Edgar Slusser, *The Farthest Shores of Ursula K. Le Guin* (San Bernadino, Cal.: Borgo Press, 1976). Subsequent references indicated parenthetically. See Charles Nicol, "Finding Le Guin's Right Hand," *Science-Fiction Studies* 4 (March, 1977): 86, a review of Slusser's pamphlet.
56. T. A. Shippey, "The Magic Art and the Evolution of Words: Ursula Le Guin's Earthsea Trilogy," *Mosaic* 10 (Winter, 1977): [147]–63. A much less sophisticated essay is Sneja Gunew, "To Light a Candle Is to Cast a Shadow: The Shadow as Identity Touchstone in Ursula Le Guin's Earthsea Trilogy and in *The Left Hand of Darkness,"* SF Commentary 48/49/50 (October/November/December, 1976): 32–38.
57. Susan Wood, "Discovering Worlds: The Fiction of Ursula K. Le Guin," in *Voices for the Future,* vol. 2, ed. Thomas D. Clareson (Bowling Green, Ohio: Bowling Green University Popular Press, 1978). Ms. Wood very kindly supplied me with a copy of her typed manuscript.
58. Le Guin, *The Left Hand of Darkness,* new ed. (New York: Ace, 1976), p. 34.

KAREN SINCLAIR: SOLITARY BEING: The Hero as Anthropologist

1. All page references to Ursula K. Le Guin's works come from the following editions: *Rocannon's World* (New York: Ace, 1966), not the Ace Double edition; *City of Illusions* (New York: Ace, 1967); *The Left Hand of Darkness* (New York: Ace, 1969); *The Word for World Is Forest* (New York: Berkley, 1972), the hardcover edition; *The Dispossessed* (New York: Harper & Row, 1974).
2. John Huntington, "Public and Private Imperatives in Le Guin's Novels," *Science-Fiction Studies,* November, 1975, pp. 237–43. Huntington has written: "The typical Le Guin hero is a visitor to a world other than his own; sometimes he is a professional anthropologist; sometimes the role is forced on him; in all cases he is a creature of divided allegiance" (p. 237). Similarly, Donald Theall, "The Art of Social-Science Fiction: The Ambiguous Utopian Dialectics of Ursula K. Le Guin," *Science-Fiction Studies,* November, 1975, pp. 256–64, has noted: "In each case the separateness of the outsider makes him an observer as well as a participant. . . . Yet even in this respect Le Guin employs the techniques of ambivalence" (p. 257).
3. Georg Simmel, "The Stranger" in Kurt Wolff, ed., *The Sociology of Georg Simmel* (New York: Free Press, 1950).
4. Alfred Schutz, "The Homecomer," *American Journal of Sociology* 50 (1945): 507.
5. Jan Pouwer, "Translation at Sight: The Job of a Social Anthropologist." Inaugural address, Victoria University of Wellington, 1968, p. 7.
6. Claude Lévi-Strauss, *Tristes Tropiques* (New York: Atheneum, 1968), p. 58.
7. This situation appears repeatedly in Le Guin's work. In *Planet of Exile* we learn through a Romeo and Juliet, Jakob and Rolery, how their two groups are

joined only by mistrust and suspicion. But Jakob and Rolery, each somewhat aloof and removed from the allegiances and blindnesses of their respective communities, can overcome their differences to find one another and to offer a hope for mutual respect between the two alien cultures. The importance of such figures is underscored, for the survival of their cultures depends on their ability to cooperate with one another.

8.   Donald Theall has suggested that the name "Ai" is a pun on "eye," "I," etc. "The Art of Social-Science Fiction."

9.   Douglas Barbour, in "Wholeness and Balance in the Hainish Novels of Ursula K. Le Guin," *Science-Fiction Studies,* Spring, 1974, pp. 164–73, has written: "Very few SF books have succeeded as well as *The Left Hand of Darkness* in invoking a whole environment, a completely consistent alien world, and in making the proper extrapolations from it (p. 167).

10.   David Porter, "The Politics of Le Guin's Opus," *Science-Fiction Studies,* November, 1975, p. 245.

11.   Donald Theall has made a similar point. He writes: "The communication between Ai and the hero of the action, Estraven—who saves Ai's life and opens Gethen up to the Ekumen—only comes about through a long and difficult process of understanding. . . . Eventually, after a long period of isolated companionship while fleeing across a great glacier, Ai comes to recognize how gender had become an impediment to communication with Estraven and how, sharing a constant threat of death, he has learned to overcome this and love Estraven" (p. 258).

12.   Ibid., p. 260.

13.   Judah Bierman, "Ambiguity in Utopia: *The Dispossessed,*" *Science-Fiction Studies,* November, 1975, p. 249.

14.   Porter, p. 244.

15.   Ian Watson, "The Forest as Metaphor for Mind: *The Word for World Is Forest* and 'Vaster Than Empires and More Slow,'" *Science-Fiction Studies,* November, 1975, p. 231.

PETER T. KOPER: SCIENCE AND RHETORIC IN THE FICTION OF URSULA LE GUIN

1.   All page references to Ursula K. Le Guin's works come from the following editions: *Rocannon's World* (New York: Ace, 1966), not the Ace Double edition; *City of Illusions* (New York: Ace, 1967); *The Left Hand of Darkness* (New York: Ace, 1969); *The Lathe of Heaven* (New York: Avon, 1973); *The Dispossessed* (New York: Avon, 1975); *The Wind's Twelve Quarters* (New York: Bantam, 1976); *A Wizard of Earthsea* (New York: Bantam, 1975).

2.   Aristotle, *Rhetoric,* trans. Lane Cooper (New York: Appleton-Century-Crofts, 1960), p. 7.

3.   Ibid., p. 17.

4.   Ibid , p. 8.

5.   Kenneth Burke, *A Rhetoric of Motives* (Berkeley: University of California Press, 1969), especially chapter 1, "The Range of Rhetoric."

6.   The terms are those of Kenneth Burke in *A Grammar of Motives* (Berkeley: University of California Press, 1969), p. xv.

7.   Darko Suvin, "SF and *The Left Hand of Darkness,*" *seldon's plan* 7 (February-March, 1975): 6–17.

8.   Robert Scholes, "Science Fiction as Conscience: John Brunner and Ursula K. Le Guin," *New Republic* 175 (October 30, 1976): 39.

9.   Banks Mebane, "The Novels of Ursula K. Le Guin," *Double: Bill* 21 (Fall, 1969): 24.

10.   Stanislaw Lem, "Lost Opportunities," trans. Franz Rottensteiner, rev. Bruce Gillespie, *SF Commentary* 24 (November, 1971): 24.

11.   Ibid., p. 22.
12.   Le Guin, "Is Gender Necessary?" *Aurora: Beyond Equality,* ed. Susan Anderson and Vonda McIntyre (New York: Fawcett, 1975), quoted in Robert Plank, "Ursula K. Le Guin and the Decline of Romantic Love," *Science-Fiction Studies* 3 (March, 1976): 42.
13.   René Descartes, *Discourse on Method,* trans. Laurence J. La Fleur (Indianapolis: Bobbs-Merrill, 1956), p. 12.
14.   Francis Bacon, *The New Organon and Related Writings,* ed. Fulton H. Anderson (Indianapolis: Bobbs-Merrill, 1960), p. 48.
15.   Ibid., p. 52.
16.   Ibid., p. 53.
17.   Ibid., p. 121.
18.   Ibid., p. 102.
19.   Ibid., p. 103.
20.   Ibid., p. 107.
21.   Aristotle, p. 8.
22.   Aristotle, p. 11.
23.   Burke, *A Rhetoric of Motives,* p. 212.
24.   Le Guin, "A Citizen of Mondath," *Foundation* 4 (July, 1973): 21.
25.   Le Guin, "Escape Routes," *Galaxy,* December, 1974, p. 41.
26.   Le Guin, *From Elfland to Poughkeepsie,* intro. Vonda N. McIntyre (Portland, Ore.: Pendragon Press, 1975), p. 3.
27.   Le Guin, *From Elfland to Poughkeepsie,* p. 27.
28.   Cf. Darko Suvin, "Parables of De-Alienation: Le Guin's Widdershins Dance," *Science-Fiction Studies* 2 (November, 1975): 265ff.
29.   I have in mind, especially, Michael Polanyi, *Personal Knowledge: Towards a Post-Critical Philosophy* (Chicago: University of Chicago Press, 1962), and Edmund Husserl, *The Crisis of European Sciences and Transcendental Phenomenology,* trans. David Carr (Evanston: Northwestern University Press, 1970).
30.   Wayne C. Booth, *Modern Dogma and the Rhetoric of Assent* (Notre Dame: University of Notre Dame Press, 1974), chapter 1.

ROLLIN A. LASSETER: FOUR LETTERS ABOUT LE GUIN

1.   All page references to Le Guin's work come from the following editions: "The Day before the Revolution," pp. 232–46 in *The Wind's Twelve Quarters* (New York: Harper & Row, 1975), Book Club edition; "The Diary of the Rose," pp. 1–23 in *Future Power,* eds. Jack Dann and Gardner Dozois (New York: Random House, 1976), Book Club edition; *A Wizard of Earthsea* (London: Gollancz, 1973); *The Tombs of Atuan* (London: Gollancz, 1972); *The Farthest Shore* (London: Gollancz, 1973).
2.   "Conversation with Ursula K. Le Guin," by Charles Bigelow and J. McMahon, (Portland) *Oregon Times,* December, 1974, pp. 24–29; quotation from p. 28.
3.   Ibid.
4.   Julia de Beausobre, *The Woman Who Could Not Die* (London: Gollancz, 1948).

JOHN R. PFEIFFER: "BUT DRAGONS HAVE KEEN EARS"

1.   Pages vi and 181, 5, 15, 19, 42, 48, 61, 74, 92, 94, 168. "Bright" also appears on pp. 12, 23, 24, 39, 43, 61 (twice), 67, 69, 73, 76, 78, 92, 95, 110, 116, 118, 119, 123, 152, 163, 177, 178 (twice), and 180. All page references to Le Guin's works come from the following editions: *A Wizard of Earthsea* (New York: Bantam Books, 1975); *The Farthest Shore* (New York: Bantam Books, 1975).

2.   Line 609; other instances are in lines 93, 158, 214, 231, 570, 896, 997, 1177, 1199, 1243, 1517, 1802, 2175, 2313, 2553, 2777, 2803, 3140. All line references are to the definitive edition of *Beowulf* by Fr[iedrich] Klaeber (Boston: D. C. Heath and Company, 1922, 1950).

3.   See an interesting discussion along these lines by Bertha S. Phillpotts, "Wyrd and Providence in Anglo-Saxon Thought," *Essays and Studies by Members of the English Association* 13 (1927/1928): 7–27. T. A. Shippey provides an interpretation similar to mine, as well as a larger discussion of Le Guin's interest in the creative function of language in "The Magic Art and the Evolution of Words: Ursula Le Guin's Earthsea Trilogy," *Mosaic* 10, no. 2 (Winter 1977): 147–63.

4.   Klaeber, p. lxxi.

5.   A matter of great debate in the study of Anglo-Saxon poetics. But see a reliable description of the rules for the alliterative Old English line in Marjorie Anderson and Blanche Colton Williams, *Old English Handbook* (Cambridge, Mass.: Houghton Mifflin Company, 1935), pp. 227–32.

6.   See, for example, lines 2, 575, 837, 2694, and 2752.

7.   More samples are on pp. 52, 55, 70, and 71.

8.   Klaeber, p. lv.

9.   Indeed, "Dreams Must Explain Themselves," the title of Le Guin's chatty piece on "Earthsea" in *ALGOL* 21 (November 15, 1973).

FRANCIS J. MOLSON: THE EARTHSEA TRILOGY
Ethical Fantasy for Children

1.   All page references to Ursula K. Le Guin's work come from the following editions: *A Wizard of Earthsea* (New York: Ace Books, 1968); *The Tombs of Atuan* (New York: Bantam, 1975); *The Farthest Shore* (New York: Bantam, 1975).

2.   Le Guin, *Dreams Must Explain Themselves* (New York: Algol Press, 1975), pp. 11–12.

3.   Northrop Frye, *The Educated Imagination* (Bloomington, Ind.: Indiana University Press, 1964), p. 100.

4.   Eleanor Cameron, "High Fantasy: *A Wizard of Earthsea*," *Horn Book*, April, 1971, p. 130.

5.   Lloyd Alexander, "High Fantasy and Heroic Romance," *Horn Book*, December, 1971, p. 579.

6.   I am thinking primarily of Lawrence Kohlberg and his ideas. See, for instance, "Stage and Sequence: the Cognitive-Developmental Approach to Socialization," in D. Goslin, ed., *Handbook of Socialization: Theory and Research* (Chicago: Rand McNally, 1969); and "Stages of Moral Development as a Basis for Moral Education," in C. Beck and E. Sullivan, eds., *Moral Education* (Toronto: University of Toronto Press, 1971).

7.   Bruno Bettelheim, *The Uses of Enchantment: The Meaning and Importance of Fairy Tales* (New York: Alfred A. Knopf, 1976), p. 52.

8.   Geoff Fox, "Notes on 'Teaching' *A Wizard of Earthsea*," *Children's Literature in Education*, May, 1973, p. 63.

9.   Ibid., p. 64.

10.   Le Guin, pp. 12–13.

11.   Ravenna Helson, "Fantasy and Self-Discovery," *Horn Book*, April, 1970, p. 122.

12.   Le Guin, p. 13.

ELIZABETH CUMMINS COGELL: TAOIST CONFIGURATIONS
The Dispossessed

1.   All page references to Ursula K. Le Guin's works come from the following editions: *The Dispossessed* (New York: Avon, 1975); *The Wind's Twelve Quarters* (New York: Harper & Row, 1975).

2. Theodora Kroeber, *Alfred Kroeber: A Personal Configuration* (Berkeley, Cal.: University of California Press, 1970), p. 261.

3. Ibid., pp. 231–41.

4. Scholars are still disputing over what is history and what is legend in the life of Lao Tzu, including even his authorship of the *Tao Te Ching*. Suffice it to say that two of Le Guin's major sources date the work in the period of the Warring States, although they do not agree on the dates for this period. Holmes Welch's most generous dates are 771–221 B.C., Joseph Needham's are the fourth to third centuries B.C. See Holmes Welch, *Taoism: The Parting of the Way* (Boston: Beacon Press, 1966), pp. 1–3, 18–19; Joseph Needham, *Science and Civilisation in China* (Cambridge: Cambridge University Press, 1962), 2.1, 33–36.

Chuang Tzu is more consistently dated in the fourth to third centuries B.C. See Welch, p. 90; Needham, pp. 35–36; Burton Watson, trans., *Chuang Tzu: Basic Writings* (New York: Columbia University Press, 1964), p. 1.

5. Gene Van Toyer, interview with Le Guin, *Vertex*, December, 1974, p. 96.

6. Le Guin, "A Response to the Le Guin Issue," *Science-Fiction Studies* 3 (March, 1976): 45.

7. Among the more notable of these are: Douglas Barbour, "Wholeness and Balance in the Hainish Novels of Ursula K. Le Guin," *Science-Fiction Studies* 1 (Spring, 1974): 164–73; David L. Porter, "The Politics of Le Guin's Opus," *Science-Fiction Studies* 2 (November, 1975): 244–45. Barbour also has published a very brief note on *DIS;* see Douglas Barbour, "Wholeness and Balance: An Addendum," *Science-Fiction Studies* 2 (November, 1975): 248–49. See the Bittner essay in this volume for a comprehensive review of Le Guin criticism.

8. Darko Suvin, "Parables of De-Alienation: Le Guin's Widdershins Dance," *Science-Fiction Studies* 2 (November, 1975): 271.

9. Ibid.

10. Van Toyer, p. 96.

11. Elizabeth Cummins Cogell, "Taoism in Ursula K. Le Guin's 'Vaster Than Empires and More Slow'" (paper delivered at the annual meeting of the Science Fiction Research Association, Miami, Fla., November 14, 1975).

12. Dates of composition are given in parentheses; Le Guin, personal correspondence, September 13, 1976.

13. Because of the wide variance in translations and explications of the ancient Taoist books and commentaries, special attention will be given to the following sources which Le Guin, in personal correspondence (August 13, 1976), has stated she has studied: Joseph Needham, *Science and Civilisation in China;* Burton Watson, trans., *Chuang Tzu;* Holmes Welch, *The Parting of the Way.*

14. Needham, p. 57.

15. Wing-Tsit Chan, ed. and trans., *The Way of Lao Tzu (Tao-te ching)* (Indianapolis: Bobbs-Merrill, 1963), p. 144. All translations in the text are Chan's unless the *Tao* passage was quoted in Welch or Needham; then their translations are used. Le Guin has stated that she devises her own version of particular passages by "collating about five different translations, all of which are totally different." See Charles Bigelow and J. McMahon, interview with Le Guin, *Oregon Times,* December, 1974, p. 26.

16. Needham, p. 36.

17. Watson, p. 6.

18. Welch, p. 54.

19. Homer H. Dubs, quoted in Chan, p. 8. Additional parallels can be found in a source Le Guin has used. See J. T. Fraser, ed., *The Voices of Time: A Cooperative Survey of Man's Views of Time as Expressed by the Sciences and by the Humanities* (New York: George Braziller, 1966).

That Chinese philosophy prefigured modern physics is clearly explained in a recent publication—Fritjof Capra, *The Tao of Physics* (Berkeley: Shambhala Publications, 1975).

20. Needham, p. 75.
21. Lao Tzu, ch. 34, in Needham, p. 37.
22. Needham, p. 37.
23. Ibid., p. 162.
24. Henri Bergson, *An Introduction to Metaphysics* (Indianapolis: Bobbs-Merrill, 1955), pp. 21–49.
25. Needham, p. 97.
26. Lao Tzu, ch. 16, in Welch, p. 65.
27. Welch, pp. 60–63.
28. Ibid., p. 68.
29. Ibid., p. 78.
30. Arthur Waley, *Three Ways of Thought in Ancient China* (Garden City, N.Y.: Doubleday, 1956).
31. Needham, p. 103.
32. Lao Tzu, ch. 57, in Chan, p. 201. See also chs. 9 and 38, pp. 115 and 167.
33. Ibid., ch. 53, in Chan, p. 194.
34. Ibid., ch. 18, in Chan, p. 131.
35. Watson, p. 3.
36. Needham, p. 68.
37. Ibid., p. 71.
38. Lao Tzu, ch. 66, in Chan, p. 218.
39. Welch, p. 20.
40. Needham, p. 59.
41. At least two female models for Odo should be noted: Emma Goldman, of whom Le Guin writes (*WTQ,* p. 285), and Theodora Kroeber, Le Guin's mother. Note that the central letters of her mother's first name are "odo." For comments relevant to her mother, see Le Guin, "The Space Crone," *The CoEvolution Quarterly,* Summer, 1976, pp. 108–11.
42. Welch, p. 33.
43. Ibid., p. 28.
44. Chan, p. 190.
45. Welch, p. 10.
46. Ibid., p. 36.
47. Ibid., p. 23.
48. Ibid.
49. Lao Tzu, ch. 46, in Chan, p. 181.
50. Chuang Tzu, ch. 18, in Watson, p. 111.
51. Chuang Tzu, ch. 6, in Watson, p. 75.
52. Lao Tzu, chs. 22 and 66, in Chan, pp. 139 and 218.
53. Lao Tzu, ch. 15, in Welch, p. 49.
54. Chuang Tzu, ch. 4, in Watson, p. 57.
55. Ibid., p. 59.
56. Needham, p. 75.
57. Ibid., p. 76.
58. Ibid.
59. Chuang Tzu, ch. 2, in Watson, p. 36.
60. Elizabeth Cummins Cogell, "Falk-Ramarren's Search for His Original Nature: Ursula K. Le Guin's Taoism" (paper delivered at the annual meeting of the Missouri Philological Association, Warrensburg, Mo., February 19, 1976).
61. This statement is borrowed from Theodora Kroeber, who writes of her husband, "To tell anything of him is to become aware of the pattern and the configuration which are at the heart of the person and the personality." Kroeber, p. vii.
62. I am indebted to Dr. Wayne Cogell, associate professor of philosophy, University of Missouri-Rolla, for consultation on the philosophical concepts in Taoism.

LARRY L. TIFFT AND DENNIS C. SULLIVAN: POSSESSED SOCIOLOGY
AND LE GUIN'S DISPOSSESSED: From Exile to Anarchism

1.   Murray Bookchin, *Post-Scarcity Anarchism* (San Francisco: Ramparts Press, 1971), pp. 33–34.
2.   All page references to Ursula K. Le Guin's work come from the following editions: "The Day before the Revolution," pp. 232–46 in *The Wind's Twelve Quarters* (New York: Harper & Row, 1975, Book Club edition);*The Dispossessed,* (New York: Avon, 1975).
3.   Le Guin, "A Response to the Le Guin Issue (SFS #7)," *Science-Fiction Studies,* March, 1976, p. 46.
4.   Colin Ward, *Anarchy in Action* (New York: Harper & Row, 1974), p. 11.
5.   Darko Suvin, "Parables of De-Alienation: Le Guin's Widdershins Dance," *Science-Fiction Studies,* November, 1975, p. 267.
6.   For a history of the development of appreciation as a concept, the development of phenomenological sociology, see David Matza, *Becoming Deviant* (Englewood Cliffs, N.J.: Prentice-Hall, Inc., 1969). It is interesting that in sociology little attention is paid to personal biography; people who write sociology have personal biographies and change over time. Matza worked through his interactionism, through his phenomenological, appreciating phase, reinstating human volition, and then into marxist critique. See the interview series in *Issues in Criminology,* especially Joseph G. Weis, "Dialogue with David Matza," *Issues in Criminology* 6 (Winter, 1971): 33–53. Also see James T. Carey, *Sociology and Public Affairs: The Chicago School,* vol. 17, Sage Library of Social Research (New York: Sage Publishers, 1975).
7.   George Fisher, "Anarchism As a Sociology: Lost and Found," paper presented at the annual meeting of the American Sociological Association, New York City, September 1, 1976, draft, page 2.
8.   See Le Guin, "The Day before the Revolution," p. 237.
9.   Larry L. Tifft and Dennis C. Sullivan, *The Struggle To Be Human: Criminology, An Anarchist Perspective,* unpublished manuscript, 1976. Much of what follows is elaborated in this work.
10.   Paul Goodman, *Growing Up Absurd: Problems of Youth in the Organized System* (New York: Random House, Vintage ed., 1957), p. 41.
11.   Leo Tolstoi, "Appeal to Social Reformers," in Waldo R. Brown, ed., *Man or the State* (New York: Huebsch, 1919), pp. 109, 113.
12.   Noam Chomsky, *Problems of Knowledge and Freedom: The Russell Lectures,* "On Changing the World," (New York: Pantheon Books, 1971), pp. 60–62.
13.   Kropotkin, *Ethics: Origin and Development* (New York: Dial Press, 1924), p. 97.
14.   See Daniel Guerin, *Anarchism: From Theory to Practice* (New York: Monthly Review Press, 1970) for an excellent review and bibliography. We also suggest L. I. Krimerman and Lewis Perry, *Patterns of Anarchy* (New York: Doubleday, 1966); and the works of Godwin, Kropotkin, Goldman, Berkman, Proudhon, Bakunin, Malatesta, Voline, Goodman, Ward, Dolgoff, and Bookchin.

A SELECTED LE GUIN BIBLIOGRAPHY

[For works of Le Guin criticism, see the Bittner essay in this volume; for interviews with Le Guin, see the Le Guin biography by De Bolt.]

BOOKS

City of Illusions. (New York: Ace, 1967, 1974). Set in Le Guin's Hainish universe.
The Dispossessed. (New York: Harper & Row, 1974; New York: Avon, 1975). Hugo and Nebula winner; runner up for the John W. Campbell Memorial Award. Set in Le Guin's Hainish universe.
The Farthest Shore. (New York: Atheneum, 1972; New York: Bantam, 1975). National Book Award winner for children's books. Third book in the Earthsea trilogy.
The Lathe of Heaven. (New York: Charles Scribner's Sons, 1971; New York: Avon, 1973). Hugo and Nebula nominee.
The Left Hand of Darkness. (New York: Ace, 1969, 1976). Hugo and Nebula winner. Set in Le Guin's Hainish universe.
Orsinian Tales. (New York: Harper & Row, 1976). National Book Award nominee for fiction. Collection of eleven stories: "The Fountains," "The Barrow," "Ile Forest," "Conversations at Night," "The Road East," "Brothers and Sisters," "A Week in the Country," *"An die Musik,"* "The House," "The Lady of Moge," "Imaginary Countries."
Planet of Exile. (New York: Ace, 1966, 1974). Set in Le Guin's Hainish universe.
Rocannon's World. (New York: Ace, 1966, 1974). Set in Le Guin's Hainish universe.
The Tombs of Atuan. (New York: Atheneum, 1971; New York: Bantam, 1975). Newbery Honor Book; National Book Award nominee for children's books. Second book in the Earthsea trilogy.
Very Far Away from Anywhere Else. (New York: Atheneum, 1976).
The Wind's Twelve Quarters. (New York: Harper & Row, 1975; New York: Bantam, 1976). Collection of seventeen stories, with a foreword, and introductions to each story by the author: "Semley's Necklace" ("Dowry of the Angyar"), "April in Paris," "The Masters," "Darkness Box," "The Word of Unbinding," "The Rule of Names," "Winter's King," "The Good Trip," "Nine Lives," "Things" ("The End"), "A Trip to the Head," "Vaster Than Empires and More Slow," "The Stars Below," "The Field of Vision," "Direction of the Road," "The Ones Who Walk Away from Omelas," "The Day before the Revolution."

A Wizard of Earthsea. (Berkeley, California: Parnassus Press, 1968; New York: Ace, 1968; New York: Bantam, 1975). *Boston Globe-Horn Book* Award for Excellence. First book in the Earthsea trilogy.

The Word for World Is Forest. (New York: Berkley, 1976). Originally appeared in *Again Dangerous Visions,* ed. Harlan Ellison (New York: Doubleday, 1972). Hugo winner; Nebula nominee. Set in Le Guin's Hainish universe.

SELECTED SHORTER FICTION

"An die Musik." *Western Humanities Review* 15 (Summer, 1961). Le Guin's first published story, one of the *Orsinian Tales.*

"April in Paris." *Fantastic,* September, 1962. Le Guin's first sale, the second story she published.

"The Author of the Acacia Seeds and Other Extracts from the *Journal of the Association of Therolinguistics."* *Fellowship of the Stars,* ed. Terry Carr (New York: Simon & Schuster, 1974).

"The Day before the Revolution." *Galaxy,* August, 1974. Nebula winner; Hugo nominee. A companion story to *The Dispossessed,* which can be read as a prologue to the novel. Set in Le Guin's Hainish universe.

"The Diary of the Rose." *Future Power,* ed. Jack Dann and Gardner R. Dozois (New York: Random House, 1976). Nebula nominee (withdrawn by the author).

"Dowry of the Angyar." *Amazing,* September, 1964. (Author's title, "Semley's Necklace"). This story helped generate *Rocannon's World;* Le Guin believes it to be characteristic of her early science fiction and fantasy. Set in Le Guin's Hainish universe.

"The Eye Altering." *The Altered I,* ed. Lee Harding (Melbourne, Australia: Norstrilia Press, 1976).

"Gwilan's Harp." *Redbook,* May, 1977.

"The Masters." *Fantastic,* February, 1963.

"Mazes." *Epoch,* ed. Roger Elwood and Robert Silverberg (New York: Berkley, 1975).

"The New Atlantis." *The New Atlantis,* ed. Robert Silverberg (New York: Hawthorn Books, 1975). Hugo and Nebula nominee.

"Nine Lives." *Playboy,* November, 1969. Nebula nominee. Le Guin believes it to be as near to "hard" science fiction as her stories get. Editorial revisions removed, and returned to original form in *The Wind's Twelve Quarters.*

"The Ones Who Walk Away from Omelas." *New Dimensions 3,* ed. Robert Silverberg (New York: Doubleday, Science Fiction Book Club, 1973). Hugo winner.

"The Rule of Names." *Fantastic,* April, 1964. This story helped generate the Earthsea novels.

"Schrödinger's Cat." *Universe 5,* ed. Terry Carr (New York: Random House, 1974).

"Vaster Than Empires and More Slow." *New Dimensions 1,* ed. Robert Silverberg (New York: Doubleday, 1971). Hugo nominee. Set in Le Guin's Hainish universe. Revised in *The Wind's Twelve Quarters.*

The Water Is Wide. (Portland, Oregon: Pendragon Press, 1976). Story published as chapbook.

"Winter's King." *Orbit 5,* ed. Damon Knight (New York: Putnam's, 1969). Hugo nominee. This story helped generate *The Left Hand of Darkness.* Revised in *The Wind's Twelve Quarters,* with the feminine pronoun used for all Gethenians. Set in Le Guin's Hainish universe.

"The Word of Unbinding." *Fantastic,* January, 1964. This story helped generate the Earthsea novels.

OTHER SELECTED WORKS

""The Child and the Shadow." *Quarterly Journal of the Library of Congress* 32 (April, 1975): 139–48. Based on a lecture presented at the Library of Congress, November 11, 1974, in observance of National Children's Book Week.

"A Citizen of Mondath." *Foundation* 4 (July, 1973): 20–24. Brief autobiographical statement on how Le Guin became a fantasy and science fiction writer.

"The Crab Nebula, the Paramecium, and Tolstoy." *Riverside Quarterly* 5 (February, 1972): 89–96. Guest of Honor speech given at the Vancouver science fiction convention, February, 1971.

"The Dark Tower and Other Stories by C. S. Lewis." *New Republic,* April 16, 1977, pp. 29–30.

Dreams Must Explain Themselves. (New York: Algol Press, 1975). Collection containing: a story, "The Rule of Names"; a map of Earthsea; Le Guin's "National Book Award Acceptance Speech"; an essay by Le Guin, "Dreams Must Explain Themselves"; and an interview with her by Jonathan Ward. Essential reading on the genesis of the Earthsea books.

"Escape Routes." *Galaxy,* December, 1974, pp. 40–44. A summation of various talks on science fiction given by Le Guin.

"European SF: Rottensteiner's Anthology, the Strugatskys, and Lem." *Science-Fiction Studies* 1 (Spring, 1974): 181–85.

From Elfland to Poughkeepsie. (Portland, Oregon: Pendragon Press, 1973). Lecture given in conjunction with the second annual Science Fiction Writers' Workshop, University of Washington, summer, 1972. Includes an introduction by Vonda N. McIntyre.

"Is Gender Necessary?" *Aurora: Beyond Equality,* ed. Vonda N. McIntyre and Susan Janice Anderson (Greenwich, Conn.: Fawcett, 1976), pp. 130–39.

"Myth and Archetype in Science Fiction." *Parabola* 1 (Fall, 1976): 42–47.

"No, Virginia, There Is Not a Santa Claus." *Foundation* 6 (May, 1974): 109–12. Review of *Red Shift* by Alan Garner.

"On Norman Spinrad's *The Iron Dream.*" *Science-Fiction Studies* 1 (Spring, 1973): 41–44.

"On Theme." *Those Who Can,* ed. Robin Scott Wilson (New York: Mentor, 1973), pp. 203–9. This essay describes the germination and composition of "Nine Lives."

"Prophets and Mirrors." *The Living Light* 7 (Fall, 1970): 111–21.

"Science Fiction and Mrs Brown." *Science Fiction at Large,* ed. Peter Nicholls (London: Gollancz, 1976), pp. 13–33. (Also New York: Harper & Row, 1977). Speech given at London's Institute of Contemporary Arts in 1975.

"Science Fiction As Prophecy: Philip K. Dick." *New Republic,* October 30, 1976, pp. 33–34.

"The Space Crone." *Co-Evolution Quarterly,* no. 10 (Summer, 1976), pp. 108–10.

"The Stone Ax and the Muskoxen." *Vector* 71 (December, 1975): 5–13. Reprinted in *SunCon Convention Journal* 1 (no month, 1976): 6–12. Le Guin Guest of Honor speech delivered at the 33rd World Science Fiction Convention, the Aussiecon, held in Melbourne, Australia, in August, 1975.

"Why Are Americans Afraid of Dragons;" *PNLA Quarterly* 38 (Winter, 1974): 14–18. Reprinted as "This Fear of Dragons," *The Thorny Paradise,* ed. Edward Blishen (Harmondsworth: Kestrel Books, 1975), pp. 87–92. Speech given at the 1973 PNLA Conference, Portland, Oregon.

Wild Angels. (Santa Barbara, California: Capra Press, 1975). Collection of poems. Contents: "Wild Angels," "Coming of Age," "There," "Footnote," *"Hier Steh' Ich,"* "Song," "Archaeology of the Renaissance," "From Whose Bourne," "March 21," "The Darkness," "Dreampoem," "The Young," "The Anger," *"Ars Lunga,"*

"The Molsen," "The Withinner," "Offering," "Arboreal," "Dreampoem II," "A Lament for Rheged," "The Rooftree," "Some of the Philosophers," "Snow," "Flying West from Denver," "Winter-Rose," "Mount St. Helens/Omphalos," "For Robinson Jeffers' Ghost," "For Bob," *"Für Elise,"* "For Ted," "Elegy *for Reese,"* "Tao Song."

CONTRIBUTORS

James W. Bittner. Instructor of English at the University of Northern Iowa. His Ph.D. (expected from University of Wisconsin 1979) dissertation is on the fiction of Ursula Le Guin. He has published on Le Guin in *Science-Fiction Studies,* and is currently at work on a full descriptive bibliography of her works.

Elizabeth Cummins Cogell. Instructor in English, University of Missouri-Rolla. Member of Phi Beta Kappa and recipient of a Fulbright scholarship, she holds an M.A. from the University of South Dakota, where her thesis concerned the influence of science on Mark Twain's work. Author of "Setting As Analogue to the Characterization of Native Species in Ursula K. Le Guin's Hainish Stories" in *Extrapolation,* she has presented several papers on Le Guin at meetings of the Science Fiction Research Association. Women in literature and the apocalyptic novel are additional research interests.

Joe De Bolt. Professor of sociology, Central Michigan University. Ph.D. from the University of Connecticut; specialist in the sociology of small groups and in social change, with publications in the *Canadian Review of Sociology and Anthropology, Sociological Focus,* and *Psychological Reports.* His works on science fiction include *The Happening Worlds of John Brunner* (Kennikat), "The Modern Period" (with John Pfeiffer) in *Anatomy of Wonder,* and *John Brunner: A Primary and Secondary Bibliography;* in addition, he teaches a course on the sociology of science fiction and is at work on a book in that area.

Peter T. Koper. Assistant professor of English, Central Michigan University. Holds a Ph.D. from Texas Christian University, where he did his dissertation on the rhetoric of Samuel Johnson, Edmund Burke, and William Blake. In addition to rhetoric and composition, he specializes in eighteenth- and early nineteenth-century literature.

Rollin A. Lasseter. Formerly assistant professor of English, North Carolina State University-Raleigh, where he taught courses in fantasy and myth in literature, and in primitive and oriental literature; currently residing in South Bend, Indiana. His publications are chiefly poetry, in *Sewanee Review* and elsewhere; but a book-length study of gnosticism and romantic poetry is in progress, as is a long essay on Tolkien. Interested in "the symbols of the inner journey of human beings, the religious thing, in West and East." Has a Ph.D. from Yale.

Barry N. Malzberg. Under his own name and the pseudonym of K. M. O'Donnell, the author of about 80 books and over 150 short stories, predominantly science fiction and mystery. These include *Beyond Apollo,* winner of the John W. Campbell Memorial Award, and *Herovit's World,* essential reading for anyone wanting to understand the genre writer's world. Also edited *Amazing* and *Fantastic* science fiction magazines in 1968. Graduate of Syracuse University; Schubert Foundation playwriting fellow and Cornelia Ward creative writing fellow. A major contributor to science fiction's widened stylistic and thematic horizons of the late 1960s and early 1970s, his recent works include *The Best of Barry N. Malzberg, Down Here in the Dream Quarter,* and, with Bill Pronzine, *The Running of Beasts* and *Justice.*

Francis J. Molson. Professor of English, Central Michigan University. A Notre Dame Ph.D. and a specialist in children's literature, he contributed the section on juvenile science fiction in *Anatomy of Wonder.* Other works include a forthcoming critical study, *Frances Hodgson Burnett* (Twayne), and essays in *Children's Literature, Elementary English,* and *The Journal of Popular Culture.* He teaches a course on fantasy and science fiction and is at work on bibliographies of children's literature in those areas.

John R. Pfeiffer. Professor of English, Central Michigan University. A pioneer in the rise of academic interest in science fiction: initiated a science fiction course while teaching at the U.S. Air Force Academy; wrote *Fantasy and Science Fiction: A Critical Guide;* special editor of the *Shaw Review* for a number devoted to "GBS and Science Fiction"; wrote "Black American Speculative Literature: A Checklist" for *Extrapolation;* contributed to *The Happening Worlds of John Brunner* (Kennikat); collaborated (with Joe De Bolt) in "The Modern Period" in *Anatomy of Wonder.* In addition, he is the bibliographer of the *Shaw Review* and is working on a book, *Bernard Shaw: An Annotated Bibliography of Writings about Him,* for Northern Illinois University Press. Ph.D. from University of Kentucky.

Karen Sinclair. Assistant professor of anthropology, Eastern Michigan University. A Brown University Ph.D., she did fieldwork in the Caribbean and New Zealand, the latter supported by Fulbright and National Science Foundation grants. Currently working on the life history of a Maori woman. Teaches courses in science fiction and anthropology, and on the anthropology of women.

Larry L. Tifft. Associate professor of sociology, Central Michigan University. Author of numerous articles on crime, police, and criminal justice in various criminological and sociological books and journals, including *Crime and Delinquency, Journal of Police Science and Administration,* and the *American Sociological Review,* he recently completed (with Dennis C. Sullivan) a book on criminology from an anarchistic perspective. Earned a Ph.D. in sociology from the University of Illinois-Urbana.

Dennis C. Sullivan. Teacher and sometime poet, presently living in Voorheesville, a small rural town in upstate New York. He is currently coordinating the writing activities of the Here and Now Writing Collective, which is preparing a paper, "Anarchism: Sociology of Welcome." Also, collaborated (with Larry T. Tifft) on a book on criminology from an anarchistic perspective.

INDEX OF PERSONS

Adams, Richard, 201n
Aldiss, Brian, 35, 201n
Alexander, Lloyd, 129–131, 207n
Anderson, Fulton H., 206n
Anderson, Marjorie, 207n
Anderson, Susan Janice, 201n, 206n
Aristotle, 70, 73, 75, 205n, 206n
Arnold, Matthew, 38-39, 203n
Atheling, William, 37
Atwood, Margaret, 45, 49

Bacon, Francis, 74-75, 81, 84, 206n
Bakunin, Michael Alexandrovich, 180, 210n
Ballard, J. G., 6, 7
Barbour, Douglas, 36, 42, 200n, 203n, 205n, 208n
Barth, Barry, 198n, 200n
Beck, C., 207n
Bergson, Henri, 158, 209n
Berkman, Alexander, 210n
Bettelheim, Bruno, 131, 207n
Bickman, Martin, 45, 204n
Bierman, Judah, 40, 42, 43, 61, 205n
Bigelow, Charles, 198n, 199n, 206n, 208n
Bittner, James W., 202n, 208n, 215
Blish, James, 202n
Blishen, Edward, 200n
Boas, Franz, 14, 15
Bond, James, 77
Bookchin, Murray, 210n
Booth, Wayne C., 85, 206n

Borges, Jorge Luis, 8, 26
Bradbury, Ray, 5, 9
Brontë, Charlotte, Emily, & Elizabeth, 33
Brookmire, Paula, 198n, 199n
Brown, Waldo R., 210n
Bruner, Jerome, 33
Brunner, John, 6, 26, 39, 202n, 205n, 215, 217
Burgess, Anthony, 202n
Burke, Kenneth, 70, 76, 205n, 206n

Cameron, Eleanor, 32, 33, 129, 200n, 207n
Campbell, John W., 20, 22
Capra, Fritjof, 208n
Carey, James T., 210n
Carr, David, 206n
Castaneda, Carlos, 202n
Chan, Wing-Tsit, 208n
Chauvin, Cy, 202n
Chekhov, Anton Pavdovich, 26
Chomsky, Noam, 210n
Clareson, Thomas D., 200n, 204n
Clarke, Arthur C., 9
Clement, Hal, 6
Cogell, Elizabeth Cummins, 208n, 209n, 215
Cogell, Wayne, 204n, 209n
Compton, D. G., 20
Cooper, Lane, 205n
Cooper, Susan, 129
Cornillon, Susan Koppelman, 201n

Dann, Jack, 206n
Davidson, Avram, 32
de Beausobre, Julia, 105, 206n
de Belges, Jean Lemaire, 17
De Bolt, Joe, 200n, 215, 217
de la Mare, Walter, 33
Delaney, Samuel R., 6, 202n
Descartes, René, 73-75, 84, 206n
Dick, Philip K., 20, 22, 27, 39, 40, 44
Dickens, Charles, 27
Dillard, R. H. W., 203n
Disch, Thomas, 6, 202n
Dolgoff, Sam, 210n
Donoghue, Anthelme, 203n
Dostoevsky, Feodore, 48
Dozois, Gardner R., 206n
Dubs, Homer H., 156, 208n
Dunsany, Edward John, 16
Durkheim, Emile, 191

Eisenstein, Alex, 203n
Eliot, George, 37
Elliott, Robert C., 44, 200n, 203n
Ellison, Harlan, 14, 198n

Fisher, George, 210n
Fox, Geoff, 34, 201n, 207n
Fraser, J. T., 208n
Frazer, Lady, 16
Frazer, Sir James G., 33, 48
Frye, Northrop, 129, 207n

Gerstenberger, Donna, 44-45, 49, 203n
Gillespie, Bruce, 201n, 205n
Godwin, William, 46, 210n
Goldman, Emma, 163, 209n, 210n
Goldmann, Lucien, 39
Goodman, Paul, 154, 163, 210n
Goslin, D., 207n
Guerin, Daniel, 210n
Gunew, Sneja, 204n

Heinlein, Robert, 9
Helson, Ravenna, 147, 207n
Herbert, Frank, 39
Housman, A. E., 48
Huntington, John, 40-42, 204n
Husserl, Edmund, 206n
Huxley, Aldous, 44, 46
Huxley, T. H., 48

Ishi, 14

Jago, Wendy, 33-34, 201n
James, Henry, 154
Jameson, Frederic, 41

Jonas, Gerald, 203n
Joyce, James, 90
Jung, Carl, 33

Kaufman, Jerry, 202n
Kellog, Robert, 37
Ketterer, David, 35-37, 201n
Kidd, Virginia, 20, 25
Klaeber, Friedrich, 207n
Klein, Gérard, 38-40, 203n
Kluckholn, Clyde, 15
Knight, Damon, 20, 199n
Kohlberg, Lawrence, 207n
Koper, Peter T., 216
Kracaw, Theodora, 14
Krimerman, L. I., 210n
Kroeber, Alfred, 14-15, 17-18, 153,
     198n, 208n
Kroeber, Clifton, 14, 16
Kroeber, Karl, 14, 16, 200n
Kroeber, Theodora, 14-15, 17, 198n,
     199n, 208n, 209n
Kroeber, Theodore, 14, 16
Kropotkin, Pëtr, 22, 46, 154, 162-63,
     191, 210n

La Fleur, Laurence J., 206n
Lalli, Cele Goldsmith, 19
Landers, Clifford, 198n, 199n, 200n
Lasseter, Rollin A., 216
Lecorps, Leila, 203n
Le Guin, Caroline, 17, 24
Le Guin, Charles, 17, 20-21, 23-24
Le Guin, Elisabeth, 17, 24
Le Guin, Theodore, 19, 24
Lem, Stanislaw, 20, 22, 34-38, 72, 80,
     201n, 205n
L'Engle, Madeleine, 129, 131
Levin, Jeff, 40, 200n
Levi-Strauss, Claude, 39, 41, 51, 204n
Lewis, C. S., 32-34, 129, 130, 201n
Lewis, Naomi, 33, 200n, 201n
Locke, John, 84
Luttrell, Hank, 202n
Luttrell, Lesleigh, 200n, 202n

McCarthy, Eugene, 21
McClintock, Michael, 200n
McCormack, Win, 198n, 199n, 200n
McGovern, George, 21
McIntyre, Vonda N., 201n, 206n
McMahon, J., 198n, 199n, 206n, 208n
Mailer, Norman, 43
Malaguti, Ugo, 200n, 203n
Malatesta, Errico, 210n
Malinowski, Bronislaw, 48

Malzberg, Barry, 26, 216
Mannheim, Karl, 38-39, 203n
Marciano, 15
Marx, Karl, 191
Matza, David, 210n
Maybeck, Bernard, 15
Mebane, Banks, 71-72, 200n, 205n
Mendel, Anne, 198n, 199n, 200n
Miller, Walter, 67, 202n
Molson, Francis J., 216
Moorcock, Michael, 6
Moore, Marianne, 31
More, Thomas, 43, 44
Mullen, R. D., 203n

Needham, Joseph, 155, 156, 158, 166, 208n, 209n
Nicholls, Peter, 34, 201n
Nicol, Charles, 204n
Nudelman, Rafail, 40-41
Nye, Robert, 200n

Oppenheimer, Robert, 15
Orwell, George, 46

Padgett, Lewis, 16
Pagett, Carlo, 203n
Panshin, Alexei, 201n
Paul, Terri, 200n, 204n
Perry, Joan, 202n
Perry, Lewis, 210n
Pfeiffer, John R., 216-17
Phillpotts, Bertha S., 207n
Pirsig, Robert M., 202n
Planchat, Henry-Luc, 200n, 203n
Plank, Robert, 43, 70, 72, 203n, 206n
Plath, Sylvia, 202n
Polanyi, Michael, 206n
Porter, David L., 40, 42, 56, 205n, 208n
Pouwer, Jan, 51, 55-56, 204n
Proudhon, Pierre-Joseph, 46, 210n
Purdy, James, 202n

Rabkin, Eric, 202n
Rasmussen, Catherine, 200n
Remington, Thomas J., 45, 200n, 202n, 203n, 204n
Roos, Stephen K., 200n
Rottensteiner, Franz, 205n
Russ, Joanna, 35, 38, 48, 200n, 201n, 202n

Sanders, Scott, 202n
Sargeant, Pamela, 201n
Scafford, Roger, 199n
Schein, Herman, 19

Scholes, Robert, 37, 70-71, 200n, 202n, 205n
Schultz, Alfred, 50, 204n
Schweitzer, Darrell, 204n
Sheldon, Alice, 202n
Shelley, Mary, 96, 163
Shippey, T. A., 47-48, 204n, 207n
Siciliano, Sam J., 202n
Silverberg, Robert, 6, 26
Simmel, Georg, 50, 204n
Sinclair, Karen, 217
Skinner, B. F., 44
Slusser, George Edgar, 46-47, 204n
Smith, Cordwainer, 18
Smith, G. O., 6
Smith, Sheryl, 201n
Spencer, Herbert, 48
Spenser, Edmund, 79
Spinrad, Norman, 6, 39
Spivak, Charlotte, 200n, 204n
Stevenson, Robert Louis, 90, 92, 94
Stewart, George R., 69
Sullivan, Dennis C., 210n, 217
Sullivan, E., 207n
Suvin, Darko, 36-37, 40, 43, 69-71, 153-54, 200n, 202n, 203n, 205n, 206n, 208n, 210n
Swift, Jonathan, 35, 43, 46

Taylor, Angus, 44, 202n, 203n
Theall, Donald, 40, 43, 58, 204n, 205n
Tifft, Larry L., 210n, 217
Tiptree, James, Jr., 38, 40, 202n
Tolkien, J. R. R., 32-34, 129, 201n, 216
Tolstoi, Leo, 16, 196, 210n
Turner, George, 35, 37-38, 49, 201n, 202n, 203n
Tylor, Edward B., 48
Tzu, Chuang, 36, 153, 157, 169-175, 208n, 209n
Tzu, Lao, 36, 153, 156-57, 159-62, 166-69, 172-73, 208n, 209n

Van Toyer, Gene, 208n
Voline, 210n
Vonnegut, Kurt, 5, 9

Waley, Arthur, 209n
Walker, Paul, 198n, 199n, 200n, 202n
Ward, Colin, 210n
Watson, Burton, 156, 165, 208n, 209n
Watson, Ian, 38, 41, 44, 202n, 203n, 205n
Weis, Joseph G., 210n
Welch, Holmes, 156, 168-69, 173, 208n, 209n
White, Ted, 201n

Williams, Blanche Colton, 207n
Wolff, Kurt, 204n
Wolk, Anthony, 44, 198n, 199n, 203n
Wolk, Susan Stanley, 198n, 199n
Wood, Susan, 48, 200n, 204n

Woodcock, George, 46, 204n
Woolf, Virginia, 26
Yeats, William Butler, 183
Yost, Daniel, 199n
Zelazny, Roger, 39, 202n

INDEX OF WORKS BY URSULA K. LE GUIN

"American SF and the Other," 40
"An die Musik," 17
"April in Paris," 19, 66-69, 73

"Child and the Shadow, The," 34, 201n
"Citizen of Mondath, A," 199n, 200n, 201n, 206n
City of Illusions, 19, 32, 36, 38, 47, 52, 53-55, 78-80, 153-54, 159, 176, 200n, 204n, 205n
"Coming of Age," 31
"Concerning the Lem Affair," 199n
"Crab Nebula, the Paramecium, and Tolstoy, The," 200n

"Day before the Revolution, The," 8, 22, 32, 47, 99, 114, 163, 192, 210n
"Diary of the Rose, The," 22, 90, 99, 105, 106, 206n
Dispossessed, The, 6, 8, 22, 26-27, 32-33, 36-38, 40-50, 60-62, 81-82, 89, 91, 109, 114, 151, 154-79, 182, 185-87, 190-94, 200n, 203n, 204n, 205n, 207n, 210n
Dreams Must Explain Themselves, 11, 48, 128, 134, 198n, 199n, 200n, 207n

"Escape Routes," 200n, 206n

Farthest Shore, The, 21, 31-34, 48, 83-84, 89-91, 105-113, 116-17, 134, 145-48, 206n, 207n
From Elfland to Poughkeepsie, 77, 206n

"Is Gender Necessary?" 201n

Lathe of Heaven, The, 6, 8, 20, 33, 36, 38, 42, 46, 52, 80-81, 89, 153-54, 176, 200n, 202n, 205n
Left Hand of Darkness, The, 5, 8, 20, 22, 25-26, 29, 32-38, 41-45, 47, 49, 52, 55-60, 63, 67, 70-73, 79-81, 90-91, 154-55, 159, 176, 200n, 205n

"Masters, The," 19, 66-69

"New Atlantis, The," 23, 43, 47, 90, 105, 109
"Nine Lives," 20, 24, 26, 45

"Ones Who Walk Away from Omelas, The," 8, 21-22, 32, 85, 90
Orsinian Tales, 5, 8, 23, 31-32, 45

Planet of Exile, 19, 32, 36, 38, 47, 52, 78, 83-84, 99, 176, 200n, 204n

"Response to the Le Guin Issue (SFS #7), A," 203n, 208n, 210n
Rocannon's World, 19, 32, 36, 38, 47, 50, 52-53, 67, 77-79, 99, 155, 176, 200n, 204n, 205n
"Rule of Names, The," 19

"Space Crone, The," 209n
"Stone Ax and the Muskoxen, The," 199n, 200n

"This Fear of Dragons," 200n
Tombs of Atuan, The, 14, 20-21, 32-33, 48, 83, 96, 98-105, 116, 134, 140-45, 207n

"Vaster Than Empires and More Slow," 8, 20-21, 41, 45, 84-85, 154, 205n, 208n
Very Far Away from Anywhere Else, 23, 31, 33

Water Is Wide, The, 31
"Why Are Americans Afraid of Dragons," 200n
Wild Angels, 14, 31, 199n
Wind's Twelve Quarters, The, 23, 45, 66-67, 85, 155, 163, 172, 199n, 202n, 205n, 207n, 209n
"Winter's King," 20, 90, 201n
Wizard of Earthsea, A, 19, 20, 32, 33-34, 36, 48, 83-84, 87, 89, 91-98, 115-127, 133-34, 200n, 205n, 207n
Word for World Is Forest, The, 7, 21, 23, 32, 36, 38, 41, 45, 48, 50, 52, 60, 62-64, 84, 204n, 205n
"Word of Unbinding, The," 19